The Essential Guide for Competent Teaching Assistants

Meeting the National Occupational Standards at Level 2

Second Edition

Anne Watkinson

with contributions by

Carol Connell, Carole Jones, Peter Nathan, Ian Roper and Debbie Schofield

Routledge
Taylor & Francis Group

LONDON AND NEW YORK

First edition published 2003 by David Fulton Publishers Ltd

Second edition published 2008
by Routledge
2 Park Square, Milton Park, Abingdon, Oxon OX14 4RN

Simultaneously published in the USA and Canada
by Routledge
270 Madison Avenue, New York, NY 10016

Routledge is an imprint of the Taylor & Francis Group, an informa business

Typeset in Sabon by RefineCatch Ltd, Bungay, Suffolk
Printed and bound in Great Britain by CPI Antony Rowe, Chippenham, Wiltshire

British Library Cataloguing in Publication Data
A catalogue record for this book is available from the British Library

Library of Congress Cataloging in Publication Data
Watkinson, Anne.
   The essential guide for competent teaching assistants : meeting the national occupational standards at
level 2 / Anne Watkinson. – 2nd ed.
      p. cm.
   Includes bibliographical references and index.
   1. Teachers' assistants   I. Title.
LB2844.1.A8W377   2008
371.14′124–dc22   2008009765

ISBN 10: 0-415-46048-4 (pbk)
ISBN 13: 978-0-415-46048-4 (pbk)

£19.99

The Essential Guide for Competent

Teaching Assistants

Second Edition

This indispensable textbo ... rt all teaching assistants working towar ...

This new edition is fu ... new materials required to meet the 20(... ng Workforce Remodelling and the Eve ... VQs, or other teaching assistant awards ...

This accessible compani ...

- actively engages the re ... the theoretical background to school-l ...

- gives insight and infor ...

- helps teaching assistan ... room support

- emphasises that teachi ... ng supported by the school.

Contributions from specia ... te, relevant and the best practice. All phase ... idary years, and references are made to sou ...

The Essential Guide for ... both study and everyday practice. It will a ... nagers supporting teaching assistants in their ...

Anne Watkinson is an ex-head teacher and LEA senior advisor who now works independently as a consultant on the role and development of teaching assistants. She has worked in this capacity for the Department for Children, Schools and Families as well as for the Training and Development Agency for Schools.

Contents

Preface

This book aims to provide the basic underpinning knowledge to support teaching assistants (TAs) in all phases of schooling when undertaking study at Level 2 on the National Qualification Framework. It supports the *National Occupational Standards for Teaching and Learning in Schools*. These are the revised standards relevant to TAs which are operative since March 2008 and which can be accessed from the standards website: www.ukstandards.org. The first edition underpinned the first set of TA standards published in 2001. The revision and thus the second edition reflect the changes in the standards and in schools since then, such as Workforce Remodelling and the Every Child Matters agenda. They also reflect both the greater variety of jobs that TAs do and the actual level at which they are working in schools. This second edition is therefore greatly expanded from the first edition, having several sections of material previously studied at Level 3. It also recognises the changes in use of ICT in the general population and in schools; all TAs will need to be computer literate now.

It assumes that you, the TA, are already working in a school and wish to learn more about the job you are doing. If you are considering undertaking a Level 2 qualification, references to the new standards are made throughout, but it will equally be useful to those not undertaking formal courses. It contains ideas for you to try out and some examples of TAs at work. In actively learning about the work you do, you will gain in confidence and understanding of the purpose of the tasks you are asked to undertake. If you wish to undertake any activities in your school, it is important that you talk over any practical issues with someone in authority in the school but it is also valuable to discuss any issues of interest to you with another professional. This may be a colleague, your line manager, or the class teacher with whom you are most closely associated. If you are unsure about these people, approach the person who appointed you, a senior manager, or in a primary school, the headteacher. The school may then appoint someone to be your mentor, so that you can discuss any issues which arise as you read or use the book. If you are undertaking any course, it is essential to have some kind of mentor within your school.

Involving you, the reader, in your own learning will help you understand how pupils learn, how to develop skills to support the teacher and various aspects of the curriculum. It firmly embeds practice of the TA within a whole-school context, enabling you to understand your role in supporting the school, and taking appropriate responsibility for aspects of care, health, safety and well-being of pupils with whom you come into contact, and to play your full part in the school team. However, some of the new standards are very specific and skills based. For these you will need practical training on the job and access to specialist understanding and knowledge beyond the scope of a single book. Increased knowledge will give you confidence to use your initiative and experience appropriately, to support teachers usefully, to help pupils learn and access the curriculum. Undertaking active learning with the school support will enable you to become part of the learning community of the school, fulfilling the school policies and participating in the formation of the whole-school ethos. You will also be developing professionally.

Acknowledgements

I would particularly like to thank:

Carol Connell, Assistant Principal – Inclusion (SENCO), The Colne Community School for her additions to and oversight of the SEN part of Chapter 7;

Carole Jones, Primary Strategy Consultant, School Improvement and Advisory Service, Essex County Council for the English section of Chapter 10;

Peter Nathan, School Improvement Adviser, London Borough of Brent and Independent Consultant for the EAL sections of Chapters 5, 7, 8 and 10;

Ian Roper, Lead Senior Adviser for Mathematics and Numeracy Strategy Manager, School Improvement and Advisory Service, Essex County Council for the mathematics section of Chapter 10; and

Debbie Schofield, Team leader ICT and Curriculum Development Adviser for ICT, School Improvement and Advisory Service, Essex County Council for her additions to and oversight of the ICT part of Chapter 11.

I could not have written the book without them.

I would also like to thank:

The Colne Community School for permission to publish some of their IEPs;

Jill James, head teacher of Colne Engaine C of E (Voluntary Aided) Primary School and her staff for allowing me time to discuss their work with them and watch them, and I thank them and the children for allowing me to photograph their school so freely;

Dee Weedon and the students of Manningtree High School for allowing me to use their photographs, Gary Smith, head teacher of Market Field School for his help; and

the many other schools and TAs, whose practice and friendship has been a constant inspiration throughout my work with them.

As ever, I thank my husband, Frank, for his endless patience and encouragement, domestic help and support with my ICT systems.

Photographs

Figures

Tables

Abbreviations

ADHD	Attention deficit hyperactive disorder
AE	Adult Education
ALS	Additional Literacy Support
ASD	Autistic spectrum disorder
BECTA	British Education Communication and Technology Agency
CLL	Communication, language and literacy
CPD	Continual professional development
CRB	Criminal Records Bureau
DCFS	Department for Children, Families and Schools
DSP	Designated Senior Person
DT	Design and technology
EAL	English as an additional language
EFL	English as a foreign language
ELS	Early Literacy Support
EMA	Ethnic Minority Achievement
ESL	English as a second language
FE	Further Education
FLS	Further language support
GCSE	General Certificate of Secondary Education
GTC	General Teaching Council
HLTA	Higher Level Teaching Assistant
HMI	Her Majesty's Inspectorate
ICT	Information and communication technology
IEP	Individual education plan
IiP	Investors in People
INSET	In-service education and training
IQ	Intelligence quotient
JD	Job description
KS	Key stage
LA	Local Authority
LEA	Local Education Authority
LGNTO	Local Government National Training Organisation
LMS	Local Management of Schools
LNS	Literacy and numeracy strategies
LSC	Learning and Skills Council
MDA	Mid-day assistant
MLA	Managed learning environment
NC	National Curriculum
NLS	National Literacy Strategy

NNS	National Numeracy Strategy
NOS	National Occupational Standards
NVQ	National Vocational Qualification
Ofsted	Office for Standards in Education
OMS	Oral and mental starter
PE	Physical Education
PGCE	Post Graduate Certificate of Education
PPA	Planning, preparation and assessment
PSHE	Personal, social and health education
QCA	Qualifications and Curriculum Authority
QTS	Qualified Teacher Status
SATs	Standards assessment tests (or tasks)
SDP	School Development Plan
SEAL	Social and emotional aspects of learning
SEN	Special Educational Needs
SENCO	Special Educational Needs Co-ordinator
SET	Southend, Essex and Thurrock
SIP	School Improvement Plan
STL	Standards for teaching and learning
TA	Teaching Assistant
TASCC	Teams around schools, children and community
TDA	Training and Development Agency
TES	Times Educational Supplement
VAK	Visual, auditory and kinaesthetic
Y	Year group
Y3LS	Year 3 literacy support
ZPD	Zone of proximal development

CHAPTER

1

Introduction

The reason for this book

TEACHING ASSISTANTS (TAS) are big news. Over the last ten years, their importance has been recognised and their number increased dramatically. There are very few schools, if any, that do not have them, although schools may call them by different titles and utilise them in different ways. The government has put considerable resources into the recruitment, training and support of systems for professional and career development, including facilitating pathways to teaching for those who wish it. National Occupational Standards (NOS) for Level 2 and Level 3 assistants were introduced in 2001 and a Higher Level Teaching Assistant (HLTA) status introduced in 2003. The rewriting of the NOS (TDA 2007) has coincided with the embedding into schools of a number of important initiatives, so the time is right for a second edition of the book to support assistants in their work.

The first set of standards seemed complicated and were written as a result of study of the varied role of TAs, consultation with focus groups and advisers. The role has not become easier to define in the intervening years: TAs have undertaken more responsibilities as well as operating effectively at the various defined levels. There are now learning mentors, cover supervisors and senior TAs in addition to the HLTAs. It is still not compulsory for TAs to have any qualifications at all on appointment, but increasingly the TAs themselves as well as school managers are recognising the value of training and celebrating the training with qualification recognition. The place of vocational qualifications as distinct from purely academic ones has also been more widely recognised by school leaders, who were used in the past to dealing with either qualified teachers or 'non-teachers'. Training, qualifications and career development including pathways for those who wish to become teachers are now well established, recognised as valuable and growing. There are nationally recognised training and qualifications available for all categories of school support staff.

Since the first edition of this book, the literacy and numeracy strategies have gone into secondary schools, and a primary strategy is attempting to give schools greater freedom to define their own curriculum. The very title of the introductory document *Excellence and enjoyment* (DfES 2003a) indicated the need to release schools from the strait-jacket which the subject strategies had become. The secondary curriculum as a whole has been reviewed and the revised one already published to be in place for September 2008. This emphasis on curriculum content and the accompanying testing regime has narrowed horizons for school teaching staff, but this has not brought about a narrowing for the TAs. The introduction of Workforce Remodelling (DfES 2003b), an attempt to lighten the workload for teachers, has increased the schools' dependence on assistance, not only from TAs but also from administrative staff. ICT (information and communication technology) has become increasingly dominant in the last few years, not only because of the development of the technology itself, but also because of government funding. Most classrooms now have interactive whiteboards, schools and classrooms are linked with the internet through wireless connections, and all teachers and some TAs have their own laptops. TAs are now expected to be computer literate and often to communicate with other staff and deal with school matters electronically. Policies and procedures are available on an intranet, along with plans and resources.

There has also been a move towards more joined-up thinking between service providers for those dealing with children and young people. Some high-profile child abuse cases, notably that of a little girl, Victoria Climbié, highlighted that lack of communication between Local Authority (LA) departments was a major factor in the failure to support the child. A very important document called *Every Child Matters* (ECM) (DfES 2004a) outlined the philosophy which was felt desirable. Instead of focusing on the curriculum and its delivery, it focused on the needs and rights of children. Children are defined as those younger than 18 years old. The details of this initiative and its implications for local government, and more particularly for schools and their staff, will permeate this edition. It focuses on the softer outcomes of child care and education rather than hard-edged, testable, target-orientated ones. It underlines the fact that while schools are more than children's homes and education is more than care, unhappy children cannot learn. Low self-esteem, poverty, ill-health and the like prevent children from reaching their potential. This has now been followed by a ten-year Children's Plan (DCSF 2007a).

Along with the major ECM initiative have come several smaller ones which all make their impact felt in schools. Short inspections, focused on the school's own self-evaluation; moves to look at the value a school adds to its pupils' achievements rather than crude test and examination result lists; providing for children before and after school hours; attempting to assess for and personalise learning rather than stick with the 'one size fits all' model have all contributed to a more autonomous climate for school governance. School budgets have been increased in real terms, enabling them to be more adventurous with staffing and resource provision. School buildings have improved, including making provision for TAs in the staffroom. It is rare now to find the teaching and support staff separation that was common ten years ago, although, sadly, it does still exist.

It is not necessary for a beginning TA starting out in their career to understand all these initiatives but you do need to recognise that government initiatives and change are facts of life. The more you listen to the talk around you and become part of the school culture, the more easily you will be able to participate and contribute. You will be able to support children and adults in your school better if you understand the context of their actions. While working at Level 2 is largely going to be a practical job, the more you understand why you are asked to do something, the better you will do it. One of the most marked characteristics of TAs is their job satisfaction. Apart from the hours fitting in with family life, it is why most TAs are prepared to accept a lower salary. 'They love the job.' Understanding the purpose of your tasks will enable you to do them more satisfactorily, effectively and enjoyably, to support the teachers and the school better.

Who the book is for

The book is intended for those of you who have recently started in the job, or who are working as volunteers and are keen to understand more about the role. The NOS Level 2 define what a competent TA, 'whose responsibilities are limited in scope,' should be able to do (LGNTO 2001:) Level 2: 2. If you read all of this book, do many of the activities, and enrol for a Level 2 course at a local study centre, you will be in a good position to get a Level 2 award, showing your competence to be a good TA. This award would prove to any prospective employer that you know what you are doing, know what the job entails (whether you are working in the primary or secondary sector, or in a middle school system), whether you are to support a named pupil or carry out a specific curriculum programme. It is likely that you will need some specific and specialist training in your school, particularly for many of the optional standards, in addition to reading this book and attending a course if the pupils you work with have particular needs. It is important for TAs in any school to understand the characteristics of the development of average children, to recognise that pedagogic expertise applies in all sectors and that curriculum entitlement is for all children, whatever schools they attend. Also, undertaking a study in the generalist areas of school work will stand you in good stead should your job change, or if when working in a special school you want to enter mainstream schools. Whether you stay in your current school or change, you should still know the basic principles which underpin the general ways in which education and schools work. The new standards recognise that there are specialisms within mainstream school, such as SEN, curriculum areas, different phases or settings, or mentoring or roles and for these specialisms you will need specialist expertise to support you.

Only you can learn about your job. Knowledge and understanding cannot be fed to you without you digesting it, taking it in and using it. You must take personal responsibility for your continuing professional development. You may want to show off your acquisition by undertaking assignments for others to read or even enter them into some kind of awards system, but fundamentally, all adults are still learners, and responsible for their own learning and progress. If you have not studied since leaving school, you may need to consider your own study skills to help you adjust, but dipping into some of the ideas in this book will help you on your way.

How this book can be used

This book can be read and acted on in the sequence in which it is written, which may take some time if you stop and reflect on ideas, or carry out some of the activities, but even then it is not intended to be a course on its own. You cannot take a vocational course successfully without actually working at the job: that is what they are designed for. Many of the specialist optional standards are very practical and will involve hands-on training from an expert or professional in the area in order to complete the standard. This book can only be a taster for those standards. You should also make sure that someone in the school is aware that you want to better yourself, increase your knowledge and understanding of the way in which you can support teaching and learning. Sharing with others your ideas and thoughts on the content is also important. If you wish to undertake work towards awards then seek out a local provider, preferably with the guidance and possibly even with the financial support of your school, and register for an accredited award. This book can then be your back-up text. If you undertake an award you will find that you do not have to cover all the content of this book to gain the award but you may find that the parts you are not covering for the award are still relevant to the job you are doing.

The real intention of the book is that it can be a foundation reference book. Use the index to find what you need, read that bit, do any associated activities and make any notes for your own future reference. Discuss the reading with others in the school or on your course and remember anything you feel is important to use in your daily work. Not everything you will want to know will be found in this book – few books can ever provide such reference. The new standards cover a wide area to provide for the possible range of activity of today's TAs. There will be a few references to other specialist texts, some of which should either be in your school resource collection or one of the teachers may have it at home or it is downloadable from the net. Your best option is to seek out the member of staff responsible for the area in which you are particularly interested, talk with them, share ideas and ask their advice and help with resources and further reading.

The book is not written to follow the standards, but as a textbook to support working in schools. This is deliberate. While there are references to working in the early years, including with babies from birth to 3, the main context of the book will be that of compulsory schooling age, that is from 5 to 16 years old. The standards are called *Supporting Teaching and Learning in Schools (STL)*. The intention is that reading this will give you a grounding in the way good schools work to support teaching and learning in an holistic way. If you are working in an early years' setting the principles of good practice still apply – you are working with other people's children. The hope is that you will understand the general principles of teaching and learning and of school organisation from this book rather than have a step by step guide to completing a particular unit for your award. Thus the book should be of wider and longer use than just supporting the NOS.

Chapter 2 starts from yourself, gives you ideas on ways in which you can help yourself to learn and undertake professional and personal development and some practical ways to proceed. Reading Chapter 2 should help you set yourself in the context of your job and your school, and begin a way of recording your thoughts and information. Then progress to the chapter or section that you feel most relates to your needs. Remember, you do not work in isolation. It is essential that all that you do in school fits in with the way things are done in that school, and that you play your part as a member of staff, whether or not you are paid to work in the school. It may feel sometimes that teachers come to school to shut themselves away from their colleagues in a classroom with children, so relationships with other adults are unimportant, but this is not so. Good schools operate as whole schools, there is consistency between classes in behaviour management, there is coherence to the curriculum and there is the spirit of a learning organisation permeating the establishment. This is increasingly important with the enhanced and recognised role of support staff. Relationships between adults and pupils, between all stakeholders of the school – the parents, governors and increasingly other professionals and the community – all underpin the school's effectiveness. Chapter 3 explores the importance of relationships and how this underpins work in any area or organisation. It gives you some understanding of the people involved in a school.

One of the ways in which the role of TAs has been described is to outline how they support the pupils, the curriculum, the teachers and the school. To do all this you also need support and that should not be forgotten. Chapter 4 deals with all the issues about working in a school that you will have to take note of, gives the school context of which you must become aware, and explores the structures, systems and procedures that go to make up a school, guidance to which you must conform and ways in which you can participate. If the school is to operate as a whole, almost like a living organism itself, with different parts having distinct functions but all parts needed to make the thing work, grow and succeed, then you must play your part and support the systems.

One of the changes in the new standards that is very significant is that the level of understanding required at Level 2 is clearly higher than previously and there is consistent and heavy emphasis on understanding about learning itself. Thus there is a lot of new material in this book from the previous edition, chapters are fuller and there is an additional chapter on learning, Chapter 5. Some of the additional material has been taken from the first edition of the Level 3 book which shows immediately the raise in levels required. Another welcome inclusion is that of early years' practice which reinforces the importance of understanding how children learn: 'child development' was always a requisite for those working with younger children but tended to be ignored in the rush to emphasise subject knowledge in the past few years. Alongside these two, and again linked with them, is the greater recognition of the importance of emotional intelligence, and the need for more freedom to investigate, explore, create and perform.

Chapters 6 and 7 cover the supporting pupil strand, Chapter 8 is on supporting the teacher and Chapters 9 to 11 deal with supporting the curriculum in its various guises. Such is the need for expertise here that some material has been contributed by experts in their subjects whom I have acknowledged earlier. They show how you can support the curriculum objectives while working with pupils under the direction of the teachers. Chapter 12 looks forward.

There are activities for you to try, shown in framed boxes. These can be photocopied to work on separately and changed to suit your circumstances if you wish. Try out some of these exercises to give you examples of things mentioned in the text you are reading and this will help you internalise the meaning. In addition, you will find some mini case studies. Some of these are fictional, but all of them are based on good practice that I have seen in the many schools I have worked in or visited. Even where the stories are factual, all the names have been changed to preserve the participants' anonymity. After you have tried out the ideas for yourself, you will begin to recognise examples of good practice for yourself within your own school, and may be able to write a few scenarios of your own. You can see that to get the best from the book it is important to work through it with someone experienced in the ways of your school to share your ideas and feelings with – the need for an in-school mentor. It could be that you find examples of ways of working that puzzle you or are quite different from those described here. It is then vital that you have someone with whom you can discuss the matters, to find out why things are done in that way in your school. There will be a good reason for the differences, which will provide yet another learning point for you. All schools are different, even if they are in the same geographical area, of the same size and age, and take in similar aged children. People make them different, just as homes in a row of similar houses are all different.

The National Occupational Standards

The original standards for TAs were consulted on and tried out over a period of well over a year before they were published. These new standards were also widely consulted on and, of course, the experience gained with the original ones was invaluable. The standards were designed 'to be suitable for all staff in England, Scotland, Wales and Northern Ireland who work with teachers in classrooms supporting the learning process in primary, special and secondary schools' (LGNTO 2001, Introduction: 2). The new standards' title *Supporting teaching and learning in school* reflects this better than the job title by which the original standards were known. Teaching/classroom assistant was the generic title used to cover all the variety of names used by schools. The term preferred by the then DfES (DfES 2000) is 'teaching assistant', but Scotland, having its own education system, preferred classroom assistant, hence the dual nomenclature in the original standards. The way this role fits in with others in schools as it is understood by the Training and Development Agency (TDA) is shown in Table 1.1.

TABLE 1.1 The support staff framework as seen by the TDA

Administration	Learning support	Pupil support	Site staff	Specialist and technical
Exam officer	Cover supervision			
Finance	Early years	Behaviour/ guidance/		
General	Special needs	support		ICT
administration	Sports coach	Care staff		Librarian
	Teaching assistant/	Midday supervisor/	Catering staff	Science/ design
	bilingual support	playworker	Premises staff	and technology

The shortened form TA will be used in this book to cover all supporters of teaching and learning in the classroom. Many references will be made to Acts of Parliament and codes of practice which are sometimes changed for use in Scotland, Wales & Northern Ireland. Some differences between the four countries may be noted in the text, for instance in referring to the requirements of the National Curriculum (NC), but not all, so do check. The other main difference in the development of these new standards was that the management of the development was with the TDA, not the employers' organisation which is the National Training Organisation for local government employees. This has meant that people involved in the teaching and learning were heavily involved from the outset of the revisions. Some of the new units for TAs are in fact not new except to be included in this award. They come from the child care, playwork or social work sectors, for instance, and reflect the diversity of the role a TA can be called upon to play.

'National Occupational Standards are descriptors of best practice for a particular function' (LGNTO 2001, Introduction: 3). However, because they follow a pattern set out for all occupations, the format and language used are often unfamiliar to the newcomer. Because they are vocationally based, they set out to define competence – what the person fulfilling that role 'can do'. Sometimes they are referred to as 'can do' statements. But no job is just about doing; for all of them some kind of underpinning knowledge and understanding is required, so the standards give statements both about performance – 'performance indicators' – and knowledge.

In order to allow for different levels of competence and understanding, NOS are given in different levels. These correspond to the National Qualification Framework: see Table 1.2. If you want to know more about this go to www.qca.org.uk where you will find further information and links to awarding bodies. All nationally recognised qualifications (at least in England, Wales and Northern Ireland) now figure somewhere in this framework.

TABLE 1.2   The National Qualifications Framework

National Qualifications Framework (NQF)		Framework for Higher Education Qualifications (FHEQ)
Previous levels	*Current levels*	*Levels and examples*
Level 5	Level 8	D (doctoral) Doctorates
	Level 7	M (masters) Master's degrees, postgraduate certificates and diplomas
Level 4	Level 6	H (honours) Bachelor's degrees, graduate certificates and diplomas
	Level 5	I (intermediate) Diplomas of HE and FE, foundation degrees and higher national diplomas
	Level 4	C (certificate) Certificates of HE
Level 3 A-levels		
Level 2 GCSEs Grades A*-C		
Level 1 GCSEs Grades D-G		
Entry level		

Level 1 defines the kind of job that is routine and repetitive such as may be found on a factory floor. It is quickly recognised that when one is dealing with people rather than things, and especially when dealing with children or young people, nothing is ever repetitive. In fact one of the joys of working in a school is that no two days are ever the same. So there is no Level 1 in educational standards. Level 2 is seen as the basic level and is equivalent to the higher GCSE or O-level grades in its knowledge requirements. Level 3 is the more advanced level, for those working across a range of responsibilities within an institution; study for a national vocational qualification (NVQ) at Level 3 equates to that of A-levels. Those seeking HLTA status were envisaged to be at a Level 4 ability (any training course should reflect this) and of course the foundation degrees for TAs are at Level 4. Qualified Teacher Status (QTS) implies not only graduate status, but also the professional qualifications needed by a teacher. Some degrees in teacher training institutions lead to the acquisition of both, and some require the recipient to take a further year's study to obtain a Postgraduate Certificate of Education (PGCE) or other teaching qualification. All newly qualified teachers have to undergo a period of at least one year's induction, which is monitored before they are fully accredited as qualified teachers. More details of these higher levels in the teaching profession can be found at www.tda.gov.uk. It is on this website that you will also find detailed guidance on how to use the standards and gain NVQs or equivalent qualifications.

This Level 2 book is intended for those of you who are at entry level and just want to be a good TA, at least to start with. The Level 2 standards set the level you should be aiming to attain. That is why the book is for those wishing to be 'competent TAs'. This is the level a school leaver wishing to be an apprentice TA will study at. If you feel you are already competent, you have already attained these standards and been in post for years or have other relevant qualifications, you should consider working towards Level 3. The Level 3 book *Becoming an experienced teaching assistant* (Watkinson 2003) will also be available in a second edition towards the end of 2008.

The standards are divided into units, some of which are considered essential for any TA in any kind of school. If taking an NVQ, these units would be considered 'mandatory'. Some even appear in both Level 2 and Level 3. Each level also contains some optional units, but this book will cover all the possible units for Level 2, as it is impossible to determine who would want information on which units. At Level 2, obtaining the NVQ would require showing evidence for the seven units of competence, five of which are mandatory units and candidates can choose two further optional units. These are listed below.

The new units at Level 2

Mandatory: 5 units

STL 1	Provide support for learning activities
STL 2	Support children's development
STL 3	Help keep children safe
STL 4	Contribute to positive relationships
STL 5	Provide effective support for your colleagues

Optional units (Select 2)

STL 6	Support literacy and numeracy activities
STL 7	Support the use of information and communication technology for teaching and learning
STL 8	Use information and communication technology to support pupils' learning
STL 9	Observe and report on pupil performance

STL 10   Support children's play and learning
STL 11   Contribute to supporting bilingual/multilingual pupils
STL 12   Support a child with disabilities or special educational needs
STL 13   Contribute to moving and handling individuals
STL 14   Support individuals during therapy sessions
STL 15   Support children and young people's play
STL 16   Provide displays
STL 17   Invigilate tests and examinations

The unit starts with a brief summary description of who the unit is for, what it is about, what it contains, what other units the unit in question may be linked to, where it may have originated from and its status in the qualification. Then follows a really useful glossary of terms for the unit. Each unit has at least two elements, and some have three. These are sections covering different aspects of that part of the TA role and they give what you would need to show in order to prove your competence in that area of your work. Each element is subdivided into 'performance indicators' which are numbered P1, P2, and so on. Each unit also has a list of the knowledge and understanding which you need in order to be considered to be working at this level. These are numbered K1, K2 and so on. Some of the K numbers are subdivided again into a, b, c, d, etc., parts. Some of the knowledge sections are subdivided according to key stage. Each numbered phrase defines the area and has to be evidenced in any qualification process. Some standards also have a separate list of the scope of activity which the standard covers. See Figure 1.1.

In other words, the NOS are very detailed, covering 99 pages for Level 2 and about 300 pages for Level 3. Hence they are not reproduced in this book, and you must get a separate copy for yourself from the standards website (www.ukstandards.org.uk). The NOS element titles are given in Table 1.3 along with some indication of where you might find material in this book to support the contents.

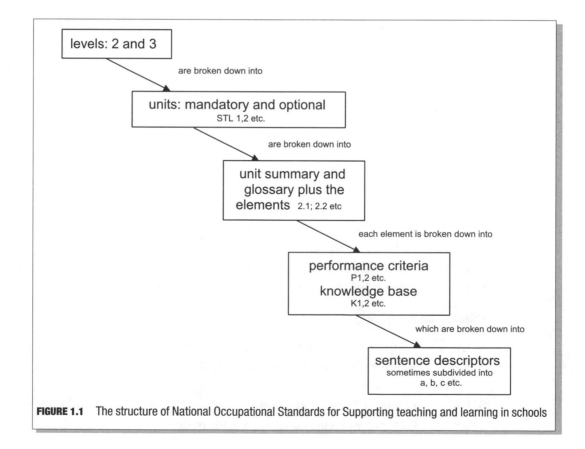

FIGURE 1.1   The structure of National Occupational Standards for Supporting teaching and learning in schools

TABLE 1.3 Level 2 units and standard with chapter references

Unit no.	Unit title	Element no.	Element title	Main chapter sources
1	Provide support for learning activities	1.1	Support the teacher in planning learning activities	8 with a little in Chapters 3,4 and 5
		1.2	Support the delivery of learning activities	
		1.3	Support the teacher in evaluation of learning activities	
2	Support children's development	2.1	Contribute to supporting children's physical development and skills	5 and 6 with a little in Chapters 3,4 and 8
		2.2	Contribute to supporting children's emotional and social development	
		2.3	Contribute to supporting children's communication and intellectual development	
		2.4	Contribute to planning to meet children's development needs	
3	Help keep children safe	3.1	Prepare and maintain a safe environment	6 with some in Chapter 11
		3.2	Deal with accidents, emergencies and illness	
		3.3	Support the safeguarding of children from abuse	
		3.4	Encourage children's positive behaviour	
4	Contribute to positive relationships	4.1	Interact with and respond to children	3 with a little in Chapters 6 and 8
		4.2	Interact with and respond to adults	
		4.3	Communicate with children	
		4.4	Communicate with adults	
5	Provide support for your colleagues	5.1	Maintain working relationships with colleagues	3 with some in Chapter 2
		5.2	Develop our effectiveness in the support role	
6	Support literacy and numeracy activities	6.1	Support pupils with activities to develop literacy skills	10 with a little in Chapters 5 and 8
		6.2	Support pupils with activities to develop numeracy skills	
7	Support the use of information and communication technology for teaching and learning	7.1	Prepare ICT resources for use in teaching and learning	11
		7.2	Support the use of ICT resources for teaching and learning	

(continued)

TABLE 1.3 Continued

Unit no.	Unit title	Element no.	Element title	Main chapter sources
8	Use information and communication technology to support pupil's learning	8.1	Prepare for using ICT to support pupil's learning	11
		8.2	Support pupil's learning through ICT	
9	Observe and report on pupil performance	9.1	Observe pupil performance	8
		9.2	Report on pupil performance	
10	Support children's play and learning	10.1	Participate in activities to encourage communication and language	5 with a little in Chapters 8 and 11
		10.2	Provide opportunities for children's drama and imaginative play	
		10.3	Encourage children to be creative	
		10.4	Support physical play	
		10.5	Encourage children to explore and investigate	
11	Contribute to supporting bilingual/multilingual pupils	11.1	Contribute to supporting bilingual/multilingual pupils to develop skills in the target language	A little in each of Chapters 5, 7, 8 and 10
		11.2	Support bilingual/multilingual pupils during activities	
12	Support a child with disabilities or special educational needs	12.1	Support a child with disabilities or special educational needs by providing care and encouragement	7 with a little in Chapter 6
		12.2	Provide support to help the child participate in activities and experiences	
		12.3	Support the child and family according to the procedures of the setting	
13	Contribute to moving and handling individuals	13.1	Prepare individuals, environments and equipment for moving and handling	7 with a little in Chapter 4
		13.2	Enable individuals to move from one position to another	
14	Support individuals during therapy sessions	14.1	Prepare and maintain environments, equipment and materials prior to, during and after therapy sessions	7 with a little in Chapters 3 and 4
		14.2	Support individuals prior to and within therapy sessions	
		14.3	Observe and provide feedback on therapy sessions	
15	Support children's and young people's play	15.1	Create a range of environments for children's and young people's play	A little in Chapters 4, 6, 8 and 11

(*continued*)

TABLE 1.3 Continued

Unit no.	Unit title	Element no.	Element title	Main chapter sources
		15.2	Offer a range of play opportunities to children and young people	
		15.3	Support children's and young people's rights and choices in play	
		15.4	End play sessions	
16	Provide displays	16.1	Set up displays	8
		16.2	Maintain and dismantle displays	
17	Invigilate tests and examinations	17.1	Prepare to run tests and examinations	8
		17.2	Implement and maintain invigilation requirements	

Even if you are not going to take the qualification, they will provide useful reference material and food for thought and discussion. There is much repetition and cross referencing inherent in the standards, for instance the need to understand legal frameworks or to refer to other adults or to use appropriate language will appear in many standards. The first edition of this book had detailed NOS references given in square brackets in the text to every criterion in the standards, but such is the detail of the new ones that this is not possible here. I will, however, refer to a unit, element and criterion statement by number for all the mandatory standards and will do so for other standards where there is clear cross referencing. Some standards, however, are so specialised that you must contact a specialist to work through each criterion with them. The aim is for this book to be of more general use to those working in schools rather than a direct support for gaining the evidence for any one unit. Hopefully, should you be undertaking a course or compiling a portfolio (see Chapter 2 for details of this way of keeping your work together), this book will ease your burden.

These standards are not themselves NVQs. They are, however, used as the structure and content of NVQs. The examination boards produce the instructions and syllabuses for candidates and centres to follow in order to obtain an NVQ Level 2 or 3, and some are also producing their own awards based on these standards, which are not NVQs. Details of all these can be found by following links on the TDA website, in the support staff section. NVQs are a way of achieving qualifications without taking formal examinations, where your competence is assessed by your workplace performance as well as your answers to questions about knowledge underpinning that performance. Different centres have different ways of questioning candidates: some do it verbally, others do it by assignment. You should be able to opt for the most appropriate method for your way of working. Search around your area for the further education (FE) or adult education (AE) college that is offering a course using your preferred mode of learning. Video or audio tape recording of your understanding should be acceptable if writing is difficult, although in the case of TA NVQs it is difficult to see how a candidate with writing difficulties can help pupils in English which also underpins all other subjects.

Underpinning the NOS are a set of values and principles which have been agreed. In the first set of standards these were published at the beginning of the whole thing and were reproduced in full at the end of the first edition. These values and principles now permeate the whole body of the standards and so are not available as a separate entity. They include the expectations of TAs in their ways of working with people, pupils and the legal and local frameworks. They refer to the kind of professionalism expected of a person working in schools in a multicultural society in the twenty-first century.

Starting with yourself

You

Your values

WHILE MOST OF THE material in the standards covers how you relate to and work with children, young people and other adults, it is useful to understand yourself and to have thought about the kind of person you are, and how you want to be. You will already have certain values in your life. These will have come from your family background, your culture and ethnic origin, maybe your place of worship, and your life experiences. You may not have thought deeply about these values, but this starting point of a new qualification and possibly a whole new career is a good point to consider them. Your personal values are the bedrock on which you lead your life: they give you integrity and consistency which enable others to know where they stand with you and enable you to make decisions based on them rather than randomly or indecisively.

Do give yourself some time to consider your personal values separately from the principles or values which may be associated with working in a school.

- Consider the following:

    - your religious or spiritual beliefs

    - your loyalties to your family and friends

    - your need for personal space or a mentor or both

    - your physical needs to maintain a healthy life

    - your mental and emotional needs to enable you to function effectively.

- Do you need time out to read or take part in leisure pursuits?

- Where would you draw the line between voluntary and paid work?

- What things would you not do if asked, regardless of financial or other reward?

- How do you balance these various values with each other?

(Watkinson 2005 : 16, 17)

The standards look at competencies, but you should look further. Working with children and their education is not just a question of competent classroom practice, but also of commitment, energy and enthusiasm in order to achieve success for the pupils. The pupils are also in a constantly changing social situation. You must work within the law of the country but you also need to challenge stereotypes, oppose prejudice, promote equality of opportunity, respect individuals regardless of gender, marital status, colour, race, ethnicity, class, sexual orientation, disability and age. It is about having and wanting in others 'a spirit of intellectual enquiry, tolerance, honesty, fairness, patience, concern for other people and an appreciation of other backgrounds' (GTC 2002).

The NC introduction itself states that 'Education influences and reflects the values of society, and the kind of society we want to be. It is important therefore to recognise a broad set of common values and purposes which underpin the school curriculum and the work of schools' (DfEE 1999a, 1999b). All TAs should read these introductory paragraphs as well as the Statement of Values by the National Forum for Values in Education and the Community given at the end of both the NC guides. The statements quoted cover the areas of self, relationships, society and the environment, valuing:

- ourselves as unique human beings capable of moral, spiritual, intellectual and physical growth and development;

- others for themselves, not only for what they have or what they can do for us;

- relationships as fundamental to the development and fulfilment of ourselves and others and the good of the community;

- truth, freedom, justice, human rights, the rule of law and collective effort for the common good;

- families as sources of love and support for all their members, and as the basis of a society in which people care for others;

- the environment, both natural and shaped by humanity, as the basis of life and source of wonder and inspiration.

(DfEE 1999a, 1999b)

You really should consider seriously whether your own values might conflict with those of the educational world of our country, or the values of the school where you work. Most schools have thought seriously about their values and have a statement of these in their prospectus. Check. For instance, if you have a different religion from the foundation of the school where you work, this could cause you problems with celebrating festivals or with dress. Talk with someone senior at an early stage if you think there might be a problem in any field in which you are likely to work.

Your practice

Knowing yourself also includes knowing how to maintain your own health and safety when dealing with pupils and knowing your own capabilities to deal with an emergency. You could even endanger life if you overstepped your own limitations, say in the area of first aid. For instance, if you move someone who has a broken back, it can cause untold damage, and similarly you must not put butter on a burn (an old-fashioned remedy), or apply a tourniquet unnecessarily or for too long.

You should take care of your own health too. It is your responsibility to stay healthy and fit, to know how or when to move things safely so as not to damage yourself, not to go crazy with gardening in the spring and make yourself unfit for work. Taking care of your own health means eating properly and getting sufficient sleep, as well as taking normal steps if you are unwell or maintaining courses of medication prescribed for you. It means being concerned about your own habits which might be life-shortening, like smoking, lack of exercise or overeating. It is your responsibility to share any health problems you might have that might affect your work with your line manager, and that includes emotional problems as well.

Ask yourself the following:

- Do you have first aid qualifications or not? Of what sort? Are they up to date?

- What do you do if you discover nits (head lice) in a child you are working with?

- How do you work alongside a pupil with a heavy cold?

- How do you protect yourself appropriately when dealing with pupils who have wet or soiled themselves, cut themselves a little or are bleeding a great deal?

- What do you do if a pupil is violently sick in front of you?

- Do you know what to do if a pupil you have been working with has an infectious disease like German measles?

- Is your own personal hygiene as good as it should be?

- Do you know the correct way to lift heavy boxes in order to avoid back problems?

- Do you know where the ladders and trolleys are kept, and when and how they should be used?

- Have you had training in the use of tools, equipment, materials or chemicals that you are asked to use?

- Do you know how to operate hoists or wheelchairs properly if they are to be used with pupils with whom you work?

Your personality

What you are is going to make a difference to how you do the job of TA. Research shows that the personality of the TA is important in how effective they are. While you cannot change yourself radically, you can recognise the traits that are useful in this job. Try the following.

Do you have any aspects of the following traits?

- Sensitivity to others, their feelings, aspirations, what interests them and what makes them work better, whether it is pupils or other staff, will enable you to enhance their strengths as well as developing your own.

- An outgoing personality, without dominating, enables you to make friends, share ideas and contribute to the teams within the school.

- Being approachable or available means that people will look to you to help, which is the essence of your job.

- Being able to go one step further than that required in any job always 'oils the wheels' of the organisation.

- Having good manners, a careful and responsible attitude to the job not only sets a good example to pupils but shows that you are someone who understands the importance of education and caring for others.

- Patience will be needed when working with slower children, so you need kindness for those who are struggling and above all an empathy for all those who are learning – staff and pupils: you are a learner yourself.

A useful concept that has been used in educational circles in the last few years is that of emotional literacy (Goleman 1996). He suggests that we all have the capacity to know ourselves (our intrapersonal skills) and we have the ability to relate to other people (our interpersonal skills). Some people are more introspective than others and some people are very outward going. Both qualities are needed and thinking about them helps. Goleman says that if we are emotionally intelligent we:

- know our own emotional traits
- can manage these emotions
- can motivate ourselves
- can recognise these emotions in others
- can handle relationships.

Study skills

Your skills

Whether you want to be a really good TA or even use your experience to go on to train to be a qualified teacher, you will need to develop study skills if you do not have them already. These skills include those of personal organisation, recording, reading, thinking about what you are doing and sharing professional ideas. You can practise observing, note-taking, reading, writing essays or accounts, finding reference books and organising your time. Try to have somewhere in your home to keep your school things – books, artefacts, your files and folders. If you start a course of any depth you will probably need a whole shelf for the books and materials you collect. Find somewhere to study – to read or write undisturbed. TAs sometimes find themselves studying after everyone else has gone to bed, particularly if they have videos/DVDs or recorded programmes to watch as part of a course. Get some nice pens and pencils, post-it notes of various sizes and a highlighter. You will probably need ring binders, the plastic document pockets that go in them, and file paper, lined in the size you are comfortable with, and a memo pad. You may find the possession of a personal computer, possibly a laptop, will soon become an essential. If your family has a computer, this may be fine if you are happy to wait until other members have finished surfing the internet or playing games or downloading their emails or music. A computer for word processing is not essential when undertaking courses unless you are undertaking a higher level course where typed manuscripts are mandatory. This is extremely unlikely to be the case at this level. However, the use of ICT in schools is so comprehensive and all-pervading that when working in school you will soon find you want to prepare resources, look for materials on the internet and use email very regularly on your own machine. You may also want to subscribe to a broadband connection rather than dial up if that is all your family has at the moment. Some schools operate an intranet with a password system so that you can access school documentation and communication at home. It is really worthwhile putting some time and thought into these practical issues and discussing them with your family; it could save some arguments or heartache later.

If organising is a problem, try indexing any collections of things that you have at home: a collection of articles, information, handouts, pamphlets on any range of topics, especially those that might be useful for school, e.g. recipes, instructions, games with their rules or places to visit. Personal organisers can be really helpful to start with. Include a timetable of your whole day, not just your school day. When do you eat, talk with your friends or family, relax and sleep? You need to do all of these sometime, even if you do some of them together – like talk and eat, or relax and sleep. Try to build in some time just for you, even if it is only an hour a week. Most of the other skills improve as you practise them. You might find the books on study skills by Northledge (1990) and Freeman and Meed (1993) useful if you are starting afresh.

Begin small, setting yourself realistic targets like reading a certain number of pages by the end of the week or always have a dip into a relevant magazine. Most staffrooms take a copy of the *Times Educational Supplement* (*TES*) and a few teachers make time to read it, using it for job searching, but it does have a magazine section too. *Learning Support* is a magazine especially for primary TAs although many articles will have relevance for secondary ones. The subject associations have regular magazines about their subject and its teaching, and the early years' sector also has specialist magazines like *Nursery World* or *Child Education* which could well be of interest. There is a list of these with contact details at the end of the book.

Local libraries can be a mine of information on what is available in your area, and may also have useful books or booklets on self-study skills. Ask for help in using the library if you are unsure where to start. The classification system they use sometimes seems designed to confuse. If you are unused to reading, try getting your speed up by reading fiction; something that grabs you will get you into the habit. Then try skimming, a most useful tool for quickly trying to find what you want – it is how most of us read the newspaper.

If writing is more of a problem, try keeping a simple diary, not just of events, but also of ideas and personal comments. Try writing letters – we have all got out of this habit with the widespread use of telephones. Essay writing takes a bit more practice, and if you are feeling rusty and essay assignments are part of the course you are taking, ask for guidance. Make notes first, and then a draft. Think of whether to use sections or chapters, even put in headings like those in this chapter, try to ensure a beginning, middle and end, and some sort of flow or continuity. Get somebody to read your draft – somebody who is prepared to offer constructive criticism before you submit a finished essay to the assessors. Note-taking is another skill, this time not using proper sentences, just clues to what you want to remember. Try making a note after a television programme of the main characters or plot as if you were going to write that letter, or of facts from a non-fiction programme. Get a good dictionary: look in the library for one you find user-friendly. Possibly also get a thesaurus. This is a book that groups together words with slightly differing meanings. Using one begins to extend your vocabulary.

Teachers TV apparently is watched by more TAs than teachers, so it must have some material which is helpful to you all. The internet can be a bit of a snare and a delusion if you are not used to it, as you can spend an awful lot of time (and money) searching if you do not know what you are really looking for. Again, librarians can help here and most public libraries have free access to the net for users if you do not have your own. Many staffrooms now have at least one spare computer connected to the intranet and/or the web and you should be able to use this. Just ask the teachers which the most useful sites are for whatever area you need. The main school ones are also at the end of the book.

If you have a real problem with any of the skills (be honest with yourself), you could take a look at the Basic Skills courses now on offer at most adult and further education colleges and consider them before undertaking any course related to the NOS. In most schools, a Level 2 qualification in English or mathematics is not required to work as a TA. However, because of the nature of the job supporting the learning of pupils, it would be very useful, and may even become advisable in the future for all TAs to prove their competence in these basic areas. The important thing is to get your brain working, and do something for yourself.

In all these activities it is really important that you reflect on what you are doing, reading or watching. Think about it [5.2P2]. Do you agree with what is being asked of you, and if not why not? Could you do better, or do it in a different way? Do you know of something similar in a different context? Do you want to know more about any item? Questions are one of the most important learning tools we have. You will notice small children ask questions all the time. Sometimes we wish they wouldn't because they drive us mad – we don't know the answer or they ask at a time when we are concentrating on something else! But getting older children to ask questions and asking them yourself is vital. This is how you begin to become a reflective practitioner. It is also the start of your continuing professional development, which hopefully will go on all the time you are in the profession

[5K9,10,11]. Questioning and reflecting are the beginning of you 'making effective use of the development opportunities open to you' [5P6].

Keeping materials together

If you are undertaking a course, it is most likely that your tutor will give you clear instructions on how to keep notes, how to study, and how best to learn and access the knowledge required of you. In case you are reading this book alone, hopefully with the support of your school mentor or a friendly class teacher, the following are a few ideas on how to proceed.

Ring binders accompanied by card pocket files are the most useful way of collecting things together. You will need a space at home to keep your papers, and the books you will begin to accumulate, such as a shelf or plastic storage box. You may need to reorganise some of your personal life to have study time away from distractions. You will need pads to write on, both A4 and note pads or exercise books for rough jottings or observations. Your tutor may talk of portfolios.

If you have been on the DfEE and DfES induction courses, you will be familiar with the Teaching Assistant Files that come with the course attendance (TDA 2006a, 2006b). They are so comprehensive now that you will need a separate empty file for your personalised material. A detailed description of how to start a *personal file* or portfolio for yourself is given in *Assisting learning and supporting teaching* (Watkinson 2002), some of which is revisited below. You need a section purely with your personal details, and then a section for your school's details. You then can have sections for your progress in your job and for any procedure of review within your school. You can have a section for keeping your jottings or notes about courses. However, if you are studying in any depth, for an externally accredited course, such a ring file will rapidly become filled with handouts, notes on your readings, observations and other relevant materials. Such materials really need a file to themselves, separate from your personal file. This will become your *reference file*, or study file. For submission in an assessment process, you will need to extract materials from it and photocopy material from your personal file to produce an *assessment or qualification portfolio*. You cannot be assessed on materials that you have obtained elsewhere, handouts or photocopies of pages from books, as these are the work of other people, unless you annotate them with notes about how these points are relevant to you.

Your observations of people or pupils working, comments on the reading you have done or on materials or resources you have used are materials for an assessment portfolio. They show your understanding, they are evidence. One thing you should always ensure is that if you put any notes regarding pupils in your portfolio, you should anonymise or depersonalise them; that is, you should refer to the pupil by a fictitious name or just a letter. 'Depersonalised information is information presented in such a way that individuals cannot be identified' (DoH, HO, and DfEE 1999: 113). This also applies to any references to pupils or other people in any assignments that you undertake.

A useful tip is to keep a diary or notebook with these thoughts from the beginning. This means your jottings are dated, but it does not mean you have to write something every day. Then, when you are looking for evidence, photocopy the page, highlight the relevant passage and put a reference in the margin to the NOS unit element and section like the ones in this book, or a qualification item reference. This book is set out in that fashion, the bracketed numbers referring to the NOS (TDA 2007), although they are matched to the text rather than in the margin. So if you carry out any of the suggested tasks which you think might be relevant, write down what you do, what you think about the task, what you might have learnt in doing it, and then date the notes and if possible put the reference number as soon as you have completed it. Some time later, you can trawl through these notes for your qualification portfolio or for a set assignment, and may find you have already shown competence, knowledge and understanding in many of the areas determined.

For example, by completing the following portfolio suggestions you will show that you can 'reflect on your practice to identify achievements, strengths and weaknesses' [5.2: P2]. Keeping a portfolio with dated entries should provide all the evidence you will require to show your competence in this area. If you have been on one of the induction courses mentioned above, and kept your file, you will already have most of the evidence you will need for this unit element. All you will then need to do is to relate parts of the file to the standards or assessment criteria for your award. All the induction materials were mapped to the original NOS and it is most likely that this will also occur with the new ones. Thus by keeping your materials organised you will be on the way to getting your TA qualification.

Contents of a personal portfolio

Keeping a note of your personal details in one place has proved to be a very useful life skill, whatever your background or expectations. We all have a birth certificate and a National Insurance number, and some of us a marriage certificate. Most of us have at least one telephone number at home and possibly also a mobile; some of us have car details or insurance details. The beginning of a personal file is just keeping these all in one place. Use the plastic pockets designed for ring files to keep documents in. This file is exactly what it says – personal to you – and does not form part of any qualification portfolio unless you choose to copy things out of it. It is a place to keep those odd certificates – first aid, swimming or being a member of the winning pub quiz team. It is a place to record things you have done or learnt that are significant. All of us have achieved something, even if we left school without pieces of paper to prove it. Running a club or a home, bringing up children or organising a meal all take skills, understanding and knowledge. A section like this often gives food for thought when you are feeling low. You realise when you collect the evidence in one place how much you personally have achieved – very good for your self-esteem. For instance, if you are reading this book, you are literate. The first section of your portfolio may also contain your examination successes and a record of any jobs you have done, paid or voluntary. Do make sure you put dates alongside these entries. In this way, this record can be very helpful when applying for further jobs and compiling a CV (curriculum vitae, a record of your professional career).

A professional portfolio

The above collection of personal items becomes a personal/professional portfolio when you start keeping details in it from your current job. General suggestions for sections are as follows.

Section 2

Your first entry will be your job description (JD) [5K1]. While a JD is not a legal requirement, good managers will always provide one and you should ask for one. You should have seen it before you applied for the job! It should state: what you are required to do to support pupils, teachers, the school and the curriculum; to whom and for what you are responsible; and what the school will do to support you.

It is important that you understand your job description as to where your responsibilities not only start but finish. Your job description can define not only your TA role but also your role and responsibilities with regard to health, safety and security and there is much more about this in later chapters [2K2]. You should always be working under the direction of a teacher, whether or not that teacher is actually present in the room with you. So you need to know the roles and responsibilities of those with whom you work. The final responsibility for the learning of the pupil in the school is that of a qualified teacher, whether or not you have planned the activity, prepared the materials, carried out the task and fed back what happened, whether or not it is decided that you can liaise directly with the parent or contribute to the assessment report on the pupil. This is also true for HLTAs. You must also work within the limitations of your knowledge, understanding and skills, or within the limits of your job description [1K11]. It is important that you know yourself and your capabilities and do not try to undertake more than you can do, and that you only undertake things for which you have been made responsible. Nevertheless, it is hoped that you are intelligent and can use your initiative where appropriate. If you feel you can do more than you were originally employed for, talk with your line manager [5K12]. In most cases senior staff will be delighted when people offer to do more, but it could be that it is actually someone else's job already, or it is inappropriate for reasons that only they can see. Often standards or job descriptions talk of 'appropriate' support or help. You have to find out what this means for you in your situation, by asking [5.2P3]. Too often in the past things have been left to people's intuition, but it need not be so. Explicit instructions can be given and do help iron out misunderstandings before they happen.

You will then need details of the place in which you work, the context for your job. There is an excellent list in the TDA induction file (TDA 2006a, 2006b:2.2–2.7). It covers the following areas, some of which will be enlarged on in later chapters:

1 Do you know the key facts about your school setting?
   This includes items about numbers of pupils, teachers and support staff and key stages, any specialisms or defining characteristics of the school.

2 Do you know about the local community?
   This includes items about the locality itself and who makes up the community, employment patterns and community activities.

3 Do you know what the governing body does and who the governors are?

4 What regular visitors from the local authority, other services, agencies or teams come to the school?
   This includes what contact the TA may have with such people.

5 How is the school organised?
   This includes class groupings, guidance on systems and procedures, policies, resources, internet access, etc.

6 Are you familiar with school procedures?
   This refers to a school handbook and procedure on health and safety, confidentiality and child protection, security, expectations of behaviour management.

7 How does the school provide for pupils' differing needs?
   This is about access to the Code of Practice for SEN, and resources and people who can support SEN or pupils with EAL.

8 What do you know about the curriculum?
   This asks about familiarity with key stage demands of the NC, the strategies, assessment procedures and inclusion implications, SDP/SIP and accountability strategies including inspection.

9 What is your school/LA doing in relation to the ECM agenda?
   This asks questions about each of the five areas.

10 What training and development opportunities are available in your school/setting or local area?
   The secondary induction includes a separate section asking 'What do you know about qualifications?' This refers to the qualifications the school offers pupils, not what is available to the TAs.

You must recognise that going to work in a school has some big differences from being at home and also from being in most industrial or business environments. You will not be working on your own, but you will be part of various teams, within the classroom, the TA team and the whole school. You will not be producing a product, your 'customers' will not come and go (generally!), but there will be deadlines and policies to which you must conform [5]. You will be working with other people and, what is different from most other work places, you will be working with other people's children. Your relationships with these two groups are of vital importance and Chapter 3 talks about the people you work with and will enable you to understand some of the issues [5.1K2,-9]. You have to work within the legal context of school and the school's own policies. The policies and procedures of your school will make a difference to the way you work, and it is here in your file that you can collect any relevant paperwork. Chapter 4 contains a lot of information as to the relevance of various school policies and procedures to the work of TAs [5.2 and many others]. There will be guidance in many of the emergency, health and safety areas for you already in writing in the school in the form of policies. You must read these and discuss anything you do not understand with your line manager or mentor. Make a note of their answers and read Chapter 4 for more details.

Section 3

As circumstances change, your job will change, and so this should be reflected in changes in your job description. Your job description needs to be up to date. Your role can change overnight if a pupil enters or leaves the school, and so it is important that even if you do not have a document spelling out your roles and responsibilities that you are properly aware of what you are supposed to be doing, how, when, where and with whom [5.2P1]. In addition, you are entitled to a review of your work [5K13]. This performance review may be called an appraisal, and should be conducted at least annually. People in your position, when first taken on, are subject to a period of six months probation, but you should be told immediately if your work is not satisfactory and helped to put any problems right during that time – not at the end of it. It is up to you to do what is required, but most people not only want to do the minimum but also to do their best. So any review should also be an opportunity for praise as well as possible improvement points – it should be a genuine review with an opportunity for both sides to have their say. Any observations of you at work for such a review should be shared with you. A record of this process can all be kept in your file [5.2P5]. Some ideas for self-review are given next:

Constituents of the self-review

(This is not something that can be completed in one go. Do not tackle this all at once – try it a bit at a time.)

List your:

- Successes and appreciation from others
- Job satisfaction and lack of it – fulfilling your existing job description
- Relationships with pupils, colleagues and others associated with the school
- Understanding of the learning process and special educational needs
- Teaching skills and contribution to the learning objectives of the teachers
- Relevant curriculum knowledge and understanding
- Contributions to pastoral and physical care and behaviour management
- Understanding of and contributions to school life

- Professional development opportunities taken: training, courses, meetings attended, personal study undertaken, in school or out of school
- Setting and achieving of any personal targets
- Areas for change, development or improvement – adjustments to job description, and career development issues or ideas.

(Watkinson 2002: 85)

Immediately you add things like this, you can see that you are maintaining an up-to-date record of what you are doing. You should keep a note of any courses you attend, or school meetings – just dates and titles and maybe a brief comment on the relevance of the activity to you and your job. Keep the course handouts and meeting notes somewhere other than in your portfolio, as they are likely to become quite bulky.

Sometimes visiting advisers or inspectors comment on your work, sometimes parents or pupils write letters to you when they leave the school. Keep these letters or a note of comments (dated) in your file; they all add to the evidence of how your job is going.

Section 4 A performance review

While the school should provide the review system, you must take account of what is said about your performance, discuss any targets suggested for you constructively, and carry out any agreed to the best of your ability [1K4; 2.5P3,4; 5K13]. Part of the agreed targets may be to undertake more training, or attend professional development opportunities offered within the school [5K14]. Attending staff meetings about new initiatives could be suggested, for instance, or participating in the school in-service education and training for teachers (INSET) days. You should keep a record of ideas and opportunities offered and those that you might have come across [5P6, K14]. It is reasonable for the school to pay you for attending meetings in what otherwise would be your own time, and most schools pay for TAs to attend courses, and some even finance the course fees. They see it as being in their own best interest to have highly competent and trained staff, and recognise the low pay scales on which many of you operate. However, even teachers and heads undertake self-financed further study sometimes in their own time and for their own career enhancement, like taking Open University modules to gain a higher degree. It is always worth trying to negotiate something. Any outcomes from a review or appraisal should be agreed between you and the appraiser, and any targets set will become the focus for your next review [5.2P4,5]. The targets should be SMART: specific, measurable, achievable, realistic and time-related. It is up to you to maintain your part of the agreement.

You should try and take any opportunity to develop yourself. Adults remain learners all their lives, and a school functions well when all the staff form part of a learning community. Ask questions, read relevant books or parts of them, attend area TA meetings or conferences, visit other schools if you have the opportunity. You also provide a good role model for the pupils if they know you are trying to improve yourself and learn more about the job.

CHAPTER

3

Working with others

The importance of relationships

IT IS POSSIBLE that you have come into the job of TA by answering an advertisement in a local shop or paper or perhaps you are a young person looking for a worthwhile career. Traditionally, people have come into the job through being known to the school, often helping in a voluntary capacity or being employed as a midday assistant. In this latter case, the head or a senior manager spotted you and may have offered you a paid job in class for a few hours supporting a child with SEN. Secondary TAs may have followed pupils with SEN as they progressed into the upper phases from primary school. All of you will have been to school, and many of you are parents with children who are at school or who have been through the system. It is tempting to think that, because of your previous experiences, you know all about how schools work. But being an employee, part of a workforce in a particular setting, does bring different perspectives, responsibilities, needs and support. All schools are different, not just because of their locations, geographical layout or phase but because of the particular gel of that group of people. Working with this group of people has similarities to working in any team or organisation, but schools also have their own legal and organisational framework, as well as developing their own ethos and culture.

Relationships between all the people concerned are most important, and even if you feel that you are only going to relate to a few pupils and one or two teachers, understanding the complexity of the whole-school community is essential to ensuring you achieve the best for those with whom you come into close contact. By the whole-school community, I mean the pupils and their parents and carers, the teachers and support staff, the governors and the local community including the visiting advisers from the various agencies associated with a school. Standard 4 has a section for working with adults and one for children, but the general principles of maintaining positive relationships are the same.

You have a responsibility to get to know who is who, who does what and when, recognising the local and national framework within which you work, but you also need to give of yourself to the people with whom you work, to make relationships that will create working partnerships, and be part of various teams – the whole-school team as well as your own TA team or curriculum support team [5.1P1]. You will need to recognise how the policies and practice of those around you affect you and how you will affect them and their work.

The good thing is that the school also has a responsibility to support you. Increasingly, senior managers and class teachers are realising that a TA does not just happen, or appear from time to time, but given the appropriate employment support and personal and professional support can become one of the most treasured resources of the school. Being supported by the school, and by participating in the various activities – in-house training, meetings, reviews and social events – you will become part of the team [5K8]. Schools work best where they are collegial, that is where people work together for a common good, each one knowing how they fit into the whole. In this way you will receive and give friendship and increase your job satisfaction. As time goes on this will become a critical friendship. This is a term used in schools to indicate professional partnerships, which not only work but are growing through the partners being able to comment appropriately on how they are working together. It does not mean you will become critical in a denigratory way of all around you, or they of you, but that you become able to take and give constructive suggestions for improvement [5K12].

The basic principles of good relationships

There are some principles that underlie good relationships whether they are professional or social, to do with friendships or the work place, whether within lifelong partnerships like marriage or a temporary job. Basically it boils down to treating others as you would like to be treated, putting yourself metaphorically in the other's shoes. Having respect for the other person or people in the relationship will show itself in things like good manners, listening when others talk, reading messages and notices, being prepared to give and take. Good manners can have a cultural side to them: for instance using 'please' in some cultures is a sign of pleading, not politeness. Good relationships are built on a sensitivity to such differences. A mutual trust has to be built up. All those concerned in a relationship are interdependent in some way even if it seems like a very power-heavy relationship. Even these need the cooperation of the participants to work or there will be anarchy. You may have rights but you also have responsibilities; you have a certain commitment even if it is short-term. Where relationships are effective, there is a mutual accountability, whether doing the asking or being asked to complete a task of some kind [5.1P3].

Simple things like punctuality, truthfulness, honesty and reliability build up the necessary trust. Be prepared to apologise and recognise your own mistakes, and try not to repeat them. Effective communication is essential in good relationships [5.1P2; 5K3]. This not only means listening, but also giving clear, appropriate and if possible unambiguous instructions or messages; even simple things like not mumbling when in doubt will help. Be explicit (politely) about needs and misunderstandings; implicit messages can be misunderstood, causing hurt or delay [4.2P3,4]. Write things down for yourself and others where you can, being as concise as possible. You will have to understand the means of communicating in your school. It may be done electronically, or by using a notice board, a newsletter, a circulating notice book or ensuring that you attend certain meetings [4.4P3,4]. Without these links you will miss vital messages about changes to routines, celebrations or items of personal interest. Ordinary conversational rules apply such as allowing others to get a word in, yet standing firm when you are sure – assertive without being aggressive. You should also be aware of body language in others and in yourself as this can communicate unease or misunderstanding. Active listening, where you pay attention to the speaker, is important especially when you role model this with children in front of the teacher [4.1P1; 4.2P1,2; 4.3P6].

Maintaining positive attitudes such as trying to see the good in people or pupils, trying to understand, smiling where you can, all help relationships to work [4K13]. Ask for things in a positive (not a negative) manner, and give instructions similarly. Try to thank people for things wherever possible, without being a 'creep'. Good relationships use systems of collaboration rather than conflict, although this does not mean always agreeing with others. Your 'yes' is only as good as your 'no', that is, only agree to do what you know you can achieve, otherwise people will not trust you. Avoid damaging conflict and unnecessary confrontation. Aggression and attention-seeking do not get the same results as cooperation [4K8]. If you have a problem, share it and do not let it fester. If in doubt, ask [4.2P5; 4.4P5].

In organisations, there will be some kind of leadership. This may reside in one person, who then delegates down through a largely hierarchical network, or it can be a flatter organisation where more people take collaborative decisions. You will need to find out how your school operates. Historically schools have been hierarchical, with a head teacher, a deputy, a senior management team, teachers and the support staff, but many schools have tried to share leadership, giving responsibilities to others. In all relationships, there are roles and some kind of rules, whether written or not. Collaborative cultures do take more effort on the part of everyone in them, but have been found to produce more effective organisations. They prevent fragmentation of jobs and duplication, and thus have a beneficial effect on the pupils.

Think of a hotel or a shop that you know quite well where you feel well served.

- Do they know to whom to go if they cannot answer your query?
- Do they seem sure of their own role?
- Can they direct you to the appropriate service if they are busy?
- Do the staff know what other people on the staff do?
- Are they polite, interested in their job and in you?
- Why do you go back to that establishment?

The important relationships in a school

There are various professional relationships of which you will become part once you start working in the school. Being a professional may be a new concept to you. It is important that you do not treat colleagues as you would a friend or member of your family, particularly at first. You may have been working in a playgroup, where the children call you by your first name and treat you like an auntie or uncle. The people you worked with may well have been your neighbours or people you met in the antenatal class. The tendency with friends is to chat while on the job, make excuses for mistakes and take things for granted because you know them well. Once working in a school certain things will be expected of you in your relationships. You should not chat on the job, you should always try to carry out tasks to the best of your ability, and you should be reliable and punctual. You must be very careful what you discuss about what goes on in the school outside with friends or family [4K11]. Forming relationships with pupils and adults is like taking one step back from familiarity. This does not mean you are cold, withdrawn or stand-offish. Nor does it mean you do not make friendships with any school staff which continue out of school. It is about maintaining a balance, being friendly and approachable even to those people you may dislike – and there could be some [4.4P1].

Think of various places where you have contact with others in a professional capacity

- *A supermarket* Do you like it when: the cashier talks to her colleague and not to you? The shelf stackers get in the way of your trolley and think their job is more important? Customer services promises to ring you back about a query and never does?

- *A hotel* Do you like it when: the receptionist chats to each customer so long that you are kept waiting? The waiter is careless with serving? The bill is incorrect and the discussion with the manager about it takes place in front of everyone else?

- *A hospital* Do you like it when: the receptionist cannot find your paperwork? The machine operative turns up late after lunch? The equipment the doctor needs is not clean or readily available, and you have to wait while they sort it out? You feel the staff may be laughing at your condition?

- *A shop* Do you like it when: staff training about using a credit card to pay for goods takes place in front of you, on the job? Order promises are not kept? The assistant asks you irrelevant personal questions?

- Can you think of similar situations in your school, and how you could and should behave in the various circumstances?

Working closely with individual or small groups of pupils [4.1 and 4.3]

You will be given a few pupils or possibly even one with whom the school want you to work particularly. The relationship with them is crucial.

This is not a parent–child relationship although at times it may come to feel like it, especially where the pupil is physically impaired to the extent that you have to perform some intimate tasks for them [2K11.3]. It must remain professional without becoming distant. One TA described their aim as 'to do myself out of a job'. Hopefully as the pupils get older and more mature, they will be able to do more and more for themselves. This immediately means that you will need advice about how far you go in supporting that pupil, how it is best for you to intervene and when to stand back, what to do with your time if you are standing back, whom you tell if things change, what your relationships to the pupils' parents are and so on [4.1P3]. It means you need to know what the teacher's intentions are for that pupil; what you should do if things get out of hand – what the policy is for managing difficult behaviour; what you do if the pupil tells you things that worry you – what is the child protection policy; what to do if the pupil cannot do the task to which you have been allotted – what is the SEN policy; and whom you can talk to about the whole situation – the confidentiality policy [4K11].

An example of a good working relationship with a pupil

Sandra, a TA in a primary school, had been appointed to look after Jo, a child starting school, who was still not fully toilet-trained. Jo also had some learning problems and had been slow in reaching most of his physical development milestones. Both his parents were agreed they wanted him to go to the local mainstream school, and had sought help early from the local authority. Sandra talked with Jo when he first came into school and met his mother to find out about how she dealt with the toilet-training. She made sure that Jo knew how he could attract her attention if she was not working

PHOTOGRAPH 3.1 Working with an individual

PHOTOGRAPH 3.2 Working with a small group

alongside him, should he feel the need of her help. She agreed these signals with his class teacher. When in class with Jo, Sandra did many other tasks for the teacher with other children, but kept to a regular timetable with Jo, again agreed with his teacher. At these times, she and Jo departed quietly for the toilet area. During this time, whatever Jo's physical needs, she talked with him about his interests both in and out of school and listened to him. She let him return to class on his own, to help him keep his sense of self-esteem. She used the same language as his mother for bodily parts and functions and she kept a 'weather ear' open in class and in the playground to see if the other children were ever 'taking the Mickey' out of him or surreptitiously bullying him. She praised his successes in the training routines and ignored the failures, but dealt with them quietly and appropriately. Her aim was to gain Jo's confidence, yet create as much independence for him as possible. She needed to balance his need for adult help with his need to retain self-respect, especially in front of his friends and peers.

When you have a new pupil to work with of whatever age:

- Use the first name by which he or she wishes to be known.

- Make sure they know your name in school. This should be your title (Mr, Mrs or Miss) and your family name.

- It is preferable to have pupils use this name, not your first name or 'Miss'/'Sir'. If the norm is for the teachers to be addressed in this way, discuss the issue politely with your line manager or a senior manager. Mutual self-respect in using names like this helps keep the relationship on a professional yet familiar footing [4.4P1].

- Find out from the teachers why you have been assigned to the pupil.

- Talk with the pupil away from the classroom about your role, be open about what you aim to do, and help them be open with you about their likes and dislikes [4.1P5].

- Always try to let them do something for themselves.

- Praise where praise is due; do not give empty praise, they always know.

- Always treat them with respect, yet ensure you follow the school guidelines for behaviour management and other relevant policies. Just because you may be working with them on a one-to-one basis is no excuse for different rules.

- Keep in close communication with the class teachers and specialist teachers who introduced the pupil to you in the first place so that you know what you are supposed to be doing, why, and whom to tell if circumstances change [1K8; 4K12].

If you are working with children or young people on your own and are likely to be out of sight of other adults, do make sure you are aware of the school policy on child protection. You could be putting yourself into a vulnerable position where one of the children could make a false accusation against you. Most school policies in this area will recommend that you always work in sight of another adult. This is particularly important if you are in caring mode looking after a child who needs any kind of intimate help such as changing wet knickers. There is more about this subject in Chapter 6.

One of the problems – or it can be a joy – of working at a school near where you live is that you will meet pupils out of school hours. Younger pupils, usually accompanied by a familiar adult, will greet you like a long-lost friend, introduce you to whoever they are with and want to chat. While this can be endearing, it can be a trial if the child becomes too familiar with you or becomes clinging or creates a jealousy within a carer, particularly if it is the mother who has found the child difficult to handle. Older pupils may do the opposite and pretend, particularly if they are with their peers, that they do not know you. If there is a problem, share it with the pupil when you are next in a quiet place together in school and ask how you can best resolve it together [4.3P4].

Another thing to watch out for is becoming too fond of your charge [5K7]. This may not be a problem, but it could prevent you wanting to hand over responsibility for them to another TA or seeing them move from your care in a primary school to a secondary school. This is where there is a clear difference between the kind of care you can give and that of a parent. You need to be able to let go if appropriate, and move on. Sometimes this bond can be long lasting as well as quite professional, and can blossom into genuine friendship in later life outside school, with you becoming a surrogate aunt or uncle, but this is infrequent. Where the TA has moved from working in the local playgroup to working in school as their own children get older, some of the children show considerable familiarity. While this may seem like forging good relationships, it is really too cosy for school, and you need to create just a little more distance and professionalism.

It is tempting to think that being with children in school is all about telling them things so that they will learn. This should not be so. Unless the child or young person gets their mind actively engaged in the subject matter, whether from the spoken word, writing or an electronic source, it will be like Muzak in a supermarket or wallpaper – there but not received, eaten but not digested. It is a large part of your role to ensure that you 'charges' understand what is being said and can use it for future reference. The main way you do this is by asking open questions and being an active listener to the answers [4.1P2,3,6; 4K1]. If their answers do not make sense you will know that either they do not understand or they do not have the words to communicate their understanding to anyone else [2K10,14; 2K11.11; 2K12.8; 2K13.7,8]. Open questions are ones where you do not give the answer in the question. 'What stories do you like?' is likely to get a more honest answer than 'Did you like this story?'. 'What did the teacher tell us to do?' will find out about understanding better than a jollying along 'Let's go and make that model'. It may take time to gain a child's confidence so that they will talk to you and with you, so be patient. There are also non-verbal ways of communicating: for example, drawings or acting out in role play may give you clues to understanding your 'charge' [2K10.4; 4.3P1–6].

Your speech should be clear and accurate, because otherwise you might communicate incorrectly [4.3P1]. You also need to think about the vocabulary you use. This is not just about using simpler words with younger children but about using correct vocabulary in subjects like mathematics and science. You might have to do a little bit of homework here to make sure you know what the teacher is on about. If in doubt ask for guidance. It is better to 'talk straight,' but simply, with young children if they ask questions. This can be a bit daunting as the questions can sometimes be quite searching – like 'what happens when you die?' and the classic 'where do babies come from?' Do not go into great detail, be honest and make sure you know the school policies for things like sex education and religious education. When hearing children read, it is worth checking that they understand the vocabulary. If the children tell you anything that worries you or that you think the teacher should know – like parents separating, a grandparent dying – then do ensure the teacher is aware of it. There is more about children revealing sensitive topics in the Child Protection section of Chapter 6. Children value honesty and are much more likely to be cooperative with you if they sense you are both listening and interested. Again, writing or drawing might be a way they can express their feelings. If the child can share their interests and preferences with you, you have a great way in to support their needs [4.3P2–5].

Pupils of all ages are also more cooperative if they think they are in charge. Many of the performance criteria talk of using the language of choice. It avoids many potential conflict situations if children can feel they have chosen, and not just been directed to the one and only option against which they can rebel. Another theme that appears is that of considering the rights of the child. We all have rights, children included, and one is to be consulted where possible. Clearly, it is not an option just to refuse to do what the teacher wants. Take time to make sure first that the pupils understand the task that is to be done and if possible why it has to be done, then try to split the task up into parts. Then give them a choice of which bit to do first, or a choice of where it could be done, or what kind of paper to use. This technique of questioning and giving choice is most valuable when catching a pupil doing something they shouldn't. Instead of just saying 'Don't do that!' you can ask 'What do you think you are doing?', probably in a loudish tone of voice. You can explain why it is not a good idea – to run at great speed through the school, say. If the miscreant argues, you can give them options: 'Either slow down in future or you will hurt someone' and 'Either slow down in future or I will report you'. We all also have responsibilities and one of yours as a member of staff is to act as a good parent and prevent accidents or confrontation where possible. There will be times when the adult knows best and has to insist for the sake of safety.

Partnership with teachers

Whatever you do in school should be done under the direction of a qualified teacher. The status conferred on them by their qualifications means taking responsibility for the learning of pupils whether in a class or a subject. This responsibility includes managing other adults in the classroom to support that learning. However, you will often find yourself doing tasks that include teaching or working with a small group out of the sight of the class teacher. Whatever the situation, that teacher still takes responsibility for the progress of the pupils and for ensuring that your role with them is as effective as possible. This can create tensions with the teacher; either you feel underused or you are given more responsibility than you feel comfortable with [1K2].

The secret lies in the relationship with the teacher. It has to be a professional partnership, with good communication and a clear understanding of the boundaries within which you operate [5K7]. This means being explicit about how things are working, not accepting the implicit. Either you or the teacher may be wrong in making assumptions about situations. Once a good working relationship is established, with lines of communication, you may not need to meet daily or to plan specific tasks.

You will find, even in the same school, that each teacher has their own foibles, and you as a TA are likely to work with several in a week or possibly even in a day. Many schools have realised that allowing the teacher and TA continuous time together, even in some cases allocating one TA per class in a primary school, has a beneficial effect on working relationships. On the other hand, varied experiences and working with different adults can increase your understanding of the different ways of tackling similar problems, giving you a range of ideas of how to operate [5.1P1].

Whatever teacher you work with, you not only need time out of the classroom to make some sort of contact before turning up in their room, you need regular non-pupil contact time to plan together and where possible to exchange feedback [1 K1,12]. You will also need time to prepare any resources requested of you.

This may be possible during the introduction time in the lesson or the plenary (the summing up) time or in assemblies. STL 1, in its glossary, refers to planning and feedback as part of the classroom process and also refers to potential barriers to providing required support. The difficult thing may be to negotiate payment for time with the teacher without pupils present and additional preparation time. Traditionally TAs have given freely of their own time, but this is not good enough: the school managers are getting something for nothing and are really exploiting TAs' good nature and love of the job. You can see that negotiating this with senior managers could be very difficult. School budgets are tight, but you will be paid half to a third the salaries of the teachers – 'less than a shelf stacker in a supermarket' in some cases, as well as being hourly paid which teachers are not. Research has shown that unless you do have this joint planning time, your time is less well spent. If you are reading

PHOTOGRAPH 3.3 Preparing resources with the guidance of a teacher

this book before getting a job, try making it a condition of acceptance that you get some paid non-pupil contact time with the teachers you work with. If you are established, you really should try to renegotiate your contractual times. Moving your day by 15 minutes to give you time before the morning sessions and then allowing you to leave 15 minutes earlier from a lesson could make all the difference to the teaching and learning experiences you are involved with and would cost the school nothing. Secondary TAs, expected to stay with a certain pupil and go to many different lessons with different teachers, have a real problem, but really, just turning up as if you were an extra pupil, a minder, is not good enough. There is much more about this professional side of the relationship in Chapter 8.

Relationships take time and thought; they do not just happen, particularly if two people who are put together to work have little else in common. It is important that you take time to talk with and listen to the teachers you work with, spend out-of-class contact time with them, if only in the corridor on the way to or leaving a lesson. Normal chat about the weather, families, homes or hobbies can cement relationships and prove to each partner that the other is human. The school should allow you to use the same staffroom as the teachers, and this is rarely a problem now. Similarly, cloakrooms, toilet areas, car parks, all provide common ground for beginning conversations.

An example of a good relationship with a teacher

TA Kati is working in a secondary school, particularly employed to support Hassan who has learning needs. Kati is line-managed by the SENCO, and has met regularly with her and the team. She is clear about her tasks with Hassan, and attends most lessons with him. She is particularly interested in English, partly through her own interest in the subject, but also because of Hassan's learning problems. His reading and writing skills are behind where they should be, although his spoken English is fluent and extensive. After English lessons she had walked with John, the teacher, to the staffroom and got into conversation with him about how best to help Hassan. Her own love of language has come out in the conversations, and John has lent her books – both fiction which extends her own reading range, and non-fiction about the teaching of reading and writing to those with Hassan's needs. John encouraged Kati to go to the local FE college to take her A-level English, something she had not contemplated previously, leaving school at 16. Kati was able to recommend a local playgroup for John's growing family. When they both attended a course on partnership, they talked of Kati's support during a stressful Ofsted inspection and John's career advice. Kati was beginning to consider that she may go on to train as a teacher.

When starting with a new teacher, a simple checklist may be useful.

Some questions you could ask before going into a different teacher's classroom are:

- What do you particularly want me to do?
- What do I do if a pupil in your room asks to go to the toilet?
- Can I write in any pupils' books?
- What contact with parents or carers do you expect of the TA?
- Do you want me to attend consultation evenings?
- Do I take part in SEN reviews?
- Can I do anything at the request of a parent, such as change a child's reading book or search for lost equipment?
- Can I tidy the rooms? Your desks? The resources area?
- Is there anything you do not want me to do?

(Watkinson 2002: 63)

Working as a support staff member, part of a whole-school team

You will be part of a team of adults who have all sorts of roles and responsibilities. This is quite different from being a member of a class at school, where you all seemed to be part of a group with the teacher on the opposite side. Nor do schools work like offices or factories, where each has a role, and often what people do in one part of the organisation has little apparent meaning or effect on others. Even in a large secondary school, where the teaching staff alone can number 100 people, and support staff at least that again, the efficiency and effectiveness for the pupils is better where these people work as a team [5.1P4; 5K8].

Various teams make up the whole-school team: there may be teachers and support staff as two, or various support staff perhaps in teams like midday assistants (MDAs), cleaners, TAs and others. But TAs can be MDAs and so dividing lines are not necessarily clear-cut. Sometimes people have drawn images of schools as a ship, with a captain, crew, passengers and so on, sometimes as a garden centre where different plants can grow, needing different cultivation conditions and methods, or as a stage with actors out front and with backstage hands supporting their work. In the past, schools were often staffed according to a strict pupil–teacher formula and the teaching staff were apparently all that counted when head teachers referred to 'their staff'. This culture is passing and there is much greater recognition that all staff have a role to play and that their effectiveness influences that of other members of staff. The Workforce Remodelling initiative has helped that process enormously. As a member of the support staff team, it is important that you play your part; you provide the foundation on which the teachers can lean.

In order to make the whole staff operate as a team, some schools even go to the length of making everyone go on a 'team-building exercise' such as one sometimes sees in advertisements or films. More make it explicit that operating as a team is important, and a few just

PHOTOGRAPH 3.4 Support staff working together

ignore it. Teams need every member to play a part, to know when to put themselves forward for tasks and when to take instructions from others [5.1P5; 5K6]. This takes thought and sometimes patience or initiative. It will be for you to be sensitive and to judge how best you can be a team member in your school. This means you need to know where you fit in in any hierarchy, who does what and when, how the systems and structures of your school work for communication and consultation. You need to try to put as many faces to names as possible, and get to know them when you can. Go to meetings, join in discussions, participate in the staffroom chat. Do join in events and social occasions when you can, which will be in your own unpaid time. Even going to school fêtes or bazaars can help you find a place, showing you want to cooperate, to belong to the school.

Watching a team working in sport or planning an event, you can see how roles develop. Somebody will probably be a leader, some seem just followers, even sleeping partners. Some apparently quiet people turn out to be the reliable ones who do the tasks others have set, and do them conscientiously and without complaining; others make a lot of fuss, yet rarely achieve the aims of the group; some are good at ideas but awful at carrying them out; some can be bossy; and some are quite content to 'go with the flow'. An ideal team person can listen, yet contribute when they have something to say or do, and help others achieve their tasks. What are you?

Relationships with other stakeholders

The governors also form a team, and staff should be represented on that team. Parents and carers form another, although staff can also be parents of children at the school.

It is hoped that the community surrounding the school is also to be seen as a stakeholder: the shopkeepers or other employers; the religious leaders; the parish or district council; the

PHOTOGRAPH 3.5 Communication with parents

playgroup or pensioners' organisation and other clubs or interest groups may all have an interest in relating to the local school and the school to them. It is likely that part of your job may be to contact members of these other teams and you may already know them well as it is likely that you come from the local community. More support staff than teachers usually do. However, if you are wearing your TA hat, as a member of the school team, you must remember to act like one, act professionally, remembering that what goes on in school is confidential unless there is a need to know. You do not share gossip or opinions on staff or children, however tempting it may be to do so.

Being part of a TA team

With the development of locally negotiated pay scales for support staff (sometimes referred to as single status agreements), recognised levels of status for TAs have become possible. Thus there are often senior TAs in a school, even a small primary school. The advent of the HLTAs has reinforced this concept and for many HLTAs the role of team leader is part of their job description. Secondary schools have developed the idea of TA teams more fully, often making curriculum teams or year teams: you may be working with a technician, such as in science, design and technology (DT) or ICT. Most primary schools have more than one TA, even in the smallest schools, so you are likely to be part of such a group. This itself is a team. You will be doing similar types of jobs although likely to be with different pupils or age groups or, in secondary schools, possibly supporting different curriculum areas. This means you can form relationships with people who may have similar problems and joys to yourself and probably similar training needs, at least where supporting your particular school is concerned.

You may have totally different backgrounds or qualifications but you will all be part of your school team.

PHOTOGRAPH 3.6   Two TAs working together

Thus training together for new initiatives within the school makes sense. This may mean sharing resources and ideas, or even just being there for each other if personal things get a bit tough. You can support your colleagues and be supported by them. By training and meeting together as a team you are part of the learning community which is a school [5.1P6].

Working with teams which include people from other organisations or agencies

Basically this is no different from working with any other adult. The people involved in schools are therapists such as speech, physio-, psycho-, music or occupational therapists [STL 14]; consultants from the LA such as the curriculum consultants or specialist teachers; educational psychologists; possibly social workers, education welfare officers or even the police and possibly Ofsted inspectors. It is unlikely in the first instance that you will be alone with such people: you will be in a supporting role to a class teacher or the SEN coordinator (SENCO). Listen, ask about what you do not understand and remember what things are relevant to the situation. You may have kept records in a notebook or on a form. If possible, talk with the appropriate teacher beforehand about the purpose of the meeting and your role in it, and check what records you can share with anyone from outside the school. This is not likely to be a problem as the person has come to help.

Other visitors might be researchers or similar people from the local authority on fact-finding missions, but you should be fully briefed before talking with such people as to their role and yours in the particular circumstances.

As the ECM (*Every Child Matters*, discussed in the next chapter) agenda gets bedded in you will be more involved with such people: one of the main issues is about adults from different agencies working together on behalf of the child. If you work in a special school or a special unit attached to a mainstream school, there will be many visitors of this kind. In some areas there are multi-agency groups already in place, called TASCC (teams around schools, children and community), but these are still in their infancy and still have teething problems.

Roles and responsibilities

Ethical expectations

It is expected that you as an employee will abide by the expectations outlined in the handbook list given in Chapter 2. If there is a dress code, there will be a reason for it. Sometimes it will be for your safety, sometimes it is to reinforce the ethos of the school. It may be, for instance, that the school considers that respect and tidiness in staff set standards and provide a role model for pupils. All adults in a school offer a role model in their dress and behaviour as to how pupils can and should behave, and what being an adult is like.

The whole question of ethos is a difficult one to grasp; it is not often explicit, except in some religious schools, but it is about the climate and tone the school is trying to promote. It will include things like respect for individuals, expectations of behaviour, positive attitudes towards each other and the appropriate use of praise, a sense of identity and pride in the school, a recognition of the importance of the environment, effective communications and relationships, and a willingness to be involved in voluntary activities on behalf of the school. None of these are legal or organisational requirements, but they go to making the school a better place to be, and in which to learn.

Along with ethos goes the principle of quality. You should give of your best to provide the best kind of environment for learning to enable both pupils and other adults to give of their best. Personal qualities such as honesty and trust are required. For instance, if you are asked to pass on a message from a teacher to the office staff, this should be done promptly and accurately, yet recognising when is an appropriate moment to do it. An office in which there is a visiting parent is not the place to announce the particular need for support of another pupil. Written notes should be treated as written records, and should be accurate, concise, dated and legible, and treated as a confidential document unless you know otherwise. If you want to be treated as an equal you must ensure that you give the pupils you work with equal opportunities to succeed, not favouring one over another. This does not mean you give them all equal time or the same task or the same resources – the crucial word is 'opportunity'.

This principle leads to that of inclusion. It has been found that many pupils with SEN succeed better when they are included in the curriculum provided for pupils with fewer needs, so long as specialist provision is made for special needs where this takes place. How those needs are met does not necessarily mean withdrawal from mainstream classrooms or mainstream schools. Nor do statements like the above mean that there should be no withdrawal from classes and no special schools. It means that segregation socially or educationally needs to be considered seriously as to whether it is providing the best for the pupils and giving them an equal opportunity to succeed in a variety of contexts [1K3].

Another principle that underpins practice in schools is that of celebrating diversity. We are lucky in many of our schools to have pupils from many backgrounds and many cultures, thus opening up the opportunity for sharing and richness that is not otherwise easily available. Pupils in a predominantly white area may have seen establishments such as 'take-aways' in the shopping precinct as the only differences around. They will not have the opportunity to see the richly patterned fabrics of saris or hear music on African instruments, to see the interesting formations of Chinese or Arabic scripts in books or on buildings unless staff make arrangements for them to do so. Pupils in wheelchairs could be the best artists in the class, and one having difficulty in reading could be the best footballer. Working in a school means being on the lookout to see opportunities for enjoyment in everything around you, and sharing them with others.

Enquire what ethnic mix comes to your school.

- Are different languages spoken at home or in the school?

- What books are available in the school to show different cultures and ways of life?

- Are there books that show people with disabilities as heroes?

- What resources in terms of musical instruments, fabrics, pictures or artefacts does the school have?

- What recorded music is played in the school and is only Western art displayed on the walls?

- What facilities are there to accommodate differences in dress worn for cultural reasons – head covering for girls or turbans for boys?

- What is the ethnic or linguistic mix of staff?

- What relationships does the school have with the local community organisations, churches or other places of worship?

- What advisers or resources outside the school are available to the school to support understanding of multi-cultural diversity?

Some schools have what is called a 'vision statement', which is a way of explicitly recognising what the school stands for in as succinct a way as possible. This will appear in the school's prospectus and other significant documentation. Some schools even set out the vision on the wall near the entrance. Whether the vision is set out in this explicit way or not, all schools have aims about their purpose. These will usually include statements about high expectations in academic terms, about pupils' achievements, sometimes standards of behaviour or other aspects of the ethos mentioned above. When you join a school staff, you are, in a manner of speaking, 'signing up' to these expectations. Sometimes there are opportunities to discuss the statements or even to revise them, and as a member of staff you would be expected to contribute to such discussion.

Following these written or unwritten principles shows that you are, as an employee of the school, a professional. This means that you will do what is required to the best of your ability, developing your skills, knowledge and understanding to improve where you can. It may mean, while you are at work, putting personal problems to one side, even acting a part to cover up your feelings. If there is a problem that you cannot cope with, then you must tell someone about it, so early on you need to know who your line manager is. It shows that you are committed to your job.

It can happen that with all the policies and goodwill in the world, things can go wrong for you in your working relationships in school. You need to be able to handle this appropriately. One of the school's policies, the *Discipline and grievance policy*, will cover the formal way of dealing with such a problem but hopefully you never have to use this or have it used against you. There may be people you do not like, but you can do little about this in a work situation. If such a personal feeling does interfere with your work – say something has happened outside school with one of your children or a spouse or partner, which makes working relationships impossible – tell your line manager in confidence. It should be possible for timetables to be adjusted.

Difficult situations

The same would apply to your finding out about dishonesty, or even malpractice of any kind – tell your line manager and let a senior colleague deal with it. If you feel you are a victim of unfairness, always try the line manager route first, and failing that, speak to a deputy head or even to the head. Formal written complaints should not be necessary. If it does come to formalities, you would be very wise to join a union and consult its staff before embarking on such a procedure, and making sure you have their representative, or another colleague whom you can trust, present with you at any meetings. Keep copies of any written communication.

Such occurrences are so rare and inevitably sensitive that there may be support networks, resources and people who can help you to deal with improving work relationships [4K10; 5.1P7]. If this area worries you at all, make sure you mention it at an early opportunity to a mentor, someone with whom you can share your fears, but who is more experienced in the ways of the school. Most of the difficult situations which you will encounter in school will be due to problems with relationships. Pupils' problems usually can be traced to their problems with each other or their families, making life hard to cope with. Managing challenging behaviour by adults is much easier where normal relationships between adults and pupils in the school are good.

Remember that by the time you have completed an induction year, you will be much more knowledgeable and experienced, and could offer support to others coming to the job after you. Make the opportunity in any job review to discuss the other person's perception of how you are fitting into the school, and add a few notes of their comments to your evidence file.

The school structures, systems and procedures that you need to know and understand

Induction

HOPEFULLY YOUR SCHOOL will have provided a proper induction for you. At some point they may have sent you on the Department for Children, Families and Schools (DCFS) induction course mentioned in Chapter 2 as well. This chapter is about items 5 and 6 from the list, all the documents you need to look at and understand, how the legal framework in which you work affects your school and you. Hopefully someone will have been appointed to be your mentor and their understanding of how the school works will be invaluable.

Your role and responsibilities

You have to get to grips with your legal and organisational responsibilities [1K2]. You do have rights as an employee, but rights always bring responsibilities. It is likely that the organisational ones respecting your school will be your first practical priority, but all schools have to operate within a legal framework, so that will be dealt with first.

Legal framework

Acts of Parliament define the laws of our country, and the case histories, that is what goes on in the law courts, define how those laws should be interpreted. These laws and legal precedents can affect your human rights as a person, your employee rights and restrictions, and your health and safety. The Children Acts affect how you behave with the pupils in the school. Education Acts determine what is to be taught, even at times how it should be taught, and, although not in this country, when it should be taught in terms of daily or weekly routines. Recommendations are made about the ages at which things are best taught, and tests and inspections are set out to ensure that this happens, although school staff recognise that children learn at different paces and in different ways. Codes of practice, along with the DCFS and TDA publications, also give guidance, but their implementation has to be tested by the courts. Some other Acts also impinge on schools such as the Data Protection Act or Health and Safety at Work Acts.

You do not need to know these legalities in detail, except for STL 13K7 and 14K1-4 which do require some in-depth understanding of the legalities involved in dealing with specific disabilities. However, you do need to recognise that sometimes what seems an unnecessary procedure in school is actually done because the law states it shall be so and the school or you could be sued if you contravene the legality [3K2,25]. You can always question (politely) if you feel something is not appropriate; there are sometimes misinterpretations of the law or misunderstandings [3K3;15.1P8; 15K13]. This can be the case in some of the safety procedures; some can be based on assumptions or hearsay, not on fact.

But if in doubt, do what the teacher asks. Theirs is the final responsibility for the pupils in their class.

Health and safety will affect every aspect of your work. It covers things like buildings and maintenance work within the school. Say you slipped on a newly polished floor and injured yourself on a projecting door catch, both of which should have been observed by the site manager or a health and safety officer (all schools have one), the school would be liable. If you are wearing unsuitable clothes for your job – high heels in a PE lesson, or no eye shields when requested in a science lesson – you would be liable. It is up to all employees to inform someone appropriate if they see a potential hazard such as a tile coming loose or a hinge without screws. Some schools have a system, a book into which such observations can be entered, then someone responsible can initial and date when the item has been repaired or replaced. All the accident prevention, first aid and security procedures of the school will come under this heading and some are inspected by outside agencies such as the fire service. As an employee you must familiarise yourself with these procedures early on; for details see later in the chapter [3K13,15,16,19].

You should read the glossary of terms for STL 3 carefully. It defines meanings of hazards (something to cause harm), risk (the seriousness of a hazard and its likeliness to cause harm), procedures (things you must follow) and practices (routines). The introduction to this unit clearly states: 'You have day to day responsibility for maintaining a safe environment, contributing to the safety, safeguarding and protection of children/young people and ensuring risks and hazards are dealt with and reported promptly according to procedures' (TDA 2007) STL3:1. There are 25 knowledge statements in this unit, and their high number gives you some indication of its importance and depth.

The Children Acts followed some high-profile child abuse cases. The impact of these Acts is clear in school when people refer to the ECM (*Every Child Matters*) agenda, first published in a Green Paper (Clarke, Boateng, and Hodge 2003). This major initiative is going to have significant effects on the way schools relate to all the other children's services – health, police and social services for a start. It is an attempt both to ensure that children's care in the widest sense of the word matters, but also to ensure that there is joined-up thinking and that children do not fall between the nets of education, care, protection and medical provision. Most local authorities have reorganised their education and part of their social services departments under one umbrella – children's services. Health does not come under the local authority charge, so joint working is less easy to organise, but in some areas some exciting centres have been established with professionals from all the relevant disciplines working under one roof to provide support and care for children and young people, and all schools are required to make local links as strongly as possible.

In schools the ECM agenda is high-profile, and is underpinning attitudes to the formal curriculum – emotional and social well-being makes a difference to how a child learns.

The aims in the Green Paper were to achieve the outcomes that matter most to children and young people:

Being healthy: enjoying good mental and physical health and living a healthy lifestyle

Staying safe: being protected from harm and neglect

Enjoying and achieving: getting the most out of life and developing the skills of adulthood

Making a positive contribution: being involved with the community and society and not engaging in anti-social or offending behaviour

Economic well-being: not being prevented by economic disadvantage from achieving their full potential in life.

You can see this language reflected throughout the new standards, and particularly in STL 3.

Schools are *in loco parentis* (acting in place of a parent) for the time the children are in school. The ECM agenda covers how you treat children who are not your own, and your knowledge of any problem there might be out of school. As someone working closely, and sometimes intimately, with children and young people, you will need to pay close attention to the policies and procedures which affect you – more of these in the next chapter.

The Education Acts cover such areas in state-funded schools as the implementation of the National Curriculum (NC), the Local Management of Schools (LMS), inspection by Her Majesty's Inspectorate (HMI) and the Office for Standards in Education (Ofsted), and the assessment procedures for pupils. The Literacy and Numeracy Strategies (LNS) and the Strategy for Key Stage 3 are not 'statutory', that is set up by Acts of Parliament, but schools when inspected would be expected to have implemented them or show their consultation with the Local Authority (LA) as to why their school has opted out. The Code of Practice for Special Educational Needs (SEN) (DfES 2001) is guidance issued to enable the best practice to be followed to implement an Education Act (1996). The most recent Education Act (2003) brought about changes to teachers' working hours and practices, some of which have meant employing more TAs (DfES 2003c). The Workforce Remodelling exercise was to encourage the best use of support staff in support teaching and learning in schools, and the act provided the regulations.

Organisational procedures

Many of these are set up so that the school can fulfil its legal obligations; others are just to make the school run more smoothly for all concerned. Some are there simply because whoever set them up felt they would give the school certain characteristics which they wished to preserve for the school.

While you have to have a contract, job descriptions are not legally required but they are essential if everyone is to be clear about what their job is and how they are to do it. Similarly, appraisals are legally required only for teachers, but equal opportunities and good practice recommend that *all* employees have the right to at least an annual review of their job description and some kind of review of the way they are doing the job. When you are appointed, do enquire about both of these. Most TAs become concerned about their pay and conditions of work. While these have improved, particularly the latter in the last few years, there is still a way to go. These are currently down to your local management. Local pay scales will have been determined by your LA, and may well be determined nationally during 2008, but where you are put on the scale is a decision of your school's management, preferably with some kind of reference to your job requirements, responsibilities and capability to do the job. This may or may not include qualifications that you have. Your annual review should also include an element of reviewing your needs for professional development. All employees should have access to continuous professional development (CPD) both to increase their personal effectiveness and to ensure that the needs of the school are being met.

In order that you know what the various procedures are for your school, many schools produce a handbook with all procedures laid out. Often the procedures are different for teachers and support staff, as support staff do not need the curriculum details required by teachers.

The school handbook

If there is not one, do check that you have the following information. You should have details of:

- The organisational structure of the school
- The roles and responsibilities of others

- Line management and staff support systems
- The expectations that the school has regarding your behaviour and dress
- The procedures to implement the legal requirements outlined above, especially for
  - health and safety
  - fire and accident procedures
  - first aid and security
  - grievance and complaints procedures
- Relevant policies – see below
- Communication systems
- Timetables and time allocations for planning, attendance at school events etc.
- Your roles and responsibilities including the limitations of your role.

Much of the above sounds a bit mechanistic, but life in any organisation depends much more on the people in it. That is why many schools now look at the processes involved in becoming Investors in People (IiP). Not so many schools actually go for the formal recognition. It is worth asking whether the school in which you work has this award and what it means to them, or if they have considered it. Whichever way it is, the relationships between the people in the school and their understanding of its aims and policies will affect the way in which you work and how effective you can be in your job. Take advantage of such support, and ensure you carry out your job description with all its associated responsibilities.

Your personal equipment

In addition to wearing the right clothes for the purpose for which you are employed, you might like to consider equipping yourself with some of the following items. A small plastic stacker box, a toolbox with a lid or one of the open ones with a handle might be useful to carry them about the school. The school may help with providing some of the items.

A TA kit could consist of:

- Several sharp pencils
- Pencil sharpener
- Soft toilet roll or box of tissues
- Sellotape
- Ruler – the clear plastic ones are very useful
- Red, black and blue biros
- Stapler
- Hole punch
- Scrap paper for pupils to try out spellings on or make notes on
- Small memo pad
- Small and large pairs of scissors
- Two rubbers
- Paperclips
- Card folder to keep your papers in
- Clipboard with timetable and any planning sheets.

You will soon find you are carrying children's work around, and odd books as well, and even a laptop, so a large strong carrying bag or box will also be useful. Some general TA books may already be available in your school and are worth dipping into as well as using this one. The David Fulton Publishers list, now available through Routledge, includes many titles, some directly written for TAs and others for specific special needs like Down's Syndrome or Asperger's Syndrome. Look on the Routledge website for titles or ask your SENCO for ideas.

Policies

In order to maintain consistency across the school, the school staff develop policies. Most of the elements of the National Occupational Standards (NOS) refer to knowing the school policy in the area being described. Some of these are legal requirements, like having a policy on sex education, others are guidance on procedures like behaviour management, and others are there to safeguard the school against allegations of unfairness. If parents send their children to a school where a certain policy is in place, say for dealing with bullying, and then complain about what happens, if that incident was dealt with according to the policy laid down, the parents have no grounds for complaint. They can still lobby for change, but not blame the school for dealing with the incident in the way laid down by the policy. Policies are to ensure that pupils and staff are treated the same. No member of staff can complain, 'It is no good me telling them not to slide down the banisters if the deputy head does not check them!'

You must ensure that you are given copies of the most important policies which will cover areas of your work, and that you know where you can see copies of all the others [15.4P3]. The whole collection will be considerable and you will not need many of these. The possible content of and implications for some general ones are discussed below, and others concerning pupils, teaching or the curriculum are discussed in the later chapters. You will need to discuss these with your mentor or line manager, particularly where they refer to the methods to be used. Annotate your copies with a highlighter and notes as to where items especially apply to you.

The essential policies for TAs

- Any vision statement for the school or statement of faith or principles set out by the school
- Health and safety which covers:
    - General and school
    - Health and hygiene
    - Safety and security
    - Child protection
- Behaviour management which covers:
    - What constitutes 'bad' behaviour
    - Rewards and sanctions
    - Supervision
    - Restraint procedures
- SEN which covers:
    - Individual Education Plans
    - Inclusion and access [1K3, 13K1,6–8]
    - Independent learning
- Any TA policy or support staff policy

- Any employee policy covering items such as:
  - Pay, performance review, consultation
  - Discipline and grievance
- Teaching and learning – general principles
- Equal opportunities, dealing with discrimination and celebrating diversity which includes:
  - Dealing with racism
  - Multiculturalism [1K3]
- Curriculum areas or aspects that you support in depth, e.g. English, mathematics, English as an additional language (EAL) [6K1; 8K1; 11K1].

It is up to you to familiarise yourself with the relevant documents, to ask for them if you do not have them and to abide by their contents. If you do not like what you read, then participate in the meetings and consultation procedures and change things gradually and democratically. Remember there is usually a reason why the policies and procedures are as they are and you are possibly the newest member of staff. Good schools welcome new ideas and open debate but aggressive criticism does not 'win friends and influence people'.

Areas you must find out about

The induction checklist in Chapter 2 gives you a good start. Most systems and procedures will be covered by the policies mentioned above, but schools, like many organisations, have their customs which are not explicit or laid down on paper and often you have to pick these up as you go along. Be observant and sensitive.

If there is not written guidance about any of the following in the checklist, then make sure you ask about them. This area will include the use of spaces, materials or equipment and how you should behave in different circumstances. Make a note of any items that are not already in writing and keep it for reference. Highlight or mark items on the written guidance that you feel are important or wish to query. Some of them are explained in principle in the paragraphs following the list; many of them will have details that refer to your school only. If you move from one school to another, you will find there are differences in procedures of which you need to take note.

A checklist

Do you know about the following?

- Use of the staffroom
  - payment for and organisation of drinks
  - timing and location of staff breaks
  - use of teacher resource banks
- Health education policy – what to do when pupils ask awkward questions
- Child protection training
- Dealing with harassment and racist incidents
- Using the office
  - other staff and equipment
  - using the photocopier
  - personal equipment and insurance

- Communication systems
  - verbal, paper and ICT
  - meetings, newsletters, staffroom, notice boards
  - non-verbal
  - confidentiality
- The learning environment
  - access to and use of resources, equipment and materials, replacement procedures (general, curriculum-specific, written)
- Preparation requirements of teacher
  - returning things correctly – storage, location
  - monitoring
  - checking and care
  - making resources and reimbursement of possible expenses incurred
  - involving pupils
- Safety equipment, storage and maintenance
  - specific: ICT including audiovisual, science, DT and art
- School buildings and grounds
- Records
  - access
  - storage
  - security
  - data protection
- School Development Plan (SDP)
  - objectives and priorities
  - consultation procedures.

Health and safety

All employees have a duty to observe the in-house organisational requirements in this area [2K10, K11.1, 12.1,13.1]. There is considerable legislation governing health and safety at work, based on the 1974 Act and subsequent legislation such as the Management of Health and Safety at Work Regulations, 1992. These indicate that establishments must have health and safety policies and carry out risk assessments for people, equipment and off-site activities. It puts the responsibility for health and safety on employers which in the case of schools may be the LA, the governing body, trustees or owners, depending on what type of school it is. The Health and Safety Executive produce some useful information leaflets and have local offices. However, all employees have a responsibility to observe local policies and take all reasonable precautions to keep themselves and others using the premises safe. This includes being personally vigilant for potential risks to adults or pupils. It does not mean you necessarily have to mend things, or make things safe on your own, but you need to ensure that pupils in your care observe proper procedures. Your responsibilities regarding health and safety may be spelt out in your job description. The requirements for all staff in the areas of health, safety, security and supervision will be spelt out in writing somewhere [3K1].

All schools will have an appointed Health and Safety Officer among the staff, usually a teacher, often linked with union affiliation. They will advise you if you have queries, and will take any concerns you have to the appropriate quarter. The standards provide useful checklists of areas that you must attend to and find out about in your particular school. You should know about the location of first aid boxes, how to protect children and adults against accidents and how to use different equipment in emergencies. The standards apply to all pupils, whatever their special needs, to all colleagues and other adults or children who may be in the building, and to all areas of the school: in and out of the classroom, outside the school buildings and in places you might visit with pupils on an educational trip.

Even if you are not undertaking these units for accreditation purposes you should read the following and undertake some of the tasks. These items are required of all employees either by law or for the protection of all the people within the organisation. Matters of health education, caring for individual pupils and child protection issues are dealt with in the next chapter.

Emergency and accident procedures [1K10]

Before you even go to a classroom, you should know about fire alarms and procedures [3K16a]. This includes how to evacuate the building, and what to do if there is a bomb scare or an intruder. As a visitor to the school, you are usually asked to sign in so that the responsible people know who is in the building if there is an emergency. As a member of staff, it is assumed that you are on the premises if the timetable indicates that you are. You need to familiarise yourself with the fire alarm points, the whereabouts of extinguishers and fire blankets and their use. Remember that if you are in laboratories, ICT suites or locations where different hazardous liquids are about, there may be different kinds of extinguisher in use. Water should not be put on oil or electrical fires as it can make matters far worse. Carbon dioxide extinguishers or fire blankets will be available in vulnerable situations; check how and when they should be used.

Usually the fire alarm is the signal for any evacuation of the building, whatever the cause. You need to ensure that any pupils in your charge behave appropriately at such times, 'silence' and 'walking only' usually being paramount. Both of these reduce panic as well as being something positive to maintain. All rooms should have evacuation instructions. If they do not, tell someone in the office – possibly pranksters have been at work.

If you are appointed to support a pupil with special physical needs, ensure you know where all their equipment is, and what you do with them in emergencies. These could be personal to them or arise in an evacuation procedure. A wheelchair may need a special route out of some areas, like access to a lift. Alert the SENCO if you have any worries.

First aid

All schools will have at least one appointed person responsible for ensuring that correct procedures are followed and probably a trained first-aider. You need to find out who these people are and where they may be found at different times of the day. Cover of some kind should be available at all times when people are on the school premises. You do not need to have first aid training but it helps, and schools usually have simple sessions every so often which deal with resuscitation, choking, bleeding and other simple procedures which any-one can use. Be wary of getting information from the internet or books on home medicine unless you are sure of their validity, since some methods are not helpful. The Red Cross and St John's Ambulance associations run lots of courses in any community and usually will come to a specific venue to run a course if sufficient people are interested. Of course, they have a small cost. The school will have a designated first-aider who will have at least some of this training, and you will be told when and how you should use them. Common sense and experience, particularly of bringing up a family, can help you, but you must know your limitations both personally and within the procedures of the school.

There may be a school nurse visiting on occasion or, very rarely nowadays, a school doctor. Visiting therapists such as occupational, speech and physiotherapists can be very helpful in giving information as to how to cope with pupils with particular needs. There may also be religious or cultural 'dos and don'ts' with some pupils or staff, such as problems with removing certain items of clothing, and you need to be aware of these. The important thing is not to panic, but to make a quick assessment of the situation. Usually your first port of call in any emergency will be to refer to the class teacher, but very quickly in your working day, you may find yourself in a learning area out of sight of such a person. You need to know who can help and how to summon assistance [3.2P2]. The emergency aid associations also publish useful manuals about first aid, at work and at home, for adults or children, and some of these manuals are available as downloads or audio files for MP3 players. Details can be found on the Red Cross web site (www.redcross.org.uk) or the St John's Ambulance site (www.sja.org.uk/sja/first-aid-advice). While books and internet information are useful, nothing can replace actually practising on a course. It is very important to know your own limitations as doing something wrong could further endanger life. Find out where the trained first-aiders are situated, where people who deal with sick pupils are located, where first aid materials are kept and who has access to them [3K13].

You should ensure you can recognise these emergencies, and check for what to do and what not to do in all the following:

severe bleeding

cardiac arrest

shock – could be hypoglycaemic (a diabetic) or an allergic reaction – anaphylactic shock

fainting or loss of consciousness

epileptic seizure

choking and difficulty with breathing

falls – potential and actual fracture

burns and scalds

poisoning

electrocution

substance abuse

(LGNTO 2001, Level 2: 33)

Some simple rules are:

- Look for danger: you may have to deal with this.
- Remove any danger: only move the casualty if absolutely necessary.
- Assess the casualty: check for consciousness, open the airway, and check for breathing and pulse.
- Get help as soon as you can [3.2P2,3&4].

You must find the whereabouts of the school first aid kit early on. You may be interested to compare the contents of a school first aid kit with one you can buy ready-made; you will probably find fewer items as the rules governing what can be used on other people's children are strict. You must know what to do with a pupil if they have an accident, or if you have an accident.

You should also ensure you know the procedures for dealing with the results of illness as well as the sick pupils [3.2P5; K15]. The administration of medicines, including the use of asthma inhalers, will be spelt out in guidance somewhere and you must be sure what your role is in such circumstances. Remember that simple things like reassurance, maintaining some privacy and calmness will help whatever the situation [3.2P1]. Afterwards, you may need to clear up vomit, urine, faeces or blood and should find out about protective clothing for yourself, such as surgical gloves, whether to use sand, sawdust, disinfectant or not, and where to locate a site manager or other help in such circumstances. Sickness or accidents to one person can be a health risk to others.

First aid checklist

Do you know your own limitations in first aid skills?

Do you know what is expected of you by the school?

Are there any cultural or religious limitations to your possible actions of which you should be aware?

Have you found out which pupils in the school
    might be allergic to food ingredients, insect stings etc. and what you do if they have a reaction [3K14]?
    have asthma and how they cope?

Do you know:
    to whom to turn for help?
    where the first aid box is kept?
    should you use it?
    what you do when you have finished using it – whom do you tell about replacing items?

What would you do if any of the above list happened to you?
    or happened to a pupil in your care?

All incidents and accidents should be recorded somewhere in the school, along with the action taken, the time and cause, so be sure you ask about this as well when informing yourself about your appropriate action. The reporting of major incidents can then be dealt with by the appropriate person. You should record incidents in which you are involved; check the requirements for your school. Most schools have notes that can be sent home, signed by someone in authority, to tell parents or carers of incidents in school. It may or may not be your responsibility to inform parents directly; it will depend on the pupil and the nature of the incident. For instance, bumped heads are always considered important, as symptoms of concussion can develop many hours after the incident, so the parents or carers need to be on the lookout for any problem, but the note may need to be signed by a senior member of staff, not by you. Some chemicals and medical materials are not allowed in school, and all medicines should be properly secure. Do not administer medicines or apply ointments or plasters unless you are sure that it is all right to do so. Never use your own creams or lotions on a pupil. Always record your actions [3.2P5].

There may be occasions when gender is important. For instance, you may have care of a female pupil who begins to menstruate yet has not got any protection with her at school, or even one to whom the event comes as a surprise. This can occur as young as eight or nine years of age. Whichever gender you are, make sure you know the school's arrangements for accessing emergency supplies of protective clothing and disposal of soiled materials, and if you are male, identify the person to whom to go for help should this condition become apparent to you. Some physically disabled girls may need intimate help at this time. Seek clear advice before undertaking this. Check you know the school's sex education policy before entering into any discussion with a girl about the reason for menstruation or how it happens [3K20b].

If you are caring for those with physical disabilities you must get specialist advice.

Equipment, materials and buildings

It is trite, but true, that prevention is better than cure and it is part of your responsibility as a member of staff, particularly one dealing closely with children and young people, to ensure your surroundings are hygienic and safe. You will need to get to know the routines for keeping the place tidy and clean [13.1P1]. Make sure you understand how guards and covers for apparatus work and use them. Be careful about keys and door fastenings and follow procedures [3K8]. Be firm about school routines, but be careful [3.1P8]. It is not your place to criticise or denigrate family customs, but to carry out the customs recommended for your school. For instance, pupils' bags can often be a simple hazard to the passer-by whether in a designated cloakroom area or left lying about a room [3K8]. Gentle reminders to put them straight can really help, since some pupils appear to have got used to people clearing up for them – that is not your job, but the safety of others is [3.1P6]. You need to be a good role model yourself where tidiness is concerned. You need to know and understand the security procedures for your school. Many schools have entry and exit procedures for visitors, but all members of staff should be alert to strangers on the premises, particularly at informal times. If in doubt question the possible intruder, ask if you can help them or ask some other innocuous question, but tell someone in authority if you are suspicious. Always be sure to refasten things like gates to foundation stage outside play areas, and to follow exit procedures regarding burglar alarms or lighting [3K16b].

You may have to visit toilet areas to ensure they are being used properly, and you may need to ensure that young pupils wash their hands after using the toilet or before handling food [3.1P7]. Make sure you know the appropriate places for you and your pupils to eat or drink in your school [3K10]. Remember that families differ in their standards of tidiness and hygiene at home. Some religious groups have strict rules about eating particular foods, so be careful when commenting on the content of lunch bags. Some schools have healthy eating policies and even lunch box policies so make yourself aware of these. You must be aware of any procedures that you should follow when dealing with food or body fluids (blood, urine, faeces) in order to avoid contamination and infections. There may be special chemicals or protective clothing which is used in your school [3K10].

Some schools may have strict rules about handling soil or animals; most leave it to common sense, that is, wash your hands well after handling either. Fewer schools actually keep animals on the premises these days but many still do. Do familiarise yourself with their care in case your particular pupils are interested. The RSPCA has a lot of information about the proper care of animals in schools as well as at home. This includes creatures in aquaria and ponds, as well as the more obvious mammals. The Royal Society of Wildlife Trusts (www.wildlifetrusts.org.uk) gives links to 47 local trusts who would be able to advise you on setting up or maintaining wildlife areas in school grounds or on places to visit locally. Learning Through Landscapes (www.ltl.org.uk) also have publications and advice. Some people can be allergic to animal fur and even caterpillar hairs, so always ask before bringing any animals to school yourself. It is really important in all the concern over health and safety that children and young people are encouraged to experience learning outside the classroom [3K9]. Overprotection can cause a reduction in immunity to infection, a lack of understanding of our dependence on natural resources and trying to live sustainable lives, and a lack of awareness of danger and how to cope with it. It is a question of balance [2K11.6;12.6; 3K12].

Make sure you report any problems with pupils carrying out your hygiene rules or creating unsafe situations, to a teacher or to your line manager, as well as any hazard you may find in using any of the school's facilities. The named Health and Safety Officer may need to be informed [1K10; 13.1P4,10].

It is your responsibility to ensure that where you work with pupils is safe – you could be asked to take a group in the grounds where there is a pond for instance – and that any tools you work with are used safely. Making sure you always have the right number of pupils with you may seem obvious but children can go missing. Make sure you know what to do if one does [3K16c]. Pupils using tools, equipment and materials should be taught how to use them and how to put them away appropriately and clean after using them This goes for cutlery at lunchtime and pencil sharpeners as well as craft knives, complicated apparatus or equipment for handling pupils with disabilities. There may be special rules and regulations, even risk assessments associated with particular items, especially if you are helping in science, DT, ICT or art areas [12.2P7,8]. Part of safety routines will be the proper use of tools and equipment, including their care and storage. Always read and obey manufacturers' instructions and if in doubt ask for a copy of these. It will be up to you to ensure there is a minimum risk in using such apparatus. All electrical equipment should be used appropriately and safely [3K5; 13.1P4]. You may need to be trained to use specialist equipment and that may include specialist safety equipment on lathes or other power tools [13.1P3]. If in doubt about the use of any tools or equipment, ask and take note. There is more about health and safety issues in practical subjects in Chapter 11. Clearing up afterwards may also include disposing of materials [14.1P2; 15.2P4]. Does your school separate waste paper for recycling? Do you know where and how to dispose of broken glass, chemicals and other possibly toxic materials? [3.1P4; 3K19]. Be a good role model in the way you use tools and materials, the way in which you organise your own belongings. Always tell someone if you have a problem or a breakage [14.1P5].

Health and safety procedures also include ensuring security procedures are observed, being alert for strangers and keeping locked any areas or equipment that should be away from general use. Schools now contain much expensive equipment such as ICT or laboratory equipment, some of which is highly portable and desirable to thieves. Secondary schools probably have some quite dangerous chemicals, bacterial cultures and even radioactive materials in various stores [3K6]. You must make yourself familiar with the routines of any environment in which you work to maintain hygiene and safety [3.1P2]. All of us have heard of the, thankfully very rare but devastating, results of aggressive visitors to schools.

A phrase that is often used in schools is 'risk assessment'. This is not necessarily a complicated paper-based task for using dangerous chemicals or machinery but can become part of your everyday thinking. A simple example is teaching children to cross the road safely [3.1P3,6]. When in school we need to be alert for possible dangers, mentally assessing the risk of certain procedures. This does not mean not doing certain procedures which may be interesting or fun, but being sure before you undertake them that you have thought the process through [13.1P3,8; 14.1P2]. Young people should be taught the concept of risk assessment as well as keeping themselves safe [2K13.5]. Some activities need formal risk assessments before they should be undertaken, such as visits off site or use of certain chemicals. Risk assessments are routine procedures in science laboratories and DT areas [3.1P5]. Taking pupils off site is covered by particular guidance regarding health and safety, so ensure you take proper advice and follow guidelines carefully [3K24].

Keep a diary for a week about where you are working with pupils.

Note any incidents that did happen – what did you do? Could these incidents have been prevented by any action you could have taken?

Think of all the potential hazards that could have occurred during that week, e.g. spillages, falls, conflicts, injuries, breakages.

How did you avoid them happening?

Can you avoid more incidents in future by taking more care? [3.1P1,2]

Dealing with harassment and racist incidents

This is really part of any school policy dealing with equal opportunities, ethos and respect for all individuals, but when such incidents do happen, they can be very personal either to you or to the pupils with whom you work closely, and so you are immediately emotionally (if not physically) involved. Schools have had to produce a race equality policy which should clearly lay down a framework of positive strategies for ensuring the development of intercultural awareness and education against racism. Various Race Relations Acts (1976 and 2000) and the Code of Practice for Pupils with SEN all give guidance.

The harassment can take the form of physical or verbal attacks, non-cooperation or disrespect and other incidents such as use of certain language printed on clothing, badges or posters, or other more subtle incidents.

It is important that you know the key actions to take following any such incidents:

Take immediate and appropriate action to deal with the incident.

Deal with it as objectively as possible, not attacking the perpetrator in a personal manner – what is done is wrong, not the person doing it.

Notify the person indicated in the policy and complete any required documents.

Provide support for the victim, expressing your concern.

A senior member of staff may have to inform and deal with parents of pupils involved, either as victims or perpetrators.

Discuss the matter with your line manager as to who should counsel and discuss the problem with the perpetrator, explaining why the actions are not to be tolerated.

As in all cases of health and safety, prevention is better than having to deal with the incident and so following the positive policies and ethos of the school will really help. Teachers can include discussion of such matters in their curriculum planning or circle times. Also remember that the perpetrator can see ignoring such incidents as condoning them. If any incident is aimed at you personally, seek advice from your line manager in dealing with it.

Using the office: other staff and equipment

It may be tempting to use the school facilities liberally to support your own work, but time and materials all cost money and schools are usually very careful about their budgets. Do ensure you know if and when you can use the telephone, whether on school or personal business, and if there is a kitty to which you should contribute when doing so. The school administrative staff are there to help all staff with clerical work, but will have their priorities and procedures too. Ask your line manager before asking for help with typing or photocopying, and even if you are doing the photocopying, ensure that you know the procedures for obtaining more paper or ink. Never take the last packet without telling someone you have done so or replenishing the supply if you know how. The next person to use the machine is sure to be in a hurry.

If you have a personal question about salary payment or something similar, find out when is a good time to talk to the finance officer or bursar. If you want to speak to a senior member of staff or to the head, it is usually wise to make an appointment, even if informally. Make sure that any written communication you have regarding pupils is legible, accurate, up-to-date and kept in a secure place.

If you want to borrow any school equipment or bring in some of your own, such as a tape recorder or laptop, make sure you ask about insurance as well as getting permission for such a thing. Ensure that your car is insured to carry passengers for business purposes before you offer to ferry anyone anywhere.

Communication

Communication is the lifeblood of an organisation: it is what connects everybody so that the organisation can function. It operates in two ways. You must communicate with your pupils and class teachers, but also with your line manager, mentor, curriculum managers or coordinators, union representatives, administrative and caretaking staff – all those with whom you may come into contact. You may not like some of them as people, but you must not show this at work. Always remain pleasant and calm – confrontation rarely achieves the best results and conflict always has to be resolved by some sort of compromise in the end. Respond to any consultations promptly, and bring necessary matters to the appropriate person's attention. These can be any matters that may be concerning you such as the condition of toilets or a shortage of recording tapes.

If you are given written guidance, read it: read memos and newsletters, notices and handouts. File them, even if they seem irrelevant, and revise the filing every so often to throw away outdated materials. Do not issue documents or post messages on boards unless you are sure it is appropriate to do so. Messages can be verbal – if you have a poor memory, then make a note, keep a small jotter in your pocket along with a pencil or biro. Messages can also be non-verbal, so, particularly when new to an organisation, watch out for body language. You may be sitting on the chair in the staffroom that only certain people ever sit on by tradition. Be sensitive to looks or gestures. Pupils can communicate non-verbally too.

Ensure that any photocopying you do falls within the copyright laws. Most schools display a copy of these by the side of the machine, and indicate where records of numbers of copies should be recorded of extracts of published items if this is relevant.

It is your responsibility to read any policies, guidance or guidelines given to you and to follow what is stated in them. If you do not agree with any of the contents then ask your line manager how such advice came about and what the procedures are for consultation in the school. Then use the proper routes to get things changed if it is important to you [5K5]. Some documents such as the prospectus and the parental newsletters will be useful for general information on the way the school works. Attending meetings is also part of your responsibility. This may cause a problem with your child care facilities if the meeting is arranged after pupil contact hours, and you may have to negotiate to be paid for such attendance. These meetings may be of any of the teams to which you belong, planning meetings with a teacher or meetings with specialists or for your appraisal. These are all necessary to the smooth running of any organisation. Paper messages will not substitute for verbal discussions or face-to-face working.

Confidentiality

As a member of staff, a professional (and this should apply to volunteers as well), you should maintain confidentiality about all that you see or hear or read while you are in school [5.1P8]. Children may behave differently at school compared with other situations and environments. For instance, you may have known them previously in a pre-school setting, or know them in a social context, or see them with their parents. Teachers may comment on children's progress. You may wish the child received more attention at home, or was kept away from another child, but that cannot be said outside the professional dialogue with staff in the school. Parents do approach TAs about their children, thinking either that they are less busy than teachers, or even that they are a softer touch, or perhaps they know you anyway. It can be difficult not to relay gossip to a friend, when you are longing to tell someone.

If you are dealing with written records about any pupil or person in the organisation, keep the highest standards of confidentiality [14.3P7]. There are likely to be procedures for access to such records, and recognised places for keeping them. Make sure you know what these are. Pupils' and staff records will be kept under lock and key, usually somewhere centrally, although some of the running records will be in the pupils' classrooms. You must find out the systems and procedures for your school, and what your roles and responsibilities are within those. Maintain their safe and secure storage at all times, and do not leave important documents on the photocopier. It is easily done. Another trap is the use of paperclips. Single sheets of paper can easily get attached to the wrong set of documents with these.

The safe storage of data also applies to matters kept on computers. All material kept on adults or pupils on computer hard or floppy disks is subject to the Data Protection Act which means that it must all be kept securely, and the subject of the item stored should have access to what is being stored. If you are asked to enter data into pupils' records on a database, ensure you know the procedures your school adopts to conform with this Act. In principle only the minimum personal information necessary is stored, and it should be as accurate as possible and only held for as long as necessary. Individuals have a right to see what is stored about them except in very limited circumstances where 'access would prejudice the prevention or detection of crime' (DOH, HO and DfEE 1999: 115). Security measures include not just the physical security of the equipment but the existence of appropriate levels of staff access. Never divulge passwords needed for access to office equipment unless requested to do so by the senior member of staff responsible for the recording systems.

The School Development Plan

One major vehicle of management and communication within a school with which you should familiarise yourself is a School Development (or Improvement) Plan (SDP or SIP). This is the business plan of the organisation and should cover all the areas of operation of the school including the teaching assistants. This plan is produced annually, usually after a review of the previous one and frequently after consultation with all the people concerned in the plan. Sometimes a major review of the plan is undertaken – after an inspection or sometimes just triennially. These are often lengthy and rather unwieldy documents and you will not need to read all of yours. There will always be a reference copy available in schools and sometimes major parts of it are displayed in a prominent place such as the foyer or the staffroom and items are highlighted as they are achieved. There is usually a summary version for circulation. It is your responsibility as an employee to make sure you know about the parts that may affect you. Look under the staffing section, or special needs or the curriculum areas with which you are associated. The development of ICT or behaviour management strategies may affect your work, and proposals for changes to the fabric of the building may impinge upon your effectiveness. It is also your responsibility to respond if consulted in the review process [5K5]. Hopefully there will be a support staff member of the governing body somewhere, who will be representing you on the governing body. All governing bodies will have 'staff' governors but they may all be teachers. Either way, do find out who they are, how they represent you and what goes on in a Governors' meeting. Governors are responsible for the strategic direction of the school and are the body accountable for the running of the school.

Development and learning

CHILD DEVELOPMENT HAS been a neglected area of study for those in teaching in recent years. The emphasis has been on curriculum delivery rather than on how pupils learn. But understanding how children learn became an optional module of the DfES induction course at primary level even before the course was updated, and it now forms part of the Level 2 TA standards as well as the Level 3 standards. STL 1K7 appears as one sentence but represents one of the most complex subjects in education. STL 2K11, 12, 13 and 14 are all about understanding the changes that occur in children with age. Teachers and TAs must know about what they are teaching in terms of subject content, and how to 'deliver' that subject, but the characteristics of the learner matter also. It is sad that the national strategies went down the route of 'one size fits all' because all learners differ in maturity, learning styles, experiences and background before any new learning experience and these have to be taken into account. The delivery and subject matter have to be matched to the learners' ability to cope while challenging them [10.1P6; 10.2P6; 10.3P4; 10.5P8; 10K1,3]. The new materials of the strategies emphasise the need to adapt them to circumstances including the nature of the learners.

The more you know and understand about the various aspects of development, particularly in the age range in which you work, the more you will be able to support that development. It is sad that the induction materials for secondary TAs do not include some information or teaching on understanding how children learn. Not only are secondary pupils learners but we all are. Not only will some secondary pupils still be learning at a level similar to that of a primary child but learning processes are not linear. The capacity to learn is something we are born with, the strategies we need change with the subject matter, our maturity and the motivation for the learning. Many of the strategies are common to any age.

The induction material for primary TAs depends heavily on videos of children learning at various ages to 11. If you have not seen these, it would be well worth while trying to get to see them, preferably in the company of colleagues and experienced teachers so that you can discuss the content. You should also try to spend some time observing children of various ages for yourself, including children in phases different from the one in which you regularly work. Observing in a nursery class can be very beneficial for TAs working with children of any age, not just those in primary schools. Techniques and protocols to use when observing are explained in Chapter 8.

The term 'child development' is much more widely used when considering the teaching and learning of pupils in the early years, and the term itself has connotations of childhood and primary schools. It is, however, the term used to cover the area of study from birth to adulthood, whenever that it supposed to be (legally 18). When working in secondary schools or even in tertiary colleges, an understanding of how the growth processes influence the way in which the pupils learn is important. Indeed, most of us regress at times to methods learnt in childhood when undertaking new fields of study. The need to 'play around' with a new television, or 'fiddle about' with a new tool is part of all our experience. Play is not confined to the early years, but is an essential part of learning [2.2P; 2K5].

Nor can we study the learning process in isolation; not only does the physical and emotional state of our bodies influence the way we learn and the efficacy of our learning, but much of our intellectual development has a physical and emotional basis. Our social, cultural and spiritual selves also develop as we become adult, and continue to do so throughout our lives. We are made up of all these facets, each influencing the others to produce a whole person. We have to try to see our pupils as whole human beings [2K7], yet in order to study the complexity which makes up the whole, we have to look at each facet separately. If these facets get out of balance, one develops but another does not, then the pupil, or adult, becomes frustrated, even disturbed. This can be seen sometimes in very bright children who are emotionally their chronological age, intellectually ahead of their peers but socially immature.

Most children develop and grow normally and do so in a recognisable sequence which can be studied and which forms the basis of designing schools, year-based schemes of work, equipment and teaching methods. Thus, in studying development you will understand the rationale behind most of the things we do, not only in school but in all parts of our lives as shoppers, parents or home builders [2K6; 10K3]. Also, a study of what are called 'norms', the stages that researchers, medical practitioners and teachers have identified over the years, enables practitioners to understand better when things are not developing as they should. Many of you will be helping pupils with developmental delay in one area or another, and it will help if you learn more about normal development. The most obvious area to start with is that of physical development.

Physical development

A family photograph album will give you material to identify some of the norms of physical development. In the UK we are relatively well fed and clothed, with a modern medical service, and so most of us have the privilege of growing to adulthood normally. Many of you have children of your own, and have kept that height chart on the kitchen or bathroom wall and entered your family heights on each birthday. Some of you may even have kept up entries in your baby books, recording weight, first teeth, first walking and talking, toilet training milestones and so forth. Doctors and nurses have tables of norms and will check development at certain critical intervals, particularly when children are in infancy.

The milestones of puberty are also marked by bodily changes. Physically, we are able to procreate in our early teens, yet we are not fully mature until our early twenties. Some might say it is 'downhill' after that; certainly we become less fertile. Mothers may have more complications in childbirth after 30 years of age, and menstruation ceases in the forties or fifties; sperm counts tend to drop with age. Boys tend to mature later than girls in many aspects of physical and intellectual development, a fact that confuses the test statistics where girls outstrip boys at most levels of testing. We all know that diet, exercise and environmental factors affect that growth pattern. In the so-called Western world, people are living longer overall as well as being inches taller than their grandparents' generation. Understanding of disease, its causes and many cures have contributed to this longevity.

Looking at physical norms

Get out your family albums with photographs of either yourself and your family or of your children. If you have them, find your children's 'baby books'. Ask other members of your family for some remembrances. Can you identify at what age the following happened? Try following the development of one child at a time. When did they first:

- Sit up on their own

- Turn over

- Crawl

- Stand up unaided

- Walk unaided

- Kick a ball

- Ride a bicycle

- Hold a pencil

- Draw a shape

- Draw a recognisable person

- Write their name

- Catch a ball with one hand

- Skip with a skipping rope

- Tie their own shoelaces?

As you do this with several family members you will begin to see a pattern emerging. Did the boys develop later than the girls in any of these respects?

Early years' practitioners will divide the abilities mentioned above into two types – gross and fine motor skills. The fine motor skills – those using just the hands – are the ones that schools usually identify as important, except in physical education (PE) [2.1P3,4]. They will provide activities that assist the development of both areas – small fiddly things like Lego, construction toys, and table activities alongside climbing apparatus and vehicles [2K10.8;10K16]. The original Lego bricks for instance also come in various sizes, the manufacturers recognising that small hands do not have the fine muscle control needed for the smaller pieces. Unfortunately, the emphasis in these toys can be on producing a finished model rather than providing a tool for imagination and creativity.

If you are particularly interested in physical development, either because the pupils you help have some physical impairment or because you wish to specialise in an area of PE, you might like to ask a friendly nurse or doctor to let you have a look at their more specialised charts. You need to recognise the important stages in physical development, as they may impinge upon your work [2.1P1]. The new framework for early years' practitioners has some excellent descriptions of developmental stages between birth and five years old, with ideas on how the development can best be enhanced (DCSF 2007b)[2K10.7]. You also need to understand for instance that girls can start to menstruate while at primary school. Tall pupils will need larger furniture to enable them to work in comfort. Many of you will be working with children with particular physical needs for which you need to understand how best to help them. So-called clumsy children may need more help in concentrating, and others may need special furniture or equipment [STL 13].

There is a continuing debate as to whether inherited characteristics or environmental factors are the reasons for differences. Our physical characteristics are dependent on our genes, the DNA which provides the code for cell development and distribution. But anything can intervene, either in the very protein which makes up the DNA or in the cells, to influence the way in which the genes can operate. Irradiation from atomic bombs dropped in Japan at the end of the Second World War caused mutations of human genetic material which resulted in anything from death to minor physical deformity. Diet and environmental factors such as water or air pollution, housing, exercise or lack of it all have their effect. The environmental factors do not necessarily have a lifelong effect; sometimes reversal of circumstance can allow the body to catch up. You may be helping pupils who have come from countries where malnutrition was endemic; they may seem small for their age, listless and slow in learning. With proper diet and medical aid to rid the body of possible infection incurred through dirty water or bad housing, the pupil may grow and regain some of their lost ground.

There are also best times for certain development. Language acquisition appears to be easiest in the pre-school years, when children seem not only able to learn their mother tongue but also to become bilingual or multilingual with more ease. Some of the muscles of the palate used or unused in that period can make it difficult in later life to articulate certain sounds; for instance, people who have been brought up speaking in a Chinese dialect find it hard in adult life to articulate all the sounds that we use in the English language. Children seem able to learn to read most quickly between five and seven years of age. It does not mean they cannot learn to read at other ages, but the effort both they and the teacher have to exert will be greater. Some of this will be due to the maturation of the brain itself. Recognising this, there are again moves to introduce foreign language teaching into primary schools [2K10.16; 4K3; 6K3].

Some pupils are learning English as an additional language (EAL). Some of these children will have been born in this country and others will be newly arrived from all over the globe. They may come from quite affluent backgrounds or they may be refugees arriving with very little. They may be quite fluent in English or it may seem that they don't know a word. A number of important language development principles apply [10.K2].

Children who are new to school in this country who speak little English may often go through a 'silent phase' or 'listening period' [2K10.15; 2K11.12]. This means that they may seem reluctant to talk at all. This is normal and can last for quite some time although a lot can depend on the child's personality and experiences, the classroom environment and how welcome they feel. Some very young children may not speak at all for up to six months. The quicker they gain confidence, make friends and are able to join in classroom activities and the life of the school the better. During this silent phase, EAL children are learning and listening. Newly arrived EAL children will learn to speak English and within one to two years, then should be speaking at least at a conversational level. Some pupils make very rapid progress and within two to three years seem to be at the same or a higher academic level than their peers. There are numerous examples of children achieving excellent GCSE grades or SATs scores after just three years in the education system. Pupils who do this tend to come from educated families, have had a good education in their country of origin and also have a fully developed knowledge of their first language. They are able to transfer their skills and knowledge from one language to another.

Intellectual development

Intellectual development or cognitive (knowing) development and the development of learning are dependent, just like the rest of the body, on genetic and environmental factors. Learning takes place in the brain. It involves thinking either consciously or unconsciously. There are many billions of brain cells, each with many connections to other brain cells. Electrical and chemical messages are transmitted at enormous speeds when we think or do anything. Recent advances in scanning and tracking activities have opened up a major field of interest to us all. The brain cells are probably not increasing in number as we grow, just more pathways develop between them, so how do we go on learning? There have been many theories, and some of these have determined the way in which we teach and what we teach over the past century. As is the case with most research, the more we know the more we find we do not know, and currently we recognise the complexity of what goes on in the brain; no one theory fits all cases and we need to look at the variety of theories, and recognise some of the strategies that have developed from them. You will soon get to recognise the characteristics of the pupils with whom you work closely and adapt your techniques to fit them – things such as how long a pupil can concentrate without taking a break [2.3P1].

The brain is not one entity; parts regulate your heartbeat and breathing, the activities which go on even if you are unconscious. Another part controls your movements, coordination and balance, so important in learning to walk and talk. The middle part of the brain is responsible for memory, emotions and processing and managing information. The upper part of the brain, the bit that looks like an outsize walnut without its shell, has the main thinking parts and personality. The right and left parts of the cortex do different things and there are pathways between the two sides. Buried inside the midbrain are some important glands whose hormones (chemical messengers in the blood) determine our body clock, our ability to react to stimuli, to control our blood sugar and so on. So you can see how close thinking and our emotions are to controlling other functions of our body. The cells make up a complex network; if some cells die or are damaged through an accident or a stroke, it is possible that alternative pathways can be found, provided the owner of the brain continues to exercise it. Obviously, it depends on the extent of the damage and the location. If it is possible to relocate pathways, it is also possible to establish new ones – the process of learning.

Modern therapies take a much more holistic approach to mental illness, recognising that we are complex beings with body, mind and spirit, all of which can become unbalanced in different ways and all of which affect the function of each other. We all live in different social contexts, with different backgrounds, talents and needs. Luckily, most of the pupils and parents with whom we work are not suffering from mental illness, but the principle is the same. Enhancing learning is not just a matter of having the right breakfast and drinking water, although these can make a difference. As with the whole body, exercise is important. Some schools do 'brain gym', as a sort of club for certain pupils [2.3P1.c,e] but unless these strategies are applied in the classroom to learning, they will become just another thing one does in school.

Thinking – activities like brainstorming, pupils offering differing opinions, discussion, challenge – takes time, when there is a mountain of curriculum facts to be delivered to pupils [10K13]. However, without time for these thinking activities, the pupils will not develop their own understanding of the facts being put forward and will not be creative or problem solvers and grow in their learning capacity. It is a dilemma which all those working within the constraints of a set curriculum have to solve for themselves.

Learning

One definition of learning is 'that reflective activity which enables the learner to draw upon previous experience, to understand and evaluate the present, so as to shape future action and formulate new knowledge' (Abbott 1996: 1).

There is still a belief that there is a fundamental inherited intellectual capability called intelligence and that this can be measured, a child being then given an intelligence quotient (IQ). There are some inherited parameters; identical twins inherit many similar characteristics but can have quite different personalities, which affect their performance. Recent ideas on learning have been influenced by the theory of Gardner who suggests that there is not just one intelligence, but multiple strands or aspects or dimensions or domains. There are different intelligences for different things, and you can be clever in one area only or in several:

- verbal/linguistic: enables individuals to communicate and make sense of the world through language (e.g. as journalists, novelists and lawyers)

- logical/mathematical: allows individuals to use and appreciate abstract relations (e.g. scientists, accountants, philosophers)

- visual/spatial: makes it possible for people to visualise, transform and use spatial information (e.g. architects, sculptors and mechanics)

- bodily/kinaesthetic: enables people to use high levels of physical movement, control and expression (e.g. athletes, dancers and actors)

- musical/rhythmic: allows people to create, communicate and understand meanings made from sound (e.g. composers, singers, musicians)

- interpersonal: helps people to recognise and make distinctions about others' feelings and intentions and respond accordingly (e.g. teachers, politicians and sales people)

- intrapersonal: enables a capacity for a reflective understanding of others and oneself (e.g. therapists and some types of artist and religious leader)

- naturalist: allows people to understand and develop the environment (e.g. farmers, gardeners and geologists).

(Pollard 2002: 150)

Some people simplify this approach and talk of VAK learning – visual, auditory and kinaesthetic. We learn by watching, listening and doing. Again it is a useful shorthand to describe a very complex process. The debate is now as to how much we should use our knowledge and understanding of a child and their preferred learning styles to maximise their better traits or whether we should train them in the areas they are not so good at in order to enlarge their horizons. The world around us – people, social interaction, rewards, as well as the physical conditions – can influence how we learn, and the world inside us – our physical status, personality, motivation and learning style – can also affect the process [2K7]. We learn facts (knowledge), how to do things (skills), ideas (concepts), and about ourselves (attitudes). Learning together can result in greater achievements than learning in isolation. What we have learnt can lead to thinking and creating new ideas or solving problems. Learning about our own way of learning can help us to improve, and assisting pupils to look at their own processes will help them to improve.

There have been many theories on how we learn and think and how this affects the way we behave. The early theorists concentrated on training to do repetitive tasks, something we still have to do. Rote learning has its place for things like tables but is a very limited approach. Nineteenth-century schooling with its chanting and object lessons depended heavily on this kind of approach. Some saw children as empty vessels to be filled with facts – read or re-read Dickens's *Hard Times* for some great descriptions of rote learning. Rewards and punishment affect how quickly these kinds of tasks are learnt in animals. We know how important praise is when trying to encourage children to learn difficult things, and that punishment is not so effective. We also know that repeating tasks, practising skills, helps to reinforce learning [2.3P1], and we know that without using the facts, like number bonds or tables, the skill deteriorates.

Later theorists like Piaget, a biologist, realised that thinking develops like the physical body, and in stages. He was a bit dogmatic about the stages and believed that all one had to do was wait, and development would happen. 'Discovery learning' tried to follow this theory where it was believed that all one needed was a rich environment and understanding, and knowledge would just happen. However, the stages he described are really helpful to understanding what can help learning develop.

- Young children, up to about 18 months old, are in what he called the 'sensori-motor stage' where an infant is involved in developing skills of mobility and sensing his/her environment [2.3P1d].

- From 2 to 4 years is the 'pre-operational' stage – the child is concerned only with themselves (egocentric). By about 4 years they are 'intuitive' – thinking logically but unaware of what they are doing [2.3P1d].

- From 7 to 11 years old, the child can operate logically, but still needs to see and work with real objects to learn and understand – the 'concrete stage'.

- Then the child is capable of 'formal' thinking about things without the 'props' – the 'abstract' stage. This is why younger children need 'props' for their learning, things like blocks for counting, or artefacts and films about days gone by. But at times we all need props like pictures or physical demonstrations and doing things for ourselves. Small children can be very perceptive about feelings and abstract concepts. We know that even small children can have an amazing imagination [2.3P1; 2K10.7–9,16,17; 2K11.7–9,13, 14; 6K5].

Piaget ignored the context of learning, and did not ask how to facilitate or accelerate cognitive development [6K3]. Very young children have all the parts of the brain functioning, formal thinking is possible for them, but often the more sensori-motor needs dominate [2K8,9]. Piaget also believed that learning was similar to digestion. We take in food, and digest it to make it part of ourselves. He spoke of 'assimilating' ideas and 'accommodating' them; they then become part of our own mental make-up.

Another area of interest has been the connection between language and thought. Language and communication is needed in literacy and numeracy as a vehicle for development [2K10.14; 2K11.11]. There are also powerful non-verbal ways of communicating, such as a hand gesture or a smile. Body language can create discomfort or raise expectations. We should also recognise that changes of background, language or culture can create barriers to learning. It is important not to talk down to children, thinking you are using the appropriate language for their age or stage of development. You must recognise that they need to increase their vocabulary, and can take part in quite sophisticated conversations and arguments, given the opportunity. Listen, observe and discuss any findings with your class teacher [2.1P2; 2K2].

Language, aiding communication, enables people to act outside as well as within their environment, broadening their horizons, and this gives added possibilities to their development. We learn a lot from each other and our surroundings in ways that do not use words. Public places including schools give 'messages' about the kind of places they are, from things like the décor of their reception areas and the body language of their receptionists. Schools have a 'hidden curriculum'; we receive motivation and encouragement in our learning from other people [2.3P3].

Each major theorist of learning has produced ideas which are useful in helping children learn. One is the concept of a 'zone of proximal development' (ZPD), which emphasises the importance of guidance or collaboration in learning. Another suggests that if we can see the potential learning of pupils we can put in place stepping stones or 'scaffolding' to bring them to the next stage of development.

All this gives a clear role for a perceptive TA. As the pupils develop 'mastery', external guidance or scaffolding can be reduced. The important thing for the pupil is that you provide the scaffolding, not that you build the complete tower. You can help this process by searching out the patterns and putting the right pieces in place at the right time [10K19]. As with language, it is important to use the appropriate equipment for the development levels of the pupils with whom you work. By inventing codes and rules, seeking out the regularity and predictability of patterns in knowledge or skills, the teacher–pupil interaction can be speeded up. Culture and social interaction are important but work within the constraints of our genetic make-up. Discuss with the teacher the sort of strategies they

PHOTOGRAPH 5.1   Recycling playtime snack waste gives a good opportunity for cooperation and communication

use and would like you to use to promote independence, to encourage and support pupils, to enable them to make their own decisions [2.2P5; 10K19].

As learning is so difficult to see and assess in process, the emphasis has been put on the outcomes of learning – the results of assignments, tests and examinations. We count the number of right answers to our questions and believe this relates to how much the pupil knows. Such is the number-crunching facility of computers, and the related ability of communicating the numeric results in written and electronic forms, that a whole industry of league tables and target setting has grown up around the results of such tests. The arguments about selection are always interesting, whether it is for a place in a school, university or football team or for a job. Are the results of competitive examinations or tests reliable indicators of potential? Many other kinds of test have been devised, such as assessing competence by watching, or psychometric tests designed to find out hidden thoughts, but still the humble interview, talking face to face with the candidate, has a place. A teacher's assessment of pupils will include things such as attitude to learning and progress made over time as well as test results.

Another thing to bear in mind is that we learn by making mistakes, not just by being able to produce right answers. All pupils like to see a page of sums with ticks, yet this can indicate they are not being stretched enough by the questions. Many pupils, when asked to guess or estimate a quantity, will feel good if they are right or near in their guess, and even alter their incorrect guess to match the correct quantity, rather than recognise that the process of estimating is the important learning point, not the answer.

It is very important to recognise that learning is not just about accumulation of facts, it is about developing understanding, and skills not only about matters outside oneself but also about using inherited talents and aptitudes. Regurgitation of facts or showing off skills may seem the aim of examinations, but how and why you use those facts and skills are what gives satisfaction in life to oneself and enriches the world for others. Creativity can be suppressed by too much instruction, yet good artists, musicians, actors and writers all need skill development and knowledge about the 'tools of their trade' [10K13]. Children are born with an innate curiosity which can drive us as parents mad at times: the toddler into every cupboard or the eternal 'why is grass green?' questioning; but this is how we learn and develop from our own motivation. The trick is to utilise a child's interest to help them on to the next stage. We have to help them solve their own problems and not just give answers, and often it means answering a question with another one [10K8].

Learning is not a sedentary, sponge-like, absorbing activity. It is active, often physically active, always brain active. There is an old Chinese proverb, quoted in the original Nuffield Mathematics Project looking at the teaching of mathematics in the 1960s:

I hear and I forget

I see and I remember

I do and I understand [6K5].

The project concentrated on how to learn, not on what to teach. The using of knowledge, not just mathematical knowledge, its exploring and investigation is what makes it meaningful. It is important that you consider not just what you are learning but how you learn, and that you continue that process for the pupils with whom you work. STL10 knowledge indicators are much about enabling the development of this aspect of learning through various activities, from the exploring play of the baby and toddler, to the creative arts such as performance and graphic arts, to science and technology. 10K22 particularly emphasises that teaching and learning in schools and settings should not stifle this side of learning.

Questions to ask yourself

Look again at the factors which have affected a recent learning experience of your own.

- Why did you start it?
- What did you need to help you – books, an instructor, discussion with other people, time on your own, the right tools or machine, practice?
- What facts did you learn? What skills?
- How has your understanding of the matter increased?
- What mistakes did you make?
- What went wrong? Why?
- What went well? Why?
- Did a certificate at the end help?
- Did other people's views matter?
- Can you still improve?
- Would you do it again?

Now consider a recent topic you have been following with a pupil or group of pupils.

- Can you answer the same questions about their learning?

- Can they answer the questions?

- Do you or the pupils need to make any changes in the way you work together?

- Can you help your pupils understand their own learning styles better?

Emotional development

Considering that learning experience you have had as an adult, you will recognise that however bright you are and however good the supporting environment, including the teacher, if you are preoccupied by other problems, bored or insecure, your feelings get in the way. Emotional development and condition affects learning; this is sometimes called the affective domain of our brains. Part of growing up is to become able to put some of our emotions on hold when having to do other things. Younger children are less able to control their emotions and teenagers' hormones play havoc with their control systems [4K4]. You can be of great help to the learning situation by providing an understanding ear to pupils in distress. There must be a warning attached to this about dealing with confidences, and this is dealt with in greater depth in the next chapter [2K4].

A relatively new concept that has been proposed is that of 'emotional intelligence'. This follows the ideas about multiple intelligences, but really indicates that our emotional state is part and parcel of the way we think and act. Motivation is one of the greatest influences on learning. The will to achieve can overcome many physical and social handicaps. When one becomes bored, or other interests take over, it is difficult to concentrate or persevere. Even easier tasks become a chore. Setting up a home of one's own can make do-it-yourself experts of even the most impractical people. Learning to read for some is a matter of accessing information about football, keeping a pet or using a computer. One of the skills you can develop is finding out what interests a reluctant pupil and building upon that: finding the book about football, or advertisements for guinea pig food or a software manual of an appropriate reading level. Another TA skill is being able to repeat a task but change it slightly to create interest, while retaining and reinforcing the learning objective. Keep a note of changes you make and share them with the teacher; these make a useful assessment tool for them [2.4P2].

Self-confidence and self-esteem

We all have stories of the relative or teacher who was demeaning of our efforts in childhood. Sometimes the put-down can motivate a person to achieve despite the comments, but even then the memory stays of the sense of discomfort. Failure or even perceived failure can prevent us all from trying a second time. The SEAL (Social and Emotional Aspects of Learning) project material is useful in this area to discuss this with the children themselves.

Small children normally come to recognise their own identity in their first year; they understand that there are other people, some who love them particularly and others who are on the periphery of their lives. These early relationships are crucial in helping the child form a concept of themselves – a self-image. They know they are valued and they develop the self-confidence to walk and talk, which later gives them the self-confidence to accept challenges [2K10.3]. Adults who have good self-images will be a good role model for children. Confident, encouraging parents and teachers (even though they may be acting) can support learners.

Sometimes adults underestimate or overestimate a child's emotional maturity. Small children can be very sensitive to atmosphere and recognise when adults are very distressed, yet nobody talks to them about what might have happened in the family circumstances to cause the distress. Conversely, an adult can sometimes assume that the child can cope with difficult happenings without problems. The increased recognition of the need for pupils to talk to someone after traumatic events has meant an increased emphasis on the work of counsellors. You need to think about what causes emotional distress, things such as changed circumstances or instability at home, changing boundaries, people or places. Pupils with SEN or EAL may find it more difficult to understand what is happening and therefore find it more difficult to adjust to such changes [14.3P2,5].

Drama and play activities can be a very powerful way of enabling children and young people to explore and express their own feelings and those of others [4K7]. The way in which role play materials and props are provided in early years' settings can help provide a variety of scenes for the pre-school child – from domestic situations to shops, hotels, hospitals and holiday destinations. Observing children at play in these circumstances can give clues as to their joys and worries but do beware, you can misinterpret their behaviour. Scary television programmes may be being acted out, not an imminent family break-up, or it may be an active imagination at work! Opportunities for creative and exploratory drama seem to have died in many primary schools, where performances still take place but often under direct production guidance from adults. Opportunities for enhancing such play in lunch breaks with props take a bit of organising but can be done [4K4,5; 10.2P4–6].

A popular formal way of exploring feelings is the use of 'circle time'. A leader guides the group to contribute only their own comments, to listen and not respond to the comments of other members of the circle. An object of some kind is circulated and its holder is the speaker. Members of the circle are free not to speak when the object comes to them. Again, there should be a health warning. To undertake this process with the serious intent of exploring feelings and not just a glorified 'news time' is a skilled activity requiring training as children can reveal areas which need counselling. Increasingly the need and opportunities for proper counselling are being recognised in schools and many of you may be involved with it.

Small children without words to express their feelings will show their distress or temper in tantrums and their joy or excitement by running around. By the time they are of school age, able to voice their feelings and to understand circumstances, tantrums are usually under control. Communication is important as a means of self-expression and developing self-esteem [4.3P5; 4K6]. By seven or eight years of age they have a concept of the passage of time and the excitement of anticipation of things such as parties and holidays becomes more manageable. By 10 and 11 they are competent to deal with more complex situations without panicking, such as finding themselves lost in a shopping centre or falling off their bicycle in a strange place. The body's hormones – the chemical messengers – can disrupt emotional stability in puberty, creating frustrations, mood swings, even tantrums again. An apparently stable child becomes a stranger at times, yet this is the time when crucial life choices have to be made and the main external examinations are held. Teenagers or younger children can become carers themselves or be in a family with disability [12K12]. Situations like these can cause stress for the child which will affect their learning. It is important that you recognise changes for what they are, and know how to manage them.

Emotional distress may not just be signalled by tantrums. Moody or withdrawn behaviour can signify that something is wrong. Some cases of the teenage eating disorders of anorexia (not eating enough) and bulimia (eating but then inducing vomiting to stop the food being digested) may be due to emotions being unbalanced. As you will be closer to some of the pupils than many of the teachers are, you will notice such changes and you will be able to alert them to a possible problem. Do seek help if you feel that an emotional outburst calls for intervention, and tell someone what has happened even if you have dealt with it appropriately. It may happen again, and parents might need to be told [4K7,14].

Working in a school as one of the caring professionals you will find at times that your work takes over your mind when you are not at work, thinking about a child with problems, or you never have enough time to do all that you want to do, so you experience a sense of failure and get stressed. This can colour your way of dealing with the next problem – 'I can't do it' may be the thought. Feeling good about what you can do is a necessary part of the job. In teaching you cannot 'win them all' and this has to be faced, but you can do some things well. TAs have suffered quite significantly from lack of self-confidence in the past, because of your comparative invisibility in the school system and your low pay. Where you are valued by the school and your colleagues, and they make you know this, you feel good about the job. It is a job with great job satisfaction – a reason most TAs give for remaining. You are doing a most worthwhile thing – remind yourself about this when you feel low.

Then, consider how the pupils you work with feel, be an active listener, don't feel you have to 'do' anything; understanding the problem is half way to solving it [1K10; 2K12.5,13.6; 4K1]. Communicating feelings can help, letting the pupils express themselves in words, spoken or written, or in drawings or even music or some kind of supervised physical activity [10K1]. Giving them time for this may enable them to control what would otherwise be an uncontrolled and possibly dangerous outburst and to maintain their self-esteem [10K15]. Let the pupil talk; sometimes getting them to keep a diary will help them to express their needs and ideas. Do make sure that anything you do is within the school guidelines for dealing with emotional problems.

Often smaller children can draw their feelings rather than write. They can make lists or flowcharts which can be positive or negative. If they are negative, try to get them to work also on the opposite:

What I did wrong – what went well today.

What I hate about school – what I like about school.

What makes me sad – what makes me happy [4K9].

Some pupils may need some help with describing words, so you could make a collection of these in case you need them. The main theme is to look for strengths in the pupil – what they can do, not what they cannot – and build on them, and to provide the pupils with a positive role model in yourself.

Appropriate praise is important, phrases like 'well tried' rather than 'well done' if the work is still not up to the standard it should be. Encourage pupils to look for the positive in situations, in adults and in their peers [2.3P3,6]. Discourage them from 'putting down' their fellow pupils, particularly when they resort to stereotypes such as 'he can't play in the team, he's too young', 'she's stupid, she's just a girl', 'he's thick because he's in a wheelchair' or 'black people smell'. When pupils are more able to cope with expressing their feelings you can move on to more constructive ideas to help them prepare for such feelings and deal with them. Use the language of choice – 'you can either accept a situation and move on or make yourself even more miserable', 'I can help you with your reading/writing if you put in your bit of effort' [4K5]. Make sure they have telephone numbers of friends or even of helplines. In the end, you cannot live the pupils' lives for them; you can only give them the tools and strategies to make the best of what they have got.

Talk to the person in your school who is responsible for personal, social and health education (PSHE) about what strategies they use, and whether they have any books you can read or any simple tips for dealing with pupils about whom you may be concerned. Always tell the class teacher what you are doing and keep them informed of your progress (or lack of it).

Social, cultural and spiritual development

Some of the discussion about the development of good relationships in Chapter 3 is relevant to this aspect of development. Children need to develop good relationships with those around them, or life will become unbearable for them [2.2P2]. Children learn about relationships from watching and imitating people around them. The bonding between parents and babies is considered crucial and mothers are encouraged to hold new-born babies from the word 'go'. Fathers or partners are encouraged to be present at the baby's birth.

Try to spend some time in the role-play areas of a nursery or playgroup just watching the children. They will act out what they have seen at home or sometimes on television screens. They will cook and look after other children if that is what happens in their home, or shout at the other children and send one out for a takeaway if that is what they are used to [10K9]. You need to be careful when interpreting role play, as sometimes children act out their fears as well as reality, so always discuss what you see with the staff in the group [2.2P2]. Father figures or male role models in the home are still considered significant whether the children are male or female, even in this era of successful one-parent families. Educationalists are concerned that schools, particularly primary schools, are becoming increasingly female domains. Toys such as teddy bears and for the very young even a piece of blanket can become a surrogate friend. Many of us have had imaginary friends when little. It is not only relationships with parents that are important, but also having grandparents, carers, brothers and sisters. It is the quality of the care and of people that determines their significance and influence. Many babies attend day nurseries successfully from a very early age, but a key worker is usually assigned to them in these stages to ensure that the right sort of bonding and relationships develop.

As children develop they should be increasingly able to leave their mother or influential carer or the close caring of a day nursery for a while, play with other children, then become happy to spend the day at school sharing the teacher with up to 30 other children. You may have seen the way in which some children still find it difficult to adjust to not being able to demand the teacher's attention without waiting their turn [10.4P7]. During the primary years children develop firm friendships, occasionally forming small gangs or clubs for different activities. They join organisations such as Brownies or judo clubs, and can operate in teams, collaborating and sharing. All the time, they try out their boundaries, and experiment with situations. As children get older, they become much more influenced by the children around them, particularly so in the teenage years, when peer pressure can induce long-lasting changes in lifestyle and attitude. Strong friendships formed in the late teens, in the last few years at school, at college or university, or in a first job tend to be friendships for life. Hopefully by the time the pupils reach this stage they can both recognise and control their own behaviour to fit in with the society in which they live.

While you may have your ideas of what is antisocial behaviour, you must determine the school's policy for what is acceptable in the various situations. Classrooms, playground, lunch hall, laboratories, toilet areas will all have their limits of acceptability. Different cultures will have their own rules or customs of behaviour towards others, and even their own ways of being abusive. The principles of positive strategies, reinforcing and rewarding the good and providing choice and sanctions for the less acceptable, hold good [2.1P3].

The way in which different cultures have differing methods of child care – whether boys and girls are educated together, or whether girls are educated at all – clearly makes a difference to other development. The kind of clothing, food, art and music which surround a child from the early years will influence development and growth; they are part of the environmental influences on inherited characteristics mentioned earlier. The rituals and customs of daily life or religious festivals become part of our lives but also influence the kind of person we grow up to be. You must guard against forming stereotypical assumptions that, because of a person's gender or apparent ethnic origin, they will behave in a certain way or hold certain opinions. Your main objective when working with pupils whose cultural background, dialect or home language is different from your own is to appreciate the additional richness that they bring to school life. It is about reinforcing their self-image [10K21]. Their knowledge and understanding of ways different to yours, their food, clothing, art, music and traditions add a diversity and interest. Multilingual pupils have a skill that many of us do not have. There will be school policies about such celebration of cultural diversity, about how various different religious festivals might be observed, how dress codes might be modified and where additional resources might be found.

Variations in family values and practices may make pupils' responses to school work differ. For instance, it may be traditional within a family or group that females never answer before males have had their turn, or that it is not done to contradict a teacher. Thus a pupil may be reluctant to challenge ideas or comments. Homes where books are rare and conversation is limited may encourage children to feel that all books are pointless and words are not helpful to express feelings. For them the motivation to learn from the printed word is minimal and problems may be resolved by violence rather than open discussion. Understanding the background from which its pupils come obviously helps the school, and it may be your role to act as an intermediary between the parents or carers, as you know them from where you live in the vicinity of the school, and the teachers.

Spiritual and moral development are often ignored. Moral development appears to come about as part of social and cultural development. Where boundaries are clear, whether they are strict or lenient, even small children know when they are doing 'wrong'. It seems to be natural to challenge boundaries, and if these are flexible or ever-moving, the children may experience problems. The child knows they have overstepped the boundary by the reaction of the person setting the boundary. Too great a reaction can result in rebellion.

Spiritual development is not confined to the development of religious belief or participation in the practice of a particular faith. Young children experience wonder and joy, they accept mystery, they are curious, creative and imaginative, and suppression of such feelings in infancy or in the early years of school can inhibit their expression for many years to come [2.3P1]. Eight- to ten-year-olds begin to seek the meaning of things, want a purpose for doing things, and even for their own existence, and are beginning to recognise their own and others' identities as people. They get a very strong sense of injustice, and often start small action groups to raise money for worthy causes, or argue strongly for fairness in a game. It is at this age they will start asking abstract questions about beliefs, such as 'Do you believe in a life after death?' Primary age children can face death in others, in their pets and even in themselves, as terminally ill children do. They can appreciate straight but sensitive talking from adults, although many adults will feel that they need help in talking with children about such matters. Children begin to sort out legends and myths from factual evidence; for instance, recognising the myth behind the tradition of 'Father Christmas' delivering presents.

Many teenagers will fight shy of discussing their deep feelings about spiritual matters; peer pressure and fashion may dictate that such things are cissy. Yet most of them will be trying out their own beliefs in practice, and will still feel strongly about the beauty of the world around them or the expression of joy or sadness in poetry, music, art or drama.

They can get emotionally involved with the more extreme versions of religious belief or practice, as their instinct for trying new ways and for rebellion comes to the fore, but most young people come through such experiences. They develop a greater understanding of the variety of human nature, the reality of the consequences of their actions, their place in the world and their interdependence with their family and the community around them. You can be an active listener at all these stages of development but as in all such matters, ensure you know what the school policy is before you contribute too much of your own beliefs. You may be working in a faith school, or where some parents hold firm views such as those of Jehovah's Witnesses or the Exclusive Brethren. It is not your place to uphold or change any particular belief.

Schools need to help children and young people retain 'a capacity for reflection, curiosity, and a sense of awe and wonder as well as an ability to discuss beliefs and understand how they contribute to individual and group identity' (Ofsted 1993: 15) at the world about them, as well as encouraging the sense of fair play. A few moments spent in looking at some new flowers growing in the school grounds, or pointing out a rainbow formed by the edge of bevelled glass in the sunshine, the growth of the class pet, or the colours of a visiting bird or butterfly can all help spiritual growth. The intensity of the curriculum and the constraints of a timetable have tended to squeeze out not only thinking time but also reflecting time. This is not part of religious worship, although of course it can be, but is part of feeding an aspect of life that can so easily be lost. For some, poetry or music may trigger such a moment, and when planning work it is always worth trying to include something that has moved you. Different people are moved by different things, but you never know when such moments might happen.

Questions to ask yourself

- If you are now part of the way through reading this book or your course, have your feelings about learning changed since you started?

- Do your feelings or beliefs influence how you behave?

- Are you clear about the ethos and values which your school stands for and your role within them?

- Is there any conflict between your belief systems and that promoted by the school? What can you do about this?

- What do you do when pupils ask you about your feelings or beliefs?

- Do you know about the cultural backgrounds and sensitivities of the families whose children come to your school?

- What does the religious education policy for your school contain? Or the policy for collective worship?

- To whom can you go in the school to discuss any problems which may arise [2K3]?

Promoting independent learning

One of the problems you will encounter is that it is very likely that you have been appointed to help those who need assistance, and this very assistance labels the pupils as being disadvantaged in some way. It is a fine balance, and a continually changing one, between helping appropriately and enabling the pupils to achieve more of their potential and feel a sense of their own achievement. Somehow, the pupil has to maintain their own self-esteem and self-confidence and become increasingly independent of you. 'Doing myself out of a job' is part of your role. You need to discuss with the teacher the sort of strategies they use and would like you to use to promote independence, to encourage and support pupils, to enable them to make their own decisions [2.2P5]. Remember, praise for trying is as important as, if not more so than, praise for succeeding [2.2P3]. Part of all children's growth and development into adulthood is the increasing acceptance of responsibility for their own actions and their own learning. They cannot do this unless they are allowed to make decisions and sometimes mistakes.

This chapter has looked at the many facets of the learning process. Sometimes the theories and ideas seem in conflict:

- Inherited characteristics versus the influence of the environment
- Maturity versus accelerating learning
- Stages in development versus intuitive jumps of reasoning
- The biological function of the brain, the computer-type action of the brain, versus the more ephemeral things such as emotions and spirituality
- The importance of social and cultural context versus 'scientifically proven' facts
- Valuing diversity versus the need for school conformity
- Collaborative learning versus independent learning [2.3P2,4].

All these go to make up a complex process of development which results in a person being like the facets of a well-cut gemstone. Different surfaces catch the light at different times and turns of the stone. Different stones need different cutting techniques to bring out their particular brightness. It is part of your job to be alert to the nature of the learning, personality and context of the pupil you are working with; listen to them, watch them at work and encourage them to talk about their own feelings and learning [2.1P1; 2.2P1; 2.3P1;K1]. You can then assist the teacher in utilising the best learning strategy for each one and planning for their future development.

Learning through play

Play is often considered the opposite of work, and parents get worried when children are 'just playing about' in primary school and not sitting learning. Most teachers see 'playtime' as their relief time and not fully part of the formal school; indeed, some secondary schools now start early and finish at lunchtime so that they do not have to consider either school meals or supervision over the lunch break when not eating meals. While STL 15 seems at first glance more suitable for midday assistants, early years' workers and those who undertake leadership of play situations in organisations like scouts or kids' clubs, it would be well worth all Level 2 candidates just reading though the knowledge criteria for that standard. There are 29 statements under this heading and, like some of the other optional standards, there is no way a paragraph or two in this book can do justice to a very interesting and complex area.

Much of the study of play has been done by early years' practitioners but we all know that when faced with a new situation we have to play about in the widest sense with the materials, try things out for ourselves, experiment, investigate potential and ascertain what that particular subject means for us. This is true whether it is writing poetry, getting a new television or meeting new people. What is sad is that formal school has downgraded this area in the way it has. You cannot tell someone the things they will learn by playing, it is about the doing, not the seeing or listening of the old Chinese proverb. Just like any other task, play needs to be worked hard at to get the most out of it.

In a good early years' setting the curriculum is about the provision of as varied a diet of equipment and experiences as possible but not all at once, and not the same for all age groups. There should be something to stimulate each of the areas of learning described here, to support physical, linguistic, intellectual, emotional, social and spiritual development. In a nursery there are usually geographical areas that can be identified with aspects of learning. You would be able to see quiet areas with books, tables for drawing or writing, creative areas with paints and modelling media, investigative areas, constructive areas and imaginative areas with facilities for role play. Most physical provision is usually put outside, where some open-air and some covered areas can be found so that physical play can take place whatever the weather. Some nurseries have sensory areas with different surfaces to walk on, objects to bang and listen to, plants with different smells, as well as areas to dig and climb on.

Children can express their ideas, explore and investigate if left to their own devices, and it was believed at one point that the rich environment was everything [4K5; 15K1–4]. Thinking of your own exploration of a new piece of equipment, you need to be left alone to play with it. Remember the learning experience suggested in the last chapter, however, and you realise that an instructor/friend/guide's intervention at the right time is just what you needed. The main role of the teacher or leader is twofold, to vary the environment to encourage the exploration and stimulate interest, but mainly to watch the 'players' and decide how best to support their learning. This requires an in-depth knowledge of the child and a very acute sense of timing. The practitioner can intervene if play becomes too rough or too messy, can join in the game or activity, can allow the play to develop naturally or add extra dimensions to the activity.

To understand this role you need to go to a well-run nursery and watch the practitioners or play leaders at work. Their observational and record-keeping work is comprehensive, as much of the time the children are left to work/socialise with each other. The time spent on planning and preparation is also lengthy as the quality of the provision will depend on the selection and care of it, and the relevance to each child's needs as identified by the observational work [15.1P2,3].

Play is also related to age and developmental stage. Take sand play for instance. One only has to watch a small child on the beach watching the effect of the tide coming in to see the value of such items as sand and water for exploration of materials. Sometimes lip service is paid to the provision of play in the early years of the primary school by providing a sand tray or water tray with a few objects in them but unless the objects are relevant to the topic of the teacher or the interest of the child or group it is a pointless exercise, soon to become tedious and even counterproductive. Village layouts can be made, or capacity measures in dry sand or modelling equipment with wet sand provided. A sand tray in a class of older primary children, introduced as part of a geography topic for a week or two, with access to a source of water would enable the children to explore for themselves the effect of rainfall on sand. Replace the sand with soil, pebbles or clay at different times and a great deal will be learnt about erosion and geomorphic change. Use the same tray in secondary school geography, with plants, blocks for buildings, and the learning could be about the effects of man on the environment. I am sure you have also seen or been an adult on the beach with children and enjoyed endless hours trying to keep the water from destroying your carefully constructed sandcastle.

Play needs time and develops concentration: it is intrinsically motivated. All children play unless prevented by physical disability or cultural or social constraints. Educationalists see it as crucial for development of the imagination, problem solving, a healthy body and mind in the widest sense of healthy. Sometimes parents have to be persuaded of its value. Those schools which have extended their provision to include what happens in the playground have seen a decrease in conflict as well as an added dimension to the children's experience. The provision of a quiet area, some playground markings and a few skipping ropes, however, will not be enough. The supervisors need training in observation and intervention skills, they need contact with the class teachers to understand interests of the moment and to be able to feed back their concerns for social or emotional upsets. Maybe some teachers and head teachers also need persuading of the value of constructive play?

Care and support of pupils

SCHOOLS ARE FOR educating pupils, they are not children's homes or care centres. Early years' settings will seem to be more supportive than educational and the new guidance for the early years may seem to some to be too instructional, but here the overlap between education and care is even more blurred. The staff in schools are there first and foremost to enable the pupils to learn. Early years' children learn, but do so through play. In promoting learning the staff themselves are always learning and so the whole school is a learning institution. However, as school staff have a common law duty to act as any proud parent (*in loco parentis*), they do have a duty of care while the pupils are present, and while learners need a challenge, unhappy or uncomfortable people do not learn as well as happy, healthy, motivated ones. Therefore staff need to ensure that the learning environment is healthy – both hygienic and safe, as well as having the right atmosphere or climate to foster good relationships between all who work there. Mental and emotional health are as important as physical health. Learning through play in mainstream schools seems largely to have disappeared owing to the demands of the curriculum but there are moves afoot to remedy this.

General health

It was pointed out in Chapter 2 that you need to take care of your own health, but you also need to be alert to changes in your pupils. The ECM agenda is quite clear about this It covers the rights of all children – and children are those under 18 years of age by law.

Being healthy: enjoying good mental and physical health and living a healthy lifestyle

Staying safe: being protected from harm and neglect

Enjoying and achieving: getting the most out of life and developing the skills of adulthood

Making a positive contribution: being involved with the community and society and not engaging in antisocial or offending behaviour

Economic well-being: not being prevented by economic disadvantage from achieving their full potential in life.

Chapter 4 pointed you at the school policies which should be in place for all health, hygiene and medical matters and these will be updated in the light of guidance following the publication of the ECM agenda. You must make sure you have a copy of all the relevant ones and that you have read them, understand them and follow the guidelines set out in them. Sick children or adults will not work well, and may be infectious to other pupils. If you see anything that concerns you, always tell the class teacher. Sometimes children come to school with minor ailments, such as a heavy cold, and you need to be able to deal with these. It is sometimes useful, particularly with small children in winter, to equip yourself with a box of tissues or a soft toilet roll to deal with runny noses. Children do not need to be off school for a cold, but you can help prevent its spread to others. Dispose of the used materials properly. A polythene bag with you could contain the used material which could then go to an incinerator or adult toilet. Ask for advice on procedures like this.

Always reassure ill pupils, and comfort unhappy ones, and recognise that '. . . no school should have a policy of "no physical contact . . ."' (DCSF 2007c:5). However, recent years have seen school staff worried about what is appropriate in order not to be falsely accused of child abuse. Touch may be appropriate during PE, first aid procedures, if a pupil is in distress or is being congratulated, but for some pupils touching may be unwelcome because they are sensitive or for cultural reasons. Differences in gender between adult and child could be significant and even 'innocent and well intentioned physical contact can be misconstrued' (DCSF 2007c:15). So a useful rule of thumb with a child who needs comforting is to do it verbally and in an appropriate manner unless they seek physical comfort from you. A returned hug in a public place from a small child missing a parent is one thing, but the same action in a quiet corner can be misinterpreted [3.2P4].

Younger children or those with a disability may need more physical support than older ones and are less likely to be able to tell you what is wrong if they are miserable. Be sure to read the section on child protection below. You may need to summon help. Some schools have a simple card communication system where staff have access to the cards which are sent in an emergency to the office. Depending on the colour of the card, the office personnel alert the appropriate support. It could be red for a fight, green for illness and yellow for an accident, for instance. Enquire whether you are able to use such a system in your school. It may be important to help pupils not directly involved in an incident, who can suffer shock particularly if the incident is severe. This is the kind of role you can play if you have to summon expert help: you will be able to support the onlookers. This may just be reassurance or removing them from the incident site.

You need to be able to recognise if a pupil you are working with is just 'under the weather' or is really feeling ill. The important thing is to get to know the pupils with whom you are working closely, what is their normal range of behaviour and appearance, then you will recognise significant changes should they occur. As you are likely to be working more closely with the pupils than any other member of staff, you may be the first to notice.

The sort of things you may notice are:

- changes in facial colour – becoming very red or pale, becoming very hot or cold, becoming clammy or shivering – fever usually means some kind of infection;
- changes in behaviour, like not wanting to go out at break-time when they usually want to be first out;
- general distress;
- reduced concentration, which can even be to the point of falling asleep at their desk;
- scratching more than usual – ask about the school policy regarding head lice – you should not examine a head unless it is appropriate in your school; or this could be an allergic reaction
- complaining of pain which persists, including headaches and stomach pain, particularly if they are not easily distracted from mentioning it;
- rashes – these can develop rapidly and may be associated with fever in the case of infection or could be an allergic reaction;
- coughing and sneezing excessively;
- diarrhoea or vomiting – these you will have to deal with as emergencies [3.2P5,6; K14,15].

You should not try to diagnose from these conditions, although always note any unusual circumstances that you see or that the pupil mentions. They may talk of strange-tasting food, or parties, circumstances changing at home, visitors to home or recent holidays. Your role is to recognise the changes and report them appropriately, unless there is an emergency to deal with. You will soon recognise the difference between the pupils who want a brief spell in the sick room or a bit more attention, and the threat of 'I am going to be sick' which needs immediate action. Make sure you know where or to whom to send sick pupils, and to whom to report the symptoms you have noticed. You may even need to summon help rather than leave a sick pupil.

Remember too, changes in mental and emotional state can also occur, particularly if something traumatic or dramatic has happened at home which can show itself in unhappiness, mood swings, lack of concentration and attention-seeking or withdrawal from activities [2.2P1]. Some cultures and religions have different ways of dealing with illness, so if in doubt, ask. The age of the pupil will affect how well they can tell you what is wrong; once you know the pupil well you will be able to tell how reliable any information from them might be and the circumstances of the incident. Some pupils can fake illness if they do not like sports or if the weather is inclement. There may be changes in patterns of behaviour. A small child who has always come to chat stands alone, or a teenager who is usually friendly is moody or withdrawn, or a usually quiet but confident pupil follows you around. It could be just growing up, the hormones of puberty taking over, or it could signify something more significant. Either way, you need mentally to register the changes, keep an eye on the pupil over a period of time and if really concerned talk to the pupil's teacher or tutor. Such changes could signify problems at home, even abuse of some kind, self-inflicted substance abuse, or bullying within or outside the school. If the pupil will talk to you, follow the guidelines set out below regarding child protection – never promise confidentiality, always tell someone of the conversation and make a simple record of it [2.3P3].

Many TAs are appointed to help a child with special learning or physical needs. You must ensure you know the full extent of your role and responsibilities with any pupil, and all the appropriate ways to support them, and whether there are particular changes or signs peculiar to them of which you should be aware [3K4; 12K11]. For instance, sometimes pupils are on particular medication which has certain specified effects, or they may need to be given that medication at a particular time. You should familiarise yourself with any particular needs of pupils with whom you may come into contact. If these details are not readily available in the staffroom, check with your line manager. Also, there may be pupils with whom you are not directly coming into contact, but who do have specific conditions of which you should be aware. Most schools now ensure that all staff know of pupils with allergies such as peanut or bee sting allergy, or the existence of pupils with diabetes, epilepsy or other disorders. These conditions could have crises with which you may need to deal appropriately. Each individual will have their own medication or procedures for dealing with any incidents.

One condition that has become more common is asthma; approximately one pupil in four will have some kind of allergic or asthmatic condition, some much worse than others, some just manifesting as hay fever in the summer or a sensitivity to certain drugs. You should check at some early point whether you will be working with pupils who suffer from asthma, where they keep their inhalers and how they are used. Usually schools have information from the Asthma Association which you can read.

- Ask your line manager what are the four most common ailments of pupils within the school.

- See what more you can find out about these ailments.

- Find out whether these ailments are treated in the same way in all countries.
- Does your school have any pupils from the countries where customs are different?
- Find out more about any conditions that apply to pupils you are working with closely.
- Does the school have any written guidelines in any of these areas?
- Do you have a copy?

Whatever the problem, make sure you know where and when to seek help, what kind of written records are needed and to whom you should report any concerns, including whether you contact parents directly or notify someone else to do this [2.2P7; 2.3P5; 2K3,4].

Health education

The school will also have a policy to do with health education of the pupils. It is usually located in what is colloquially called PSHE – personal, social and health education. This will cover areas such as sex education, how to help pupils with personal hygiene, diet and exercise, but also emotional and mental health. It will deal with matters like self-esteem, its importance and how to promote it, bullying and coping with it, whether the school has access to people with counselling skills. While you will not necessarily be directly responsible for teaching pupils in any of these areas, your relationships with them are very important in enabling them to grow into mature, self-confident adults. A healthy school is not only hygienic and safe physically but is a welcoming and secure place with good relationships between all who work there [2K12]. Your example to the pupils is important. You can show by the way you talk to colleagues or pupils, by your tone of voice, what can be expected. You give an example in the way you listen, or are prepared to follow up problems, to get help. Even remembering names shows that you care and are prepared to bother about others. The way in which you show respect engenders respect in others [3.4P6]. If you are willing to assist with preparation of resources for teachers or get someone a cup of tea when they are fed up or overstretched, it shows you can think about them and do something practical to assist. If all staff had such an attitude, the school would be a good place to work and pupils would soon recognise it as a good place to learn.

It is highly likely that you will be asked questions by pupils, as they get to know you and you work in close proximity to a small group or to individuals. Note that primary schools only have to have a sex education policy. That policy does not have to ensure sex education is done by the school; it may indicate that it should be done at home. It is really helpful if you are able to talk with children and young people about health issues informally and possibly individually, to talk about how their bodies work in a matter-of-fact way provided you are sure you are working within school policies and the information you are giving is correct [3.3P6,K20]. Ask for help from a senior member of staff if in any doubt.

Find out

- whether you should listen without comment to the exploits of the teenagers, such as:
  - smoking on the school premises?
  - substance abuse?
  - getting drunk at the weekend?
  - declaring their sexual habits or preferences or that they are pregnant?

- what do you do if you are told of incidents of bullying, or disastrous friendships?
- whether you can talk about HIV and AIDS if they ask the questions?
- what should you do if they show you pornography?
- should you comment on a pupil's diet or exercise level to them even if they seem excessively thin or obese?
- whom you tell if the pupils are so upset about something that it is affecting the way they behave?
- simple ways to boost pupils' self-esteem [2K12.11;K13.10,12].

The SEAL project and materials have been used very successfully in some primary schools, so much so that the programme is being made available to all schools including secondary schools. The original programme offers seven themes, one for each year of primary school. It is a whole-school approach, to help children develop skills of self-awareness, managing feelings, motivation, empathy and social skills. The seven themes are:

New beginnings

Getting on and falling out

Say no to bullying

Going for goals!

Good to be me

Relationships

Changes

The secondary pack has a full programme of four themes for Year 7. More information, including some material for parents, can be found on the website www.standards. dfes.gov.uk/primary/publications/banda/seal [2.2P4; 2K10.4;K11.4;K12.3,4;13.3,4].

Some suggestions for raising self-esteem are as follows:

- Talk to everyone the same way, regardless of gender, race or background.
- Address pupils by their preferred name.
- Use positive comments: 'thank you for walking', 'well done for being quiet', including written comments if you can: 'well read today', 'I liked the story'.
- Use praise appropriately, not indiscriminately.
- Treat boys and girls equally, whether for tasks or treats or even lining up.
- Provide a good role model in gender, culture and disability, both in reality and when finding examples in teaching materials such as books and magazines.
- Use rewards, praise and congratulation systems for work, including showing it to other staff.
- Catch them being good or working hard and tell them.
- Set small achievable targets and congratulate them on achieving them.
- Have reward systems for behaviour – telling the teachers about the good as well as the troublesome.
- Value work by ensuring it is taken care of, and presented well, both by you and by the pupil.
- Encourage independence appropriate to age and maturity.
- Enable and encourage peer tutoring.

■ Use humour carefully.

■ Encourage children to value their own performance.

■ Listen to the views of pupils and act on them where possible.

■ Avoid being patronising or sarcastic as pupils recognise both.

Can you add to this?   (Watkinson 2002: 38)

Settling pupils

One area where you are likely to be involved is with pupils who are very new to the school [2K14]. This is particularly likely if you are working with children in the early years' class, sometimes called the reception class, or with Year 7s in a secondary school (Year 5s or 9s if your area has a middle-school system). The school is likely to have well-thought-out procedures, some of which will have taken place before you meet the pupils. The teachers may have visited the pupils' previous school or playgroup, or even their homes, and pupils are most likely to have had at least one visit to the school before their first 'real' day. You need to find out what these procedures are and may even accompany members of the teaching staff on their visits.

Remember

■ How you felt when you started school.

■ How you felt when you transferred schools.

■ How you felt when you started this new job.

■ How you felt if you went to a new school if you moved house as a child.

■ What helped you to settle?

■ Who helped you to settle?

■ How long did it take?

■ So – what can you do to help newcomers to your school?

All sorts of things affect a child's ability to settle in a new environment. If things are troubling them at home – say their parents have broken up, which necessitated the house move – it is not just the new school that is troubling them, but new neighbours and missing one of their parents. Making new friends can be a problem when changing schools. They may have come from another country with different customs. They may not speak our language. They may have had a period away from the school, while a parent serves with the armed services or during a return visit to their native land. The sort of thing to look out for is a child who is not mixing with others at break times, one who cries without apparently being hurt or one who is clinging on to you, a pupil of any age who cannot follow instructions or get on with their work, but does not appear to have learning problems. A young child may wet themselves, afraid to ask for the toilet, or fall asleep because they are not sleeping well at night, worried about their new school. Small children anxious at starting school are even likely to run away unless the school has made proper arrangements for the first few days.

Older pupils attending the new large secondary school after their relatively cosy, probably much smaller primary school will feel very lost. They will have to carry their bags around to various classrooms instead of having a classroom and a few well-known teachers for most subjects. Generally, an unsettled child will be fearful and tearful, but such feelings could manifest themselves in angry or even aggressive behaviour as the child is cross at being put in this strange situation. Pupils with learning problems, with a disability or with little ability to communicate either because of home language being different or through speech problems, may have a higher risk of unease with new situations, as they find it more difficult to understand what is happening. But beware of misinterpreting the reasons for difficult behaviour. Always talk matters through with the teacher if you have concerns, and respond as he or she directs.

As a TA, you can be invaluable in settling pupils in. It may be an idea to negotiate with the teachers for you just to be available for this task at the beginning of a new school year. In this way the pupils will get down to the school work much more quickly and satisfactorily. It may even be important to change your timetable for a couple of weeks to spend more time at the beginnings and ends of days ensuring the new ones know where they are going and get there happily. The teacher may ask you to liaise directly with the parents and stagger entry and exit times for the new pupils. In this way an easier transition can take place, especially if a larger number are starting together. Changing classrooms or teachers can unsettle pupils. A constant change of teacher when supply teachers are standing in for a teacher on sick leave can also be a problem. In these situations you may be the one constant person in their school lives. Do ensure you talk to the class teacher if you continue to notice signs of distress after a week or so, or to a more senior teacher if the class teacher's absence is the problem. Talk any problems through with the class teacher.

Strategies that may help to settle pupils

- Be warm and welcoming.

- Learn to recognise distressed pupils.

- Learn their names as soon as possible.

- Make sure they know the name of their class teacher or tutor and encourage the other pupils with you to befriend and help the newcomer.

- Make sure they know where they are going round the building, where their next classroom is, where their cloakroom and the toilets are and to whom they can go if they are worried.

- Smile at them when you see them in the building but are not directly working with them.

- Allow them to talk about their previous school or playschool.

- Allow them to work a little more slowly at first.

- Have patience, listen and possibly talk about your own experiences if appropriate.

- Keep to classroom routines and where possible to the layout.

- Make sure you know whether they have special educational needs or speak a different language.

- Try wording your sentences more simply if that is a problem.

- Try to learn a few words of their language, as they begin to learn our words – their words for mum and dad, for home and toilet, bag, book and table would do for a start.

- Carry the tissue box with you in case of tears.

- Ensure you tell their class teacher or tutor if they have problems after the first week.

Behaviour management

It is possible that you have been appointed to assist in the support of a pupil who has problems with conforming to the expected behaviour patterns of the school, thus disrupting the work of other pupils and not learning well themselves. But, for whatever reason you have been appointed, you must become part of the whole school's system for behaviour management. The words discipline and behaviour management always seem to have a negative connotation. If behaviour is all right we tend to ignore it, and only deal with it when things go wrong [3.4P1,2]. Any good behaviour management policy will talk of reinforcing good behaviour with praise, just as you should reward good work with praise. If

- the curriculum is interesting and absorbing
- free time provision is interesting and stimulating
- relationships are encouraging and proactive
- praise and rewards are used appropriately and frequently [12.1P5]
- the climate of the school is a positive one

then behaviour is much more likely to be acceptable and reprimands less likely to be necessary [1K9; 11.1P7]. Also, it is no good to have only certain adults maintaining discipline; pupils need to understand that all adults will reinforce the codes by which the school maintains order. Wherever possible, try to get some local training in this area.

If a situation becomes more than you should deal with, senior members of staff will always be available for you, either to refer matters to at the time or later for advice. Schools also have access to specialist teams and psychologists to whom you may be able to talk. There will be courses available both within the school INSET (in-service education and training) programme and externally delivered. Discuss with your mentor what would be most suitable for your needs. All schools have policies and procedures that all staff must follow, the important factor being consistency of approach whatever the incident [3.4P4]. Some of the policies that do not directly give guidance about behaviour management are also important in this area. For instance, if you suggest to a pupil that they have time out or if you find that you need to withdraw a pupil from class because he or she is behaving badly, you are depriving him or her of that part of the curriculum but sometimes it has to be done, as long as it is appropriate for your role and the pupil's needs. Restraining a pupil could be construed as child abuse – make sure you follow the school's policy; dealing with bullying may be in a separate policy. You must know the limits of your authority, when and to whom you refer incidents outside that authority, your particular role within the school and the roles of others. As you become more experienced you may see situations or learn of strategies that could be introduced to your school but are not currently available. Again, talk with your mentor or line manager about them, and feed them back in any in-house training sessions for discussion.

Rogers (1991) has some useful things to say about discipline and behaviour: Decisive discipline is marked by these characteristics:

- a focus on the due rights of all
- an assertive stance (Assertion is distinguished between aggression and hostility on the one hand, and passivity or capitulating to student demands on the other. Essentially, assertion communicates one's own need and due rights without trampling on the other parties' rights.)
- refusal to rely on power or role-status to gain respect

- speaking and acting respectfully even when frustrated or angry
- choosing to respond to discipline incidents (from prior reflection and planning) rather than reacting to incidents as they arise
- preparing for discipline as rigorously as for any aspect of the curriculum.

When actually disciplining, a decisive approach engages the student by:

- establishing eye contact
- speaking clearly with appropriate firmness
- speaking briefly, addressing primary behaviour and ignoring as much of the secondary behaviour as is possible
- distinguishing between the child and his or her behaviour
- expecting compliance rather than demanding or merely hoping for it
- re-establishing working relationships as soon as possible.

(Rogers 1991: 43)

You must quickly learn what is acceptable behaviour in the various areas of the school and what is not, how to identify pupils in difficulties and what is normal. Negative behaviour may be verbally or physically abusive or offensive. Racial or sexist actions or language should not be tolerated. Bullying needs to be recognised and dealt with. Try to spot signs of potential conflict – it is more easily dealt with in the early stages, then monitor developments. You must also recognise that sometimes circumstances change, both for pupils and for the school, and be alert to these changes. Changing rooms or buildings or going from inside the school to the playground or sports field can alter behaviour. In order to learn all this, you will need to understand the limits of normal behaviour and have copies of the policies and procedures for your school on dealing with what, for the school, is inappropriate behaviour. Go through them with a mentor or line manager to identify your role and appropriate strategies. Behaviour patterns develop as do other aspects of physical and mental development [2K10.6].

Emotional and social development also take place, so expectations of behaviour will vary with the age of the pupils. Physical changes such as those experienced by pupils going through puberty can alter their behaviour radically, as any parent of a child of this age will know. Peer pressure can make an otherwise well-behaved child do something out of character, such as play truant or cheek a teacher. In some cultures, some behaviour is acceptable for boys but not for girls. This can sometimes be seen in early years' settings where rough play is acceptable for boys, but girls will be admonished for similar behaviour [2K10.6]. We can all have assumptions about what is appropriate, depending on our own upbringing. For instance, many people still have the idea that young people with severe learning problems do not have sexual urges; they do, and can fall in love just like more able youngsters. The paraplegic athletes have challenged our ideas of physical capacity in recent years [3.4P5].

What is age-appropriate in an infant school pupil may be considered inappropriate in a secondary school pupil, yet some secondary pupils may behave in an infantile way, expressing their feelings or emotions in coping with a problem. While you will aim to respond to the older pupil hoping they will respond in a more mature way, in responding to their behaviour rather than to them personally you may need to modify your actions. You need to accommodate the pupil according to his or her level of development and this will probably need you to discuss your actions with your mentor or line manager and find out more about the pupil [2K10.6]. It is also important to recognise that behaviour management takes place all the time, not just when things go wrong. Thanking, smiling, praising appropriately, all contribute to positive attitudes in relationships. Encouragement is very important for all children, and for adults too [10.2P6].

Think back to that personal learning experience suggested in the last chapter, and to your own relationships. How much easier it is to work with people who recognise your effort, even if the actual achievement is small. Many of those with learning problems have poor self-esteem and this can be a real drawback when learning, although low self-esteem can affect a pupil of any ability. Let them know when they are doing well and show them how close they are to getting the desired outcome. Ask the teacher whether you can write on pupils' work and what kind of comment is acceptable. Specific remarks are much more useful: 'completed quickly' and 'clearer handwriting' say more than 'well done'. Be careful not to do too much for them (no matter how much they wheedle) [12.2P6].

One of the real problems is that children with poor learning skills can develop a kind of learnt helplessness. Being pleasant whenever possible means that when you have to correct inappropriate behaviour it has more effect. Role model how you wish children to behave, modulate your voice, walk, do not run, be punctual and polite. Keep calm (whatever you are feeling inside), listen and be consistent. Respect breeds respect [3.4P6]. We all need boundaries so rules are developed. We all have rights, but we also have responsibilities. This includes access to school facilities, equipment and materials for staff and pupils, and developing responsibility in pupils. The aim is to make pupils take responsibility for their own behaviour.

The behaviour management training in the TA Induction course (TDA 2006b, 2006c: 4.1–4.22 in the TA file) talks of the 4Rs approach: Rules, Routines, Rights and Responsibilities leading to choices which have consequences [3K21–23]. Your school may have a systematic reward system, with stickers and certificates for achievements. If so, you will need to know whether you can operate this and what for, and if not how you can best bring achievements to the attention of someone who can do the rewarding. Similarly, there may be sanctions which you can use, such as stopping a pupil misbehaving in the playground and giving them 'time out', or ensuring a particular item gets mentioned in a home dialogue or report book. Usually you are there on the spot to see to the immediate situation, but a more senior member of staff will carry out a punishment such as detention or informing parents/carers. If the situation occurs in the classroom in a lesson, you need to know what to refer to the teacher and what you can deal with. Once you know the ways of the school, you are in a strong position to say to a pupil who might argue with you, 'You have a choice – you can do what you know is right or . . .' whatever the consequence is for that misbehaviour in your school [3.4P3; 15.2P1].

Using the language of choice will [3.4P3; 15K9]

- reduce instances of conflict arising from trying to make things happen
- teach pupils a sense of responsibility
- create an important link between choice and consequence
- help to empower pupils as individuals.

(TDA 2006c: 13)

It means they save face in the process and recognises that mistakes are a normal part of learning.

Deal with matters immediately you see inappropriate behaviour. The secret is to be assertive without being aggressive or confrontational and to ensure that you are separating any inappropriate behaviour from the pupil. This enables the pupil to save face and maintain their self-esteem, which is probably low. Keep the focus on the primary behaviour, the thing that drew your attention in the first place, and actively try to build up your relationship with the pupil concerned. Always follow up on things that count: if you have said you will refer the matter to someone else or you will talk to them again on the next day, then be sure you do it. Always seek help if you need it. Try not to get yourself into a situation where you are alone with very challenging pupils. If you see a potential problem situation, make someone else aware and attempt to defuse it. Such a situation can occur with an individual if there is a shortage of equipment or a challenging piece of work; or with a group, for instance, in a slow lunch queue. Typical positive strategies include appropriate praise and encouragement. Pupils who are motivated and interested are less likely to misbehave. Giving children choices rather than just being negative is a recommended management strategy [3.4P3]. Where children can voice an opinion on provision they are much more likely to use it properly and care for it [15.1P1,2]. Do not touch or restrain a pupil in a conflict situation unless you have been specially taught the procedure for your school.

Counselling is a skill. Before you embark on any in-depth work of this kind with pupils, do take advice and if possible training to ensure you know what you are doing.

You need to find out what is appropriate for:

- classrooms. Different teachers' classrooms will vary slightly
- within other areas of the school
- outside the school premises
- laboratories or technical areas
- individuals
- groups
- whole classes

what are:

- the rules
- the rewards and sanctions that can be applied
  - by you
  - by others

what strategies are available for you to use in managing inappropriate behaviour:

- time-out places
- sources of help and referral at different times of the day
- report forms or notes
- withdrawal of privileges

how you:

- report incidents
- develop your skills of behaviour management
- seek advice.

Other pupils may have individual targets, plans and performance indicators similar to those of a pupil with learning difficulties. These may be called Target Report Cards (this will vary from school to school), Behaviour Support Plans or, in some cases, a Pastoral Support Plan. If you are likely to come into contact with such a pupil, you must acquaint yourself with these. The targets will be small, such as for the pupil to keep on task for ten minutes without interrupting anyone. Your aim will not be to take responsibility for, cure or independently change the pupil's behaviour. Some of these plans will be the equivalent of an IEP (Individual Education Plan) for behaviour, showing what you are to do, and usually any paperwork, of which you have copies, will have a space for you to comment on progress. As the pupil will know their targets, any comments about progress that you might make to the pupil can also relate to the target, such as 'You stayed on task and you didn't interrupt. Well done, let's see if you can do it again tomorrow.'

Bullying

This is a particular concern of many pupils and parents/carers. No school is without its bullies and the nature of bullying is that it will take place away from adult sight, so may be hard to detect. 'Bullying is forcing others to do, act and feel the very things a bully would never want done to him. Bullying is not accidental, it is learned.' Schools have policies for dealing with bullying issues, as they need to have 'clear, school-wide consequences' (Rogers 1994: 101). There should not only be strategies for dealing with the bully, but also for helping the victim, both in the short term and in the long term, to become more assertive. It is likely that pupils will debate the issue in class and strategies like circle time will be available to help. These are probably run by the teachers, but you may be asked to undertake training in this area to run such sessions as well as participate in discussions.

Child protection

It is essential to know about this, although it is a sensitive area. Some of you may have had close personal involvement with family or friends where problems have arisen, or feel that these matters are better not dealt with until an incident arises. You will all have been checked by the police through the Criminal Records Bureau (CRB) before you took up post. However, there are things that, as a member of staff likely to come into close physical and pastoral contact with pupils, you must be aware of. All schools will have written policies in this area and make sure all staff are trained together at least every three years, but it does not always happen. If it does not happen in your school, then suggest it. If you are at all uneasy in this area, ask for help and training [3.3P1].

There are legal and organisational requirements and implications for you when you work with other people's children. The Children Acts apply to schools as well as to the general population. The school policy should lay out clear guidelines for all staff on what to do if there is a suspicion of abuse and on how to prevent allegations against staff themselves. The latest guidance from the government is clear and available to anyone. *Safeguarding children and safer recruitment in education* give references to all the guidance and websites from which further information can be obtained (DfES 2006a) [3K25]. There should be a designated senior person (DSP) who has lead responsibility for dealing with child protection issues. Their name should be known by all staff; they are trained in what to do and where to go if help is needed. In a primary school this is usually the headteacher. There is clear guidance in the induction training of the DCFS provided by LAs so try to make sure that you are able to go on the courses.

Abuse is 'when a child is hurt or harmed by another person in a way that causes significant harm to that child and which may well have an effect on the child's development or well-being' (DfES 2004b:37). This must be compared with that which could reasonably be expected of a similar child, but the judgement and responsibility for care does not lie with the school but with Children's Social Care.

There are two main areas of sensitivity, one in recognising the signs of abuse and the other in behaving appropriately as a member of staff. Keep yourself aware of any proposals which could affect you or your work. All staff should be aware of the possible signs of abuse, and these are not always physical. It can also be emotional abuse, neglect and sexual abuse. While some of these signs can be listed, they must be considered only indicators. All sorts of personal or family events can cause changes in behaviour. Social factors can increase a child's vulnerability to abuse, but it is not restricted to certain kinds of people or behaviour [3K18].

The important thing is to tell someone senior to yourself of your concern, as patterns may emerge when several people's evidence is collated, or several different signs appear on or with the same pupil [3.3P2]. Different local authorities will issue slightly different guidance, giving local arrangements for training, case conferences and support systems. For instance the Southend, Essex and Thurrock (SET) guidance gives a useful list of signs and symptoms of abuse in a small handbook which all schools have and makes available considerable multi-service guidance on a special website: www.escb.co.uk.

Some of the lists below come from the SET guidance.

Child abuse and neglect may come about

- through inflicting harm or failure to prevent harm
- in a family, institution or community setting
- found in all social groups, regardless of culture, social class or financial position
- by those known to the family or more rarely a stranger
- by adult/s or other child/ren.

The presence of factors described under recognition IS NOT proof that abuse has occurred, but:

- must be regarded as indicators
- justify discussion
- may require consultation and/or referral.

In practice the categories overlap and an abused child frequently suffers more than a single type of abuse [3K17a and b].

Physical abuse may involve hitting, shaking, throwing, poisoning, burning or scalding, drowning, suffocating or otherwise causing physical harm to a child.

Physical harm may also be caused when a parent or carer fakes the symptoms of, or deliberately causes ill health to, a child they are looking after.

Possible indicators

- Explanation inconsistent with injury
- Several different explanations
- Unexplained delay in seeking treatment
- Parents/carers uninterested or undisturbed by injury
- Parents absent without good reason when child presented for treatment
- Repeated presentation of minor injuries
- Family used different doctors, hospital emergency departments and other health provisions
- Reluctance to give information or discuss previous injuries.

Possible signs

- Bruising
- Bite marks
- Burns and scalds
- Fractures
- Scars.

Emotional abuse is caused by persistent or severe emotional ill-treatment or rejection such as to cause actual or likely adverse effect on the emotional and behavioural development of a child under the age of 18 years. It is difficult to recognise and may need observations over time. There may be

- Parent/carer and child relationship factors
- Child presentation concerns
- Parent/carer related issues.

Sexual abuse is the actual or likely sexual exploitation of a child or adolescent under the age of 18 years by any person. This would include any form of sexual activity to which the child cannot give true consent either by law or because of ignorance, dependence, developmental immaturity or fear.

Possible indicators

- Boys and girls scared to talk
- Full account must be taken of cultural sensitivities of any individual child or family
- Difficult to recognise unless disclosure
- Behavioural indicators
- Physical indicators.

Persistent or severe neglect of children under the age of 18 years involves persistent failure to meet a child's basic physical and or psychological needs or the failure to protect a child from physical harm or danger.

Recognising neglect

- Child related indicators
- Indicators in the care provided.

Golden rules

- It is not the responsibility of education staff to interview pupils. If a pupil makes a disclosure of abuse they should listen carefully to what the pupil has to say, but should not question them in a way that puts words in their mouth
- It is important to make accurate notes about what has been heard, seen or told
- Interviewing pupils should be left to the police and social care staff, who have the necessary training to carry out this role effectively. Inappropriate interviewing may jeopardise the chances of a successful prosecution at a later date
- Concerns should always be made known quickly to the DSP, or in their absence to another senior member of staff

- Concerns should not be discussed with parents/carers until advice on how to proceed has been obtained from the DSP

- A pupil must not be promised confidentiality about any information on abuse they may choose to disclose. The member of support staff must explain that they may need to pass on information to other professionals to help keep the pupil or other children safe.

(DfES 2004b:44) [3.3P3]

Staff are vulnerable to false accusations:

- When alone with pupils

- When providing intimate care

- If restraint is needed

- When taking action if concerned about the action of a colleague

- When talking to parents or carers – care about confidentiality.

Useful websites

www.publications.doh.gov.uk/safeguardingchildren

www.teachernet.gov.uk/childprotection

www.nspcc.org.uk

Do not use any list as being definitive: you need proper training from the trained Child Protection Officers or whoever provides the training in your area. All children can have bruises from accidents or from playing roughly. It is the type of bruise and where it is on the body that can be important. Do not be obsessive or inquisitive, but just be vigilant, for instance when children change for PE or are talking informally.

Revealing

A child may reveal to you what has happened to them. You are particularly well placed for children to feel secure with you. You will work in small groups or with individual pupils for periods of time and build up friendly relations. No school staff are trained to deal with children or families in detail in child protection matters but you all have a responsibility to recognise and report to people who are. You should not question a child in these circumstances as you may ask leading questions. You should never promise not to tell anyone. Listen carefully, sensitively, caringly, inwardly note what they say and then tell the named designated member of staff as soon as possible. Make a short written record afterwards, date it and give it to this named member of staff. It is that person's responsibility to deal with it by informing Social Services or the police, who do have trained personnel for helping the children and their families on any matters that arise [3.3P4,5].

It is difficult, because you make assumptions or have memories which could prevent you from listening properly, but it is a responsibility that you take on when working in a school. If you have any doubts about what you have heard or seen, and these incidents are rarely clear cut, discuss what you have seen or heard with the class teacher, your teacher mentor, the designated teacher or the head. If you are involved further, be guided by the designated senior person in the school. These people will understand about case conferences, child protection registers, and agencies which can support vulnerable children and their families. Of course, you maintain confidentiality with the staff concerned, in all these proceedings.

The other area where you can be involved in these issues is when you are dealing with children in intimate situations. Again this often happens when TAs have been appointed to deal with pupils with physical disabilities, or very young children who have toileting accidents [2K10.3]. Nursery staff will be involved in toilet training [2K10.4]. Usually the parents know what the policy is as well, whether school staff can clean children up after toilet accidents or change underclothes. TAs are sometimes asked to work in pairs when these events occur. Always comfort unhappy children, but do it in public, not privately. Pupils need sometimes to see school as a haven, a place of safety and security which they may not otherwise have, but do not put yourself into a situation that could lead to unjustified accusation. Always be aware of, and respond to, troubled children, but recognise how to do this appropriately. Do not single them out for attention; it is better for them to come to you.

Contact

Another aspect of this can be when dealing with difficult pupils. Again, you may have been appointed just for this purpose. The proper procedures cannot be taught to you in a book. Touching pupils inappropriately, let alone restraining pupils, can get you into difficulties with parents and even with the law. The pupils concerned are usually particularly volatile, liable to act up, or react unnecessarily to being told how to behave. So do make sure you know the school policy on restraint, and if possible get appropriate training in this area. In your early days in the school, you should not be in a difficult position with a pupil swearing in your face, being aggressive or dangerous to others. Make sure you talk quickly to your line manager and sort out who does what. Most LAs have people who are specialists in this area who can help.

In all these health and safety issues it is vital that you know the policies and procedures that exist for your school. Some of these may be based on national guidance. They may seem irksome but they are written to protect the pupils and to protect you. Ensure you know about what liaison there is with parents over various incidents, what records the school requires to be kept and maintain confidentiality appropriately at all times.

Caring for children with physical disabilities

This is so likely to be the role of some TAs that it forms a whole standard in the optional STL 13. As in the restraint issues mentioned above, this is a very specialist area in which you must receive direct training from a qualified professional. This may be someone from within your school, especially if you are working in a special school, but it may be a specialist teacher or adviser from the LA or the medical profession. There are some general principles which apply whatever the condition or injury and some which will be specific to the condition. The glossary of terms at the beginning of this unit is a very useful summary of principles.

The carer aims to:

- maximise the potential and independence of the individual
- respect the rights, wishes, feelings of the individual in order to meet their needs and take account of their choices
- where necessary or possible act as interpreter and advocate for the individual
- act within the law
- treat the individual equally with their peers and not discriminate against them
- treat them with dignity, respecting privacy
- protect the individual from danger and harm
- enable access to information about themselves
- communicate with them in their preferred method and language.

This kind of care can range from the short-term care for a child who has a broken leg in a mainstream school to being a TA in a school for children with profound or multiple disabilities. The disability could be due to an accident, or to an inherited condition like cystic fibrosis or a birth trauma like cerebral palsy. You may be dealing with a wheelchair or a hoist; you may have to help a teenage girl with muscular dystrophy who cannot deal with her own menstrual needs.

All the usual precautions should be used to maintain hygiene, like washing your hands before and after any intimate procedure or making sure equipment you use is clean and in good order. Individuals with disabilities of these kinds may be more vulnerable to infection than the norm. If there is any apparatus to be used or a care plan drawn up by one of the specialists, you must make sure you understand all the instructions and follow them. Get a practical demonstration and if in any doubt refuse to undertake any procedure until you get one. You do not want to be the cause of any accident. Similarly if you can see any risk or consider something unsafe, get advice or help. When you have finished any procedure it is really important that you make sure any equipment you have used is clean and ready for the next time – it may not be you that has to deal with them.

Self-esteem is even more important for children or young people who have any disability, so talking with them, telling them what you are going to do, asking their advice on the preferred way of doing things is really important. They need to feel they are in charge of what is going on. Remember what it is like when somebody cares for you when you are unwell. It is tempting to feel sorry for yourself and even pretend to be worse than you are to get sympathy. So there is a delicate balance here between doing the right thing for an individual and getting them to help themselves.

If you are working in this way it is also more important than with children without disabilities that you understand the ways in which risk assessments work, the school policies and the legal frameworks surrounding caring for those more vulnerable. So, health and safety, accessing records and the need for appropriate confidentiality must be understood. Just as you watch for changes in any normal child, your monitoring of physically disabled pupils in your care is crucial. You may be the first to see a breakthough in someone walking unaided, or a minor deterioration which could necessitate a change of medication or equipment.

You should find out as much as you can about the condition of the pupil from websites or experts and where possible and appropriate discuss the condition both with the pupils and with their parents or other carers. Always keep in close contact with the teacher or senior member of staff who is responsible for the pupil in school and know where to get help quickly should you need it.

Providing for similarities and differences of pupils

Inclusion: principles and practice

THE MOVE FOR inclusion in education has developed from a worldwide move towards recognising human rights and counteracting segregation including apartheid and other forms of ethnic cleansing. For some, the word 'inclusion' has come to mean the wholesale closing of special schools, set up to serve the pupils in most need of special education whether their needs are physical or in areas of learning. In practice, pupils with special educational needs are increasingly being included in mainstream education, with arrangements made to ensure their special needs are met. Special schools are still providing education and sources of expertise in various areas, such as those with profound learning, behavioural or physical disabilities, including deafness and visual impairment, and increasingly these schools are working in tandem with mainstream schools. Mainstream schools sometimes also have special units (known as 'enhanced provision') attached to them with specialist staff in a limited area of disability, where pupils are included in as many mainstream school activities as possible, but withdrawn for certain specialist lessons to the unit. Often pupils are bussed to such units from a wider area than the general catchment area for only one or two years to enable the pupils to get closer specialist attention than would be possible in, say, a small rural school. The pupils then return to their own area school more able to cope with the general curriculum.

The government Green Paper *Excellence for All Children* (DfEE 1998a) set out the vision 'for increasing the level and quality of inclusion with mainstream schools, while protecting and enhancing specialist provision for those who need it' (p. 43). After consultation, *Meeting Special Educational Needs – A programme of action* (DfEE 1998b) was produced, followed by a new code of practice for those working in schools (DfES 2001). Inclusion does not just happen by a school admitting pupils with particular needs whom it has not admitted in the past: it will mean changes in attitude by some people in the school, always a lengthy process, and will require changes in the learning environment and resource provision. It may mean the appointment of special assistants to support the learner. Ramps or lifts may be needed for wheelchairs, and visual aids or computers may be needed also. The SEN and Disability Act 2001, which required every governing body of a maintained school to have an 'accessibility plan' in place by April 2003, has been extended by the Disability Equality Duty where all schools had to have a Disability Equality Scheme by April 2007.

Including pupils with SEN has sometimes meant admitting pupils with needs and then segregating them from their peers for specialist interventions. The very appointment of a special assistant can, if not managed appropriately, label a pupil as different, and this would not have occurred in a special school. Inclusion, therefore, does not just mean access to curriculum entitlement, but involves including pupils socially and emotionally and enabling them to achieve as much independence as possible, taking their needs into account. Each school should clearly state how it promotes and operates inclusive provision [12K5]. You must make yourself aware as to how you fit into this scheme of things [2K10.2;11.2; 12.2;13.2]. You may also find that you have been employed as part of a team of support assistants to work with different students during the course of a day/week. This is often done, especially in secondary schools and in some primary schools in Year 6, so that pupils do not become over-reliant on one support assistant and they are encouraged to use social skills and develop independence. It also helps you to have a range of pupils to work with since being the only assistant working with a student with challenging behaviour can be very stressful. Make sure you are clear about your role within the team and that there is opportunity for liaising with the rest of the team, daily.

Schools should also have policies saying how they will promote disability awareness and equal opportunities, and celebrate multicultural diversity. These may also have implications for your practice in dealing with individual pupils. Withdrawing a pupil from assembly for extra reading, or from PE for regular physiotherapy may or may not be the best use of the time for the pupil, and may have implications as to access to the full curriculum as well as identifying the child as being 'different'. It is essential that the pupil, parents/carers and staff including specialists are consulted [12.3P2,3;14.3P6]. You must follow the directions of the class teacher or SENCO in such matters [14.1P1]. If you find you and particular children are becoming excluded from activities by working away from the rest of the class, have a word with the teacher directing you and find out whether you can work with the group closer to the main class, or can vary the times of your sessions so that your group becomes more part of the general class work. As this might mean a reorganisation of resources or timetable, do this tactfully. If you are concerned, always discuss this with the class teacher or your mentor.

Often your role is to support social relationships between pupils with difficulties or disabilities and their more able peers, enabling them to interact and communicate as the more able peers would with each other. You can enable them to work and play together by your sensitive support, without drawing attention to the problems [12.1P6]. A continually hovering adult only makes matters worse, but appropriate intervention, a word in the right place at the right time, could help [12K4].

An example of good practice

A secondary school is on two floors and has several separate buildings. It has lifts at various points. Sometimes a TA is delegated just to ensure a wheelchair-bound pupil can get from lesson to lesson quickly enough. Midday support ensures that physically disabled pupils can have assistance with feeding in the main dining area, alongside their friends. Physiotherapy done by TAs is timetabled for lunch-hours. Children with learning problems are supported in class by TAs who help pupils of all abilities within the class. To ensure this happens appropriately, discussion meetings between all TAs and selected heads of departments are held weekly to discuss pupils' needs. Timetabling of TAs is constantly reviewed in the light of these joint meetings [12.1P1; 12.2P3; 12.3P1]. Any one student may have assistance from several TAs in a day or week. Individual teachers ensure brief joint planning sessions before lessons and informal feedback after lessons. The SENCO also has regular training sessions with the TAs and the special needs teachers also employed by the school, about appropriate techniques for supporting learning. Some TAs with specialist skills are allocated where they can best be used – a drama graduate TA to the performing arts faculty, an Urdu speaker to the English department to assist with newly arrived students from Pakistan, an ex-professional football player to the PE department. TAs are included in SEN reviews and some liaise directly with parents/carers or with specialist advisers such as the physiotherapist. Pupils are rarely withdrawn from classes but may be allocated different homework or tasks within the ordinary lessons. TAs where required oversee the homework diaries with students for whom writing is laborious. Homework facilities are available after school in the ICT suite and library for those with home study problems. Teaching staff and

TAs discuss students informally on many occasions, and discuss social and emotional needs with the students, sometimes in formally timetabled group sessions. The school employs trained counsellors part time, and some TAs are trained in basic counselling techniques by them.

Special educational needs

The Code of Practice quotes from Section 312, Education Act 1996:

> Children have special educational needs if they have a learning difficulty which calls for special educational provision to be made for them. Children have a learning difficulty if they: (a) have a significantly greater difficulty in learning than the majority of children of the same age; or (b) have a disability which prevents or hinders them from making use of educational facilities of a kind generally provided for children of the same age in schools within the area of the local education authority; (c) are under compulsory school age and fall within the definition at (a) or (b) above or would so do if special educational provision was not made for them. Children must not be regarded as having a learning difficulty solely because the language or form of language of their home is different from the language in which they will be taught. Special educational provision means: (a) for children of two or over, educational provision which is additional to, or otherwise different from, the educational provision made generally for children of their age in schools maintained by the LEA, other than special schools, in the area; (b) for children under two, educational provision of any kind. (DfES 2001:6)

The code goes on to define disability:

> A child is disabled if he is blind, deaf or dumb or suffers from a mental disorder of any kind or is substantially and permanently handicapped by illness, injury or congenital deformity or such other disability as may be prescribed. (Section 17 (11), Children Act 1989) A person has a disability for the purposes of this Act if he has a physical or mental impairment which has a substantial and long-term adverse effect on his ability to carry out normal day-to-day activities. (Section 1 (1), Disability Discrimination Act 1995, cited in DfES 2001: 7) [12K1,2].

Statementing and Individual Education Plans

In order to ensure that pupils with SEN or disabilities have as equal an opportunity of education as other pupils, special provision is made for them and TAs are often part of that special provision. However, this very fact can be counter-productive and it is up to the teacher and the TA to ensure that the provision is appropriate and does not make the pupils stand out instead of becoming more part of the school community. If you stick close by your named pupil (sometimes called the 'Velcro' model) this can label your 'charge' as being different, or the pupils can become more dependent on help rather than more independent – one of the aims of providing help. It is essential that you have a purposeful role that enables the pupil to develop independence as a learner as well as at a social level. You will need to discuss this with your SENCO and the teacher [12K4].

The Code of Practice (DfES 2001) clearly sets out the procedures for identification, assessment and provision for pupils with SEN. These need not worry you in great detail but you may well be asked to provide evidence for assessment procedures or to carry out some of the specialist provision for identified pupils. Teachers and the SENCO will have decided what action should be taken, but you should always report any concerns you have to the class teacher if nothing has been mentioned to you. There are stages in the response of the school to pupils with SEN. Some schools have an in-house system for identifying pupils of concern at an early stage within the class. The first stage in the Code of Practice is for the school to decide whether a particular School Action needs to be taken in addition to or different from the normal provision for pupils at the school [12K10]. They will have collected all sorts of

93

evidence which will be entered into the school records and have contacted the parents/carers of the pupil [12K3,8]. This action may mean some additional one-to-one tuition, often undertaken by a TA. The agreed strategies to be undertaken will usually be recorded in an IEP which will also set out targets to achieve, a timetable and process for review, and possible success or exit criteria. Some real completed IEPs are reproduced in Figures 7.1 and 7.2.

A word about IEPs: where a school has a comprehensive individual target-setting process for all students in place, then a full IEP which includes targets may not be necessary, especially for pupils on School Action or School Action Plus. It is, however, essential that provision and strategies are identified for all those working with the pupil. You will need to find out from the SENCO what the practice is in your school and where you can find all the necessary information. It may be kept as part of the SEN Profile or Learning Support Record. Pupils with a Statement of SEN will have an IEP since objectives and provision have to be met [12.2P3–5].

If the school, in consultation with the parents/carers and if possible with the pupil themselves, believes that advice or provision from outside the school facilities is required, then the next level School Action Plus is put in place. (Sometimes the TA is included in the consultation if they have valuable insight into the pupil's needs or lack of progress.) External support services will probably come to see the pupil and their records. A new IEP will usually be drawn up; the delivery of the strategies remains the responsibility of the class teacher (in primary schools) or the subject teacher (in secondary schools). The provision should, at least in part and wherever possible, be undertaken within the normal classroom setting. A pupil who has difficulty in reading may not only benefit from a Design and Technology class, through their own achievement, but may have a greater ability with tools than a pupil who can read fluently – they then experience success and have raised self-esteem. Where possible, particularly where practical work is undertaken, mixed ability

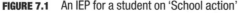

Individual Education Plan	The Colne Community School and Colne College	
Name: TG: _10_ Date: SA/~~SA+~~/~~Stmnt~~ RA: _11.0 context_ SA: _13.2_ _14.7 sight words_ English NC level/GCSE Grade ___ D _Tme D/C_ Maths NC level/GCSE Grade _E/D D/C_ Science NC level/GCSE Grade ___ _D/C_ TML/TMG _____ IEP Reviewed by: _____	Strengths • Visual memory • French • PE / Sport • Good conversational skills with adults (especially in 1:1 situations)	Needs - General & behaviour • Prompts to remain on task • Self esteem boosted. • Support with comprehension • Visual prompts

3 Short-Term Targets	Success Criteria	Strategies to be used	Outcomes _Complete for Review_	Support Provision
① • Be able to complete a table square in 3 mins. ② • Monitor own behaviour ③ • To have more positive comments than infringements at any one time	to demonstrate. Fewer infringements in PD, and full week gaps when has requested Target Report. Personal Organiser to be checked, to see 4.5 times per term.	① • Practise using stop watch. • Look for number patterns • Fill in 2,3,5 & 10's ②• ___ just to request Target Report if he feels he needs support • Staff to check for understanding of task • Set small achievable targets in class • PRAISE & REWARD		Individual/Withdrawal/Small Group By Whom: Frequency: In-class support By Whom: LSA Subjects: Sc × 4 En × 3 Specific Resources: Homework & coursework support available in L2 Tues, Wed & Thursday of each week ☑

| IEP to be reviewed:

Date: _Oct/Nov_ | Copies of IEPs
☑ Parent/Carer
☑ LS Student File | ☑ Form Tutor
☑ Subject staff
via subject links | ☐ Outside Agency
☑ LS IEP File
☑ YM>VP>P>Main File | |

FIGURE 7.1 An IEP for a student on 'School action'

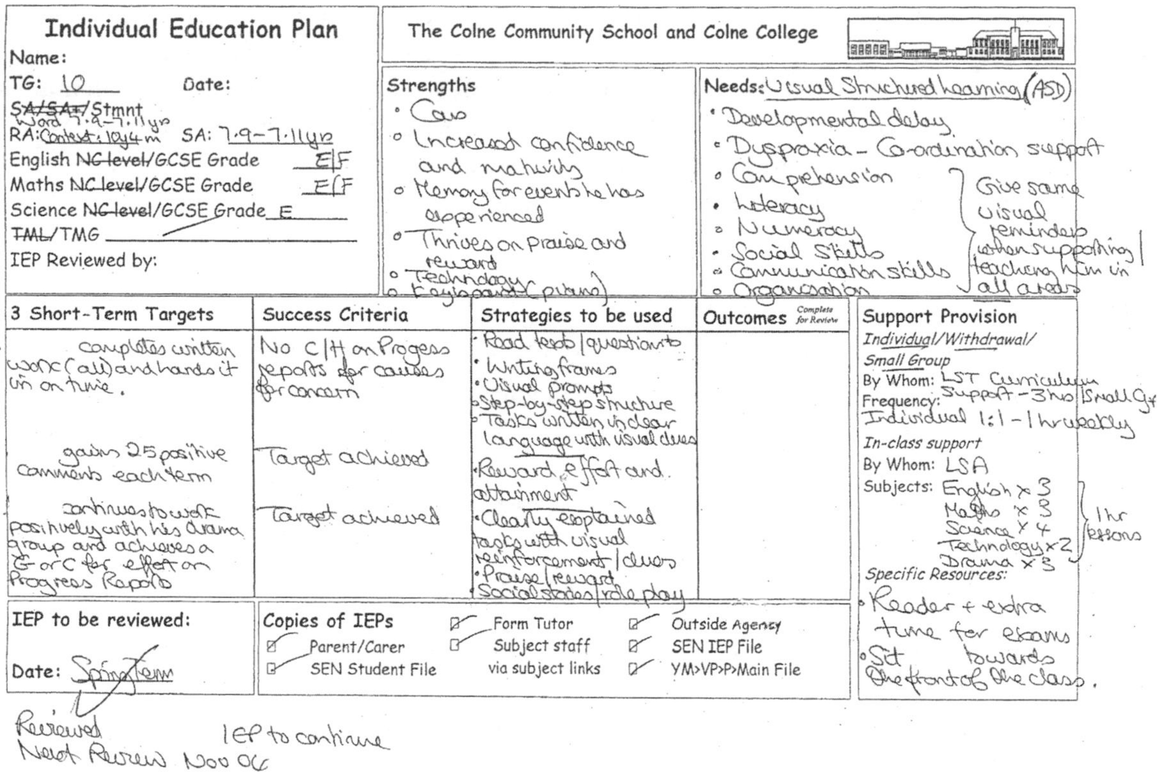

Individual Education Plan

Name:

TG: 10 Date:

~~SA/SA+~~/Stmnt

Word 7.9–7.11yrs

RA: ~~Context: 10y4m~~ SA: 7.9–7.11yrs

English ~~NC level~~/GCSE Grade E/F

Maths ~~NC level~~/GCSE Grade E/F

Science ~~NC level~~/GCSE Grade E

~~TML~~/TMG

IEP Reviewed by:

The Colne Community School and Colne College

Strengths	Needs: Visual Structured Learning (ASD)
• Cars • Increased confidence and maturity • Memory for events he has experienced • Thrives on praise and reward • Technology • Keyboard (piano)	• Developmental delay • Dyspraxia – Co-ordination support • Comprehension • Literacy • Numeracy • Social Skills • Communication skills • Organisation Give same visual reminders when supporting / teaching him in all areas

3 Short-Term Targets	Success Criteria	Strategies to be used	Outcomes (Complete for Review)	Support Provision
1. completes written work (all) and hands it in on time.	No C/H on Progress reports for causes for concern	• Read texts / questions • Writing frames • Visual prompts • Step-by-step structure • Tasks written in clear language with visual clues		Individual/Withdrawal/Small Group By Whom: LST Curriculum Support – 3hrs Small Gr Frequency: Individual 1:1 – 1 hr weekly
2. gains 25 positive comments each term	Target achieved	• Reward effort and attainment		In-class support By Whom: LSA Subjects: English x 3, Maths x 3, Science x 4, Technology x 2, Drama x 3 – 1 hr lessons
3. continues to work positively with his drama group and achieves a B or C for effort on Progress Reports	Target achieved	• Clearly explained tasks with visual reinforcement / clues • Praise / reward • Social stories / role play		Specific Resources: • Reader + extra time for exams • Sit towards the front of the class.

IEP to be reviewed:

Date: Spring Term

Copies of IEPs: Parent/Carer; SEN Student File; Form Tutor; Subject staff via subject links; Outside Agency; SEN IEP File; YM>VP>P>Main File

Reviewed ✓ IEP to continue

Next Review Nov 06

FIGURE 7.2 An IEP for a student with a statement

groups allow opportunities for sharing and discussion, role modelling and understandings to develop which otherwise are lost.

There are a very few pupils where even Action Plus change is not resulting in sufficient progress. However, where lack of progress is a cause for concern, it will be necessary, with the permission of the parents/carers and following consultation with those working with the pupils (e.g. external agencies including the school's educational psychologist), for a request to be made to the LA for a statutory assessment to be undertaken. (It should be noted that parents/carers have the right to request a statutory assessment independently of the school.) The LA will consider all the written evidence submitted by the school, and decide whether a statement of special educational needs should be made. This statement will include details of the provision needed by the pupil, and may identify extra resources that will be required. LAs have funding to allocate for such cases, and statutory (legal) duties to fulfil to ensure these resources are properly used, so monitoring arrangements have to be set up as well. If the LA decides not to issue a statement, they have to send a written note to the parents/carers telling them why. The final statement includes all the evidence submitted by the school, and the advice given from all the external agencies involved, as well as the educational placement and provision, and any non-educational needs that have to be met. There are processes of consultation, a final statement, methods of appeal and annual review systems all linked to the process. This creates a considerable amount of paper and use of time for many people and so is not undertaken lightly. A provision named in the statement is also statutory. All pupils in a special school will be there as a result of a statement being made that such a school was in the pupils' best interest. So if you work in a special school, the processes here will have been completed and annual reviews will take place for all pupils. All pupils in a special school will have statements as placing them in that school will be part of their provision.

The Code of Practice (DfES 2001) also designates four main areas of need which are likely to be recognised, but these areas quite clearly are not hard and fast [12K9]. It recognises, as LAs will recognise, that 'each child is unique . . . should reflect the particular circumstances of that child . . . that there is a wide spectrum of special educational needs that are frequently inter-related, although there are specific needs that usually relate directly to particular types of impairment' (p. 85). Individuals may well be in more than one area. In some cases, a pupil's needs are complex and also severe. The four areas are:

Communication and interaction

Cognition (knowing) and learning

Behaviour, emotional and social development

Sensory and/or physical, providing for similarities and differences of pupils.

If you are working with pupils whom you feel have special needs, when you are settled in post, with the agreement of a class or subject teacher:

- Start with one pupil whose records you have not seen.

- Note as many characteristics as you can that are similar to those of other pupils in the class, e.g. can walk, can use a pencil, does not need glasses etc.

- Then note the characteristics that make you feel they have special needs.

- Do they have needs in any of the areas above?

- What has the teacher said about them?

- What do you do to help?

Ensure you keep your notes secure, discuss all of them with the teacher and dispose of them with the advice of that teacher.

You may be helping a pupil with specific needs and should know what is required by the IEP or any behaviour plan so that you can have the same aims in your support as the teachers and other assistants [6K6; 8K14; 12.1P1; 12K6]. You may want to know more about the condition or the needs, to know how best to help that pupil. A useful brief description of the most common needs along with your possible actions and some related support associations can be found in the Induction materials TA File (TDA 2006a, 2006b:6.1–6.39). If you have not undertaken the TA Induction course, see if you can get oversight of this section as it is very helpful regarding definitions and the kind of role a TA can have when assisting those with SEN. If you did the course, but not this inclusion module, go through the TA file notes with the SENCO. It has some case studies for discussion and some brief descriptions of particular special needs: Attention deficit hyperactivity disorder (ADHD), Asperger's Syndrome, Autistic Spectrum disorders (ASD), Cerebral Palsy, Down's Syndrome, Dyslexia, Dyspraxia, hearing impairment, visual impairment. The SENCO will be a good source of information, or you can type the condition you are interested in into a search engine on the internet, or enquire at the local library. David Fulton Publishers, whose titles are now published by Routledge, have an excellent collection of very accessible books on individual disabilities. Most disabilities have associations, often with local branches to support those disadvantaged or their parents/carers. It is not necessary at an ordinary competent TA level (Level 2) to have an in-depth understanding of various disabilities or needs, unless you are undertaking STL12,13 or14, but any relevant and accurate information helps your understanding and thus your ability to support that child [12.1P1]. You also need an aware-ness of what is normal for pupils of the age range you are working with, what is unusual, and what might change or cause changes.

Supporting pupils in class

There are various ways in which you can support any pupil, whether or not they have SEN [4.1P1–6]. Some pupils just need a bit of individual attention [4K1,2]. Some are shy in large groups, some slower to understand what is required and some just take longer to do things [4K4]. Some need to repeat tasks several times before 'the penny drops'. Sometimes they come from large or busy families where few people, particularly the adults, have time to talk with them, and more particularly to listen to their point of view.

You may need to:

- repeat the teacher's instructions
- simplify a little or restructure the task indicated by the teacher
- read a worksheet
- help the pupil plan out or organise their work
- ensure the pupil concentrates on the task
- suggest where equipment or materials can be found
- suggest another way to do the task
- allow the pupil the opportunity to talk their thinking through
- listen to what the pupil has to say or ask
- get the pupil to check for errors in their work before you point them out
- ask the pupil about the task, what they have found out or learnt
- help the pupil to see what they have done well, enabling them to measure their own success
- ensure they tidy up
- or a combination of some or all of these [6.1P3,4; 6.2P3,4].

You have got to learn how to balance the pupil's need for attention with the principle of enabling all pupils to become as independent of you as possible – remember your real job is to do yourself out of a job [9K5; 12K4]. The aim is to promote independent learning. This balance is an art which you will acquire if you are sensitive. Always try to return a question with a question, even 'What do you think?' Encourage pupils to get resources rather than wait on them, to have a go at a task rather than just saying 'I can't do that'. Sometimes the individual attention is due to particular needs, largely physical, that need your help. Personal hygiene needs of a pupil should have been spelt out to you in your induction. You may need to remind a pupil to wear their glasses, or to adjust aids for hearing-impaired pupils. In these cases you should also have had training as to how to carry out your task. You may provide an escort for a pupil who has to go to see a specialist visitor, possibly even delegated to do so by the parent or carer.

It is more likely that you will be working with pupils in small groups, where individuals in need of special support are one of the group. In this way, the individual needs are less obvious, and you are able to keep an eye on your 'charge' without being oppressive. Group working can be of two kinds. Sometimes pupils just sit in a group for convenience, but actually they all have individual tasks to complete. Here it may be that you just need to keep

PHOTOGRAPH 7.1 AND 7.2 Supporting individuals without doing the task for them

PHOTOGRAPH 7.3 AND 7.4   Supporting diverse needs within the classroom

them on task. However, one of the ways to help them is to get them to finish a little before the intended time, and share their findings or what they have got out of the task. If one has to talk about one's learning, it usually makes that learning 'stick' better [4.3P1–6; 12.1P4]. Often members of the group can learn from each other or help each other in a way that promotes the learning of all parties. Sometimes groups are put together and need to work as a group. If they have to discuss something you can act as chairperson, prompting the shy and reticent, making sure everyone has an opportunity to share their ideas, and that all but the speaker listen. Being part of a group may be an individual pupil's target.

You can encourage cooperation and interaction and facilitate discussions. It is a great opportunity to role model how people can work together, and also for promoting self-esteem by suitable praise. Never go overboard on praise; pupils know when they have tried hard or when a piece of work really could be better. Your role with the group may be direct teaching – explaining a point, demonstrating a practical task or giving some new information [10K2]. You should have been briefed by the teacher and been able to prepare. There is more about working with teachers in the next chapter.

It is possible that you will be asked to work with a whole class while the teacher carries out a task with an individual. Be careful if this happens. You are not qualified or paid, and possibly not insured, to teach a whole class, although you can be an adult in a classroom in an emergency while a teacher is found. If the task is something simple, like reading a story to the class, make sure the teacher is within call or eyesight – they are responsible for the class. You may have a skill as a potter or musician which you can demonstrate to a whole class, again making sure a qualified teacher is around. It is also worth stressing at this point that it is the teacher's responsibility to differentiate work and that when you are working in a lesson your role is clear.

If problems arise, you must talk to the teacher, your line manager or the SENCO, according to the type of problem [12.1P3]. It may be that pupils have misbehaved with you, or revealed something about other pupils which is important. They may have problems with the tasks set, or just not have got on with the task properly. The fault may lie with your techniques with the pupils, or the match of task and pupil, or the emotional state of the pupil. It needs to be sorted quickly so that it does not become habitual. If you are handling or treating a child with a specific condition, you should always also talk with your teachers immediately if you notice any changes in the condition [13K9; 14.2P6–8]. If you are undertaking either STL 13 or 14 you need specific guidance and training from experts in the field.

At the end of a lesson, a week or a term, you may be asked to complete aspects of pupil records, or write a contribution for these records. Always do this under directions. Be concise and accurate [12.3P4]. Always ensure that the records or notes are kept confidentially, stored appropriately in a secure place. It is most likely that you will only do this on the school premises anyway.

Communication and interaction

The Code of Practice defines this area of difficulty as follows:

> 7:55 Most children with special educational needs have strengths and difficulties in one, some or all of the areas of speech, language and communication. Their communication needs may be both diverse and complex. They will need to continue to develop their linguistic competence in order to support their thinking as well as their communication. The range of difficulties will encompass children and young people with speech and language delay, impairments or disorders, specific learning difficulties, such as dyslexia and dyspraxia, hearing impairment and those who demonstrate features within the autistic spectrum; they may also apply to some children and young people with moderate, severe or profound learning difficulties. The range of need will include those for whom language and communication difficulties are the result of permanent sensory or physical impairment [6K6].

7.56   These children may require some, or all, of the following:

- flexible teaching arrangements

- help in acquiring, comprehending and using language

- help in articulation

- help in acquiring literacy skills

- help in using augmentative and alternative means of communication

- help to use different means of communication confidently and competently for a range of purposes, including formal situations

- help in organising and coordinating oral and written language

- support to compensate for the impact of a communication difficulty on learning in English as an additional language

- help in expressing, comprehending and using their own language, where English is not the first language.

(DfES 2001: 86)

The Code of Practice states

Children making slower progress may include those who are learning English as an additional language or who have particular learning difficulties. It should not be assumed that children making slower progress must, therefore, have special educational needs. But such children will need carefully differentiated learning opportunities to help them progress and regular and frequent careful monitoring to their progress.

(DfES 2001: 33)

There are specialist programmes to support language development, but again you need individual expert tuition to use these, for instance that mentioned in 12K7. There is a separate section later in this chapter giving more details of the needs of those for whom English is an additional language.

To communicate effectively you need to:

- Try to understand the needs of the person with whom you are speaking.

- Show and expect respect.

- Listen well.

- Speak or write clearly, with correct English grammar (you may need to slow down, but shouting does not help).

- Use vocabulary appropriate to the age and learning stage of the listener.

- Keep to the point.

- Share ideas.

- Smile and use humour and praise appropriately.

- Be relaxed, warm, friendly and supportive.

- Keep eye contact.

- Be positive.

Cognition and learning

The Code of Practice defines this area of difficulty as follows:

7:58   Children who demonstrate features of moderate, severe or profound learning difficulties or specific learning difficulties, such as dyslexia or dyspraxia, require specific programmes to aid progress in cognition and learning. Such requirements may also apply to some extent to children with physical and sensory impairments and those on the autistic spectrum. Some of these children may have associated sensory, physical and behavioural difficulties that compound their needs. These children may require some, or all, of the following:

- flexible teaching arrangements

- help with processing language, memory and reasoning skills

- help and support in acquiring literacy skills

- help in organising and coordinating spoken and written English to aid cognition

- help with sequencing and organisational skills

- help with problem solving and developing concepts

- programmes to aid improvement of fine and motor competencies

- support in the use of technical terms and abstract ideas

- help in understanding ideas, concepts and experiences when information cannot be gained through first hand sensory or physical experiences.

(DfES 2001: 86–7)

You can see that many of the requirements of the pupils with needs in this area are similar to those with communication or interactive difficulties, but the emphasis is on organisational and coordinating skills, concept development and problem solving. Many of these skills, however, are mediated through language, including specific language to handle more abstract ideas. Your role-modelling of utilising correct nomenclature for things, and your organisation will help pupils, particularly in the more technical subjects like science. Emphasise working sequentially, one thing at a time, and tidying up properly. Allow older pupils to use concrete materials – counters for number work, for instance, or draw pictures of objects if you do not have them to hand, if they are having problems with working in the abstract. Most of the strategies that are used to support the learning of pupils younger than the ones with whom you are concerned will be useful, so you can ask teachers of the younger pupils how they would tackle certain areas of the curriculum if it is appropriate to do so [6K6]. You should ask the teacher with whom you are working if this is all right, as a matter of courtesy. Many of the concepts like hot and cold or hard and soft are usually learnt through play activities in the early years. These are developed in science lessons in the properties of materials, as are the more difficult concepts like forces, electricity, growth and change. Some specific programmes have been developed to help disorganised pupils to organise themselves, but use of these is likely to be part of the pupil's SEN provision. You should receive training if asked to implement such programmes.

Behaviour, emotional and social development

The Code of Practice defines this area of difficulty as follows:

7:60   Children and young people who demonstrate features of emotional and behavioural difficulties, who are withdrawn or isolated, disruptive and disturbing, hyperactive and lack concentration; those with immature social skills; and those presenting challenging behaviours arising from other complex special needs, may require help or counselling for some, or all, of the following:

- flexible teaching arrangements

- help with development of social competence and emotional maturity

- help in adjusting to school expectations and routines

- help in acquiring the skills of positive interaction with peers and adults

- specialised behavioural and cognitive approaches

- re-channelling or re-focusing to diminish repetitive and self-injurious behaviours

- provision of class and school systems which control or censure negative or difficult behaviours and encourage positive behaviour
- provision of a safe and supportive environment.

(DfES 2001: 87)

Sensory and/or physical needs

The Code of Practice defines this area of difficulty as follows:

7:62   There is a wide spectrum of sensory, multi-sensory and physical difficulties. The sensory range extends from profound and permanent deafness or visual impairment through to lesser levels of loss, which may only be temporary. Physical impairments may arise from physical, neurological or metabolic causes that only require appropriate access to educational facilities and equipment; others may lead to more complex learning and social needs; a few children will have multi-sensory difficulties some with associated physical difficulties. For some children the inability to take part fully in school life causes significant emotional stress or physical fatigue. Many of these children and young people will require some of the following [13K10]:

- flexible teaching arrangements
- appropriate seating, acoustic conditioning and lighting
- adaptations to the physical environment of the school
- adaptations to school policies and procedures
- access to alternative or augmented forms of communication
- provision of tactile and kinaesthetic materials
- access to different amplification systems
- access to low vision aids
- access in all areas of the curriculum through specialist aids, equipment or furniture (you must have specialist training in moving and handling children with severe disabilities both in technique and rationale) [13K11–20; 14K5–16]
- regular and frequent access to specialist support.

(DfES 2001: 88)

Most of these provisions are specific to the physical impairment of the pupil and you will need specialist training in their use, even if this is fairly informal [13.1P10]. All of your support needs to be done with a view to maintaining the pupil's maximum independence within the limits of the disability [13.1P5,6]. Depending on the age of the pupil and the nature of the disability, your role might range from one-to-one assistance with a learning task to being on hand to give occasional assistance for learning or personal needs. You will find it very helpful to get information from specialist support associations about the impairment you are supporting. The other thing is that you may be in the best position to spot the early signs of an impairment, such as the need for glasses or the beginning of deafness. Do tell the appropriate teacher of your concerns, and the teacher can then discuss the matter with the parent. You also can help pupils by reminding them to use their aids. Be prepared to meet and discuss the support with any visiting agency as you are in the best position to have seen any aids or materials in use [12.2P9,10]. If you have to move or handle a physically impaired child, always talk with them about what you are doing and why, and how they can help [13.1P7; 13.2P1–6].

English as an additional language

This area of support now has a standard [STL11] to itself at Level 2. Like some of the areas mentioned above, this book cannot do justice to the complexities and ideas that you will need in order to complete this as an optional standard. You must seek out specialist training, possibly from an in-house teacher of EAL or in many areas from the LA. All the things you are considering with supporting any pupils need to be taken into account here, but with slightly different emphases. Remember, as with any pupil, your aim is to support to enable them to become independent of you. Also, stress will only reduce their ability to try new things out. Many aspects of the support of those for whom English is an additional language are the same as for supporting any child: taking advice and feeding back to the class teacher, planning, preparation, praise and feedback are needed for all school activities [11.1P2; 11.2P2,6].

Pupils for whom English is an additional language make up about 20 per cent of the total school population in England and Wales and have origins from all over the world, from Colombia to Afghanistan and from Sri Lanka to Lithuania. The EAL pupils tend to be found in schools in urban areas such as in London and Birmingham, and some boroughs, including Tower Hamlets and Hackney, have more than 50 per cent of pupils designated as EAL. Schools in rural areas, however, often have EAL pupils too and LAs such as Devon and Norfolk provide support to these pupils. This has become more common in recent years with the increase of European Union migrant workers in agriculture and a range of other industries. Not all, however, are born overseas and indeed many may have been born here to families whose first language is not English. These pupils may enter school not speaking English as they have grown up in communities in England where English is not the first language. Television may also not be in English, so little English may be used in the family home. These pupils provide a cultural and linguistic richness to schools and are sometimes our highest achievers. EAL pupils are referred to in most DCSF and Ofsted publications, and the achievement of and the provision for EAL pupils is a key focus for Ofsted in school inspections. There is advice for those of you working in the early years' sector. A recent publication from the government has recognised that this is not only a concern for the traditional centres of migrants. The increase of economic migration from recently joined European Union countries has seen families for whom EAL will be an additional problem settling in traditionally white rural areas where teachers have not been used to helping such children. This guidance *Aiming high: meeting the need of newly arrived pupils learning English as an additional language (EAL)* can be found on the website www.standards.gov.uk.

The term ESL or English as a second language was dropped some years ago because many EAL pupils speak more than two languages. For example, a child from Kenya may speak Swahili and Panjabi and be learning English as an additional or third language. The term EFL or English as a foreign language should not be used either as this usually refers either to students learning English in countries where English is not the mother-tongue, or to students coming to Britain to study English for short periods of time. The term 'bilingual' is often used to define pupils living in two languages or having access to these languages and not necessarily being fluent in them.

Not all EAL pupils are beginners in English. LAs usually have their own system for grading pupils from beginners to fully fluent bilingual pupils. Some LAs use stages of language learning with between four and seven levels, and others have moved over to additional NC step levels as recommended by QCA. You can find out about these through the EAL teacher in your school if you have one or through your LAs. It is currently thought that it takes children between five and seven years to achieve full fluency in English although there can be considerable variation depending on the pupil. Remember, full fluency in terms of schooling does not just mean being able to use conversational English but to have knowledge of academic language and the literacy and oracy skills that go with this.

EAL pupils are not a homogenous group of learners and can be put into three general groups:

- Some children may come into schools with little or no spoken English but with strong literacy skills in another language particularly if they are older. They may have received a good education in their home country and already be competent in many NC subject areas. These pupils are sometimes referred to as 'elite bilinguals', often coming from middle-class homes where there are considerable expectations and knowledge of the education system. These children may come from families who have chosen to travel abroad for business, academic or diplomatic reasons or may be from educated refugee families, forced to flee their home country.

- A further group of children are those who enter school with limited spoken English and little or no reading or writing skills in their first language. The child's home language may have low status in wider society yet there will be a strong pressure from the local community to maintain the first language and culture. The family may value education highly but not understand what is specifically needed to support a child's academic learning. These pupils are sometimes termed as coming from linguistic minorities.

- Some children will come from homes where another language is spoken by one parent and the child grows up with two languages in a bilingual family. Quite often the language of the host country (English) will predominate as the child gets older.

There is a very useful set of pages in the TA induction file in the inclusion section (TDA 2006a, 2006b: 6.40–6.77). If you are helping such a pupil, whether or not you are being employed because your own first language is that of the pupil, get a copy of these pages and go through them with the EAL teacher or SENCO to make sure you understand your role and the potential of your help in enabling those with EAL to access the curriculum. The pages can be downloaded from the TDA website. They include some useful background pages giving the history of the relevant legislation, and some useful contact addresses and references for further reading. Page 6.58 has a comprehensive flow diagram showing how English language acquisition and curriculum learning match together using:

- observation and monitoring
- visual support
- the classroom environment
- pupil grouping
- creating opportunities for talk

and by:

- valuing diversity
- planning for inclusion
- and supporting English acquisition.

Page 6.59 shows how the NC for English at Level 1 is an appropriate tool for assessing development of English. Children with EAL do not necessarily have other SEN and with help to use English will succeed alongside their peers. Also, it is important to remember that those with EAL are as disparate as any group of children in their ways of learning, background and experiences, although many may well have had a greater variety of experiences of other customs and countries than indigenous British people. The advice on assessment and recording in the latter pages of the induction materials mirrors good practice in any such activity whether or not the pupil has EAL.

If the pupil comes from a home where English is not the language of communication, they may need help in interpreting the nuance of some words, especially where the teacher has given instructions in technical language or speaks quickly. Another sensitivity you must show is towards those who come from a different culture from yourself. This is not necessarily associated with race or colour; it could be due to religion or region or even socio-economic background. The problem may not be one of actual vocabulary but of differences in meaning of different words in a different culture. This is most obvious when speaking in English with people from the US. Words like suspenders, pants and bathroom, for instance, mean different things on the other side of the Atlantic. Always discuss any concerns you have with your mentor, line manager or the teacher. Children with EAL do have one big advantage which you can use: their ability to speak or understand another language is an ability that many native-born British people do not have, so you can boost their self-esteem every time they attempt English. Remind them how difficult some of us find it to learn their language!

It will depend on the age and background of the child whether they are able to read and write in their own language as well as to speak it. Schooling may not have been readily available for them, or alternatively, they may have been quite advanced in their native country. It is usual for oral fluency to be ahead of literacy development.

When working with EAL pupils, it is important to find out as much as you can about their background to inform your expectations, particularly if you have been asked to work with a child or group of children. For example, if you are working with an 11-year-old who is at an early stage of writing development, this may be because the child has had a disrupted education because of war or lack of access to schooling rather than having a special educational need. Other children may have had an excellent education in their home country and may be very good, for example, at Mathematics – you may find the work you have been given to do with them is not at the right level and needs to be more challenging.

> It would be useful to find out more about all the EAL pupils in your school.
> What percentage of pupils in your school are EAL?
> Which countries do they come from and what languages do they speak?
>
> If you are working with EAL pupils, find out as much background information on them as you can.
> How long have they been in the UK?
> What was their previous educational experience, if any?
> Sometimes assessments are carried out in children's first language.
> Has this been done and if so what were the results, if any?
>
> N.B. The school may well have protocols about finding out information about pupils and it is important to follow these.

If there is an EAL or EMA (Ethnic Minority Achievement) teacher or department in your school (perhaps including the class teacher herself), they may know a lot about the pupils concerned. The school office should hold much useful information in the pupil files on the languages children speak, their previous educational experience and their ethnicity and religion. You will need to remember that some of this information may well be confidential so check either with the office or with a senior member of staff that it is all right for you to do this. It should not normally be a problem but it is vitally important to follow a school's protocols.

Factors affecting pupils' learning of English [11K3]

Age

It is often assumed that it is easier for younger children to learn languages than for older children. This is not necessarily the case. Some children who arrive at nursery school speaking little English can find it quite a stressful situation and can take some time to start learning English. On the other hand, older secondary age children may well already have considerable language skills in their first language which they do not have to re-learn when learning English. These skills can be transferred to English and partly explains why some EAL pupils can achieve high GCSE grades within two to three years of arriving at a school in this country.

Immersion

It is often assumed too that the best way of learning English is to be thrown in at the deep end: to be immersed in it totally. It seems logical that if the language is all around you, you must learn and learn quickly. However, many high-achieving children, for example from Chinese or Indian backgrounds, speak more than two languages regularly. They may speak English at school in lessons, speak Chinese or Indian and English at home with their parents, and watch some Chinese or Indian TV. There is no evidence of a correlation between time spent in an English-speaking environment and learning English. Indeed the evidence suggests that it is critical to have a well-developed first language and that this is a key factor in learning English. Furthermore in lessons, if you can provide a quick translation of a key word, this can help understanding of a concept and support a child's learning.

Character and emotional factors

Inevitably, a child's character is important in determining success in language learning. Children who are more outgoing and who are prepared to take risks tend to be better language learners. Shy, quieter and less adventurous children may be less successful. Further emotional issues may inhibit a child learning. If a child is unhappy because of experiences she/he has been through, is worried about friends and relatives left behind in another country or has not settled well into the school, inevitably this may get in the way of effective learning.

A safe and welcoming environment

It is important that all children feel safe and supported within their school. Because some EAL pupils have little English and some may be obviously different to other children in terms of skin colour, hairstyle or dress, they may be picked on, bullied or isolated from other children. You need to be aware of this and work with the school to follow the advice offered below on supporting children new to the school. Ensure you know the school procedures for dealing with bullying and racist incidents. Children who are bullied may suffer low self-esteem and their attendance at school may also suffer.

Teaching styles

Children who arrive in school from overseas may have had a very different experience of schooling. Some may have gone to schools with a similar education system to ours but others may be used to what might be termed a more 'traditional' system. There might have been a lot of learning by rote, little expectation that the pupil should contribute to lessons and very little pair or group work. Children may take a little while to adjust to a different system.

Beginner EAL or bilingual children

You will find that in some schools panic will set in when a child arrives who speaks little or no English. How do we communicate with him/her!? Will he/she understand anything!? In other, usually inner-city schools, staff see this as par for the course and indeed in some nurseries the vast majority of children may have little English when they arrive.

At the admission interview which should normally occur with the parent or carer, important information should be found out about the child and you should find out as much as you can [11.1P1]. Hopefully an interpreter will have attended the interview to support both the parent/carer and the school (this may have been you if you are bilingual yourself). Good admissions practice will usually mean that the child will not start school immediately so you and other members of staff can be ready for the child's arrival [11K9].

If you know what language the child speaks it may be possible for you to learn a little of that language such as greetings or 'what is your name?' You may assist the class or form teacher to identify a buddy or buddies to look after the pupil when he/she starts. This may include someone who speaks the child's language – this can obviously help the child settle in fairly quickly although sometimes the buddy child may not want to do this – be sensitive to this. Often the best buddies are those you know to be supportive and friendly. You may find out some information about the country the child has come from and, with the class teacher, conduct a short input on this with the class or form. This could also include looking at how to help someone in school if they don't speak English and how it might feel to be in that position.

If you do speak the child's language and are familiar with the culture, you might decide to prepare some school and classroom signs in the child's language or even teach the other children some greetings in the new language. You could talk to the class teacher/s and to the class about the new child's country and culture and any key differences that there may be to do with religion or food. You might find some posters for a display about the country the child has come from [11.1P3].

Having everything prepared for when the child arrives, as with any new child, is also very important. In primary schools, for example, ensure there is a place to sit, books ready and a tray labelled. In secondary schools, this may mean having exercise and text books available and a school diary. Make sure you know how to pronounce the child's name correctly and you know the child's first or calling name. Children have been known to go through school being called the wrong name or having been given an 'English' name instead. If you have been asked to support the child, it can be very useful to establish who the home contact is – and at the beginning or end of the day establish contact with the person who brings the child to school. Talk to the class or form teacher about this.

When the child starts school

This can be quite a daunting experience to start with for some children.

Try to imagine how it might feel. Spend a minute or two thinking about this, what might be different and how you might feel.

You enter an institution in a strange country, where it may be that no one or few people speak your language and you can't speak theirs. You have no friends, people may be a different colour to you and look different, you don't know the rules (written and unwritten) of the school and you don't know what to expect in lessons. It may be that you didn't even want to come here – it was your parents' decision or you had to leave! You may be missing your home and your friends.

Put yourself in the child's position or reflect on your own experiences and perhaps frustrations when travelling or living abroad and what would have helped you.

Because of this, it is important that the school is as welcoming as possible. You could:

- Be prepared (see above)
- Show the pupil around the school – where the toilets are, the dinner hall, and so on

- Introduce the child to his/her buddy and make sure the child is looked after at break and lunchtimes

- Introduce the child to a supportive child, perhaps an older child, who also speaks his/her language [11.1P6]

- Establish a home contact

- Smile and be friendly and relaxed. Talk to the child normally (don't be slow and halting) – she/he won't understand everything, but use clear simple language.

In lessons, the child may not say anything at all to start with, even if they know some English. This is quite normal and is often known as the 'silent period' – the child will be listening and learning but not necessarily speaking (see section on language development). You may be asked to work with a new arrival pupil/s on induction sessions separate from the rest of the class for the first half-term to term. These may be every day for half-an-hour to an hour, although this varies considerably from school to school. Work should be set for you to do by the class teacher or EAL teacher [11.2P1,2]. It is important that you liaise with these staff on an ongoing basis about the lessons and the progress pupils make. If you do speak the children's first language, this can be an ideal time to talk to the child in this language about how school is going and to establish a rapport. This can be a great relief for some children who may be struggling to communicate and succeed in school.

Although this section is only a start in understanding the needs of children learning EAL, *Learning to learn in a second language* is an excellent and very practical publication, a must read (Gibbons 1991). It can be very useful to compare two EAL pupils, one who is succeeding and achieving well in school and one who is not doing as well. Find out as much as you can about these two pupils and try to work out why this is the case. Remember, you should normally have high expectations of EAL pupils.

Supporting the teacher and teaching

The learning environment

THE SURROUNDINGS IN which learning takes place influence the quality of the learning. You know yourself that having things where you know you can find them – materials or tools – makes a job easier. Having the right lighting or a comfortable chair at the correct height makes a difference to how long you can persist at a task. Sharp tools are usually safer than blunt ones. A jigsaw with lost pieces is useless, blunt pencils will not produce good handwriting, paper with curled edges does not encourage good presentation. A welcoming room or building encourages its use. Appropriate warmth and breaks for refreshment or exercise all make a difference to the amount of things you can memorise, how well or how long you can practise a skill or how well you can concentrate on trying to understand something new to you. Ideas often come in the spaces between concentrated thinking, and breaks themselves can be productive.

You are responsible for all the equipment or materials you and the pupils in your care use. You should provide a role model on your care and use of them [3K19]. You will need to find out where items that you will be using are kept and how to use them properly.

This will include knowing about storage facilities, knowing what to do if you or a pupil you are with breaks or spills anything, and knowing how to dispose of waste of any kind. This goes for pencils, paper and scissors as well as televisions, audio or computer equipment, scientific equipment or chemicals, tools, toys and books [3KL5]. Check before a lesson that you have correct and sufficient materials for a task, and never leave your pupils to go to get something, particularly if they are young and away from their class base. You should have both the teacher's planning and time to access resources outside the pupil contact time, and if you don't then you should talk to your line manager about getting this. Communication before the lesson about any such queries should be the norm.

Give time towards the end of any task to clear up, clean or return equipment, check the equipment and leave the work station tidy for its next user [15K26,27]. Even reception class children can wash paint pots; you do not have to do it for them. If you are concerned about the way in which pupils handle materials, tools or equipment, if they are wasteful or destructive, first try to re-train them yourself and if there is trouble discuss it with the class teacher. Your joint care and use of all such items should become part of a routine way of working.

It may be part of your job description to care particularly for some items in school – as a librarian or technician, or attached to a particular classroom or area of the building. Where possible, with permission, involve the pupils in such a task. You may be asked to stock-check certain areas regularly such as art materials, or to tape-record broadcast programmes regularly. Be as tidy and as organised as possible so that others can access your system if you are away or ill. If the equipment has a specific use, make sure you know how to use it properly and safely, and how it is cared for. You may need to consult specific subject

PHOTOGRAPH 8.1 AND 8.2   Organised, accessible and tidy storage of materials for English in the classroom, and for creative and DT activities out of the classroom

teachers for help in this. The school grounds will also have specific uses, and maintenance procedures, so check before gaily digging a flowerbed for worms, or picking samples of leaves. One of the teachers or senior TAs should have responsibility for the use of the grounds for teaching purposes and there may be specific areas for environmental study and others for relaxation or physical activities.

During the era of 'discovery learning' it was believed that all you had to do was to expose children to an exciting environment and they would learn; it was even believed at one time that just having lots of books around and reading stories and poems would get children to read. This clearly did not work except for certain gifted children who did not seem to require instruction. However, during the era of the strategies, where instruction and structure has overwhelmed some teachers, or more often in secondary schools, less emphasis has been put on the actual classroom provision. Good mainstream infant classrooms used to resemble a good nursery classroom but perhaps with more tables: that is rare to find now. The old-fashioned nature table of the infant class had evolved into exciting interactive displays, where children could explore, touch, read up about – play with – artefacts for a variety of subjects [10K14]. Mathematics areas and music areas joined the reading corners, art materials were freely available and so on. Few classrooms now have such a learning environment. Sometimes space and the numbers of children in the room preclude expansive areas given to practical activities except at specific times, but largely primary classrooms are much less exciting places to be than they were 20 to 30 years ago. Secondary schools have always had more emphasis on specific classrooms for specific activities, confining books to a library, art media to studio areas and so on. Drama takes place in drama studios, not in role play corners. However, secondary schools have got much better at displaying students' work, making their corridors and entrance areas attractive with relevant and interesting displays to show what pupils can do.

An area which has been neglected in some schools is the use of the outside. Schools are likely to be provided originally merely with PE playing field space and plain tarmac play space, but many schools have recognised that these areas have great potential for learning. If you are working in a nursery or an early years' class there is likely to be an allocated fenced area for outside play which is usually well thought out in terms of varied provision to support the general curriculum, not just free play time. Learning through Landscapes is a charity which supports schools in the imaginative development of their outside areas. Schools have developed environmental areas with ponds and trails, outside classrooms, even herb gardens and vegetable areas. Interest in these has revived recently with the increased interest in healthy eating [10K23]. Simple things like a disused sand tray will collect water and encourage frogs and insects, and growbags or pots can be used for beans or tomatoes. Seating and quiet places along with trim trails and games equipment can transform a dead time into a useful one.

There are more details of various uses in different parts of this book, but the important thing to remember here is that all these areas need thought in their rationale, their setting up, their use and maintenance and replacement when required. It is here that you can be of great use, training pupils to treat such areas with respect but also to make the best use of them. Talking with them about the purpose of their surroundings not only draws attention to them but may inspire some to take further interest in whatever is provided. You need to make sure you know as much as you can about whatever is around you and why it was put there in the first place. The lack of maintenance because of other priorities and over-familiarity with neglected areas, inside and outside, is often the reason for their lack of usefulness.

The classroom environment

Display

Part of the reason for displays – the interactive sort that promotes enquiry and interest – is outlined above but display has other purposes [16.1P1]. It may include:

- health and safety notices, like the fire escape route, washing hands after handling certain things, or use of potentially dangerous tools;
- ideas for using equipment, like books or computers;
- ideas for work to do if set tasks are finished;
- posters giving general information or pictures of relevant interest to topics being studied;
- pupils' work showing quality presentation or good ideas, or just valuing the achievement of class members;
- three-dimensional displays of books or artefacts or models associated with the work of the pupils;
- lists of names, spellings, mathematical tables for reference or learning;
- an opportunity for collaboration and thought by a group of pupils in putting the display together.

Whatever is displayed and the manner in which it is displayed give messages to people entering the room – pupils and adults – about the purpose of the room, the nature of the work that goes on there, what is valued by the teacher and the school. If displays become

PHOTOGRAPH 8.3   A display following work on social and emotional learning

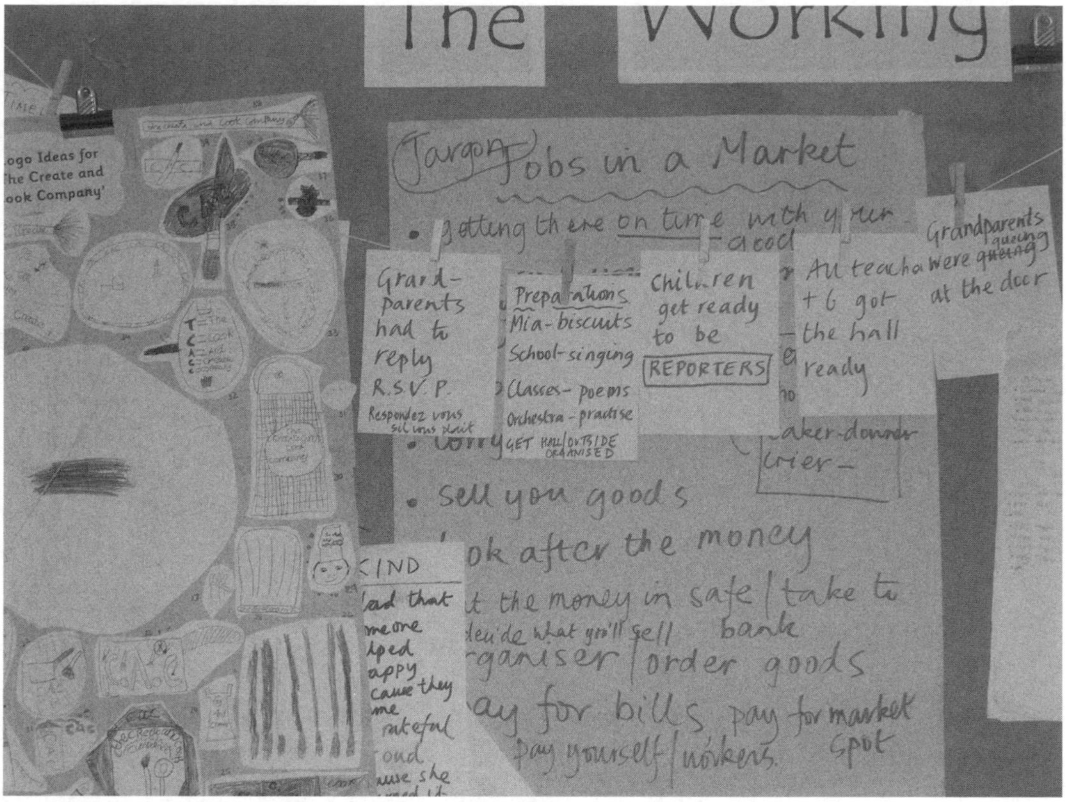

PHOTOGRAPH 8.4 A display showing work in progress

faded and tatty, the message is 'who cares?' This area is now seen as sufficiently important to justify a whole standard to itself, STL 16. In order to undertake this standard, however, you will need greater responsibility than an ordinary TA for this aspect of the school's work. The liaison required with teachers throughout the school in order to ascertain purpose and duration is considerable [P16.2P1–5]. You will need access to ordering and storage facilities, as well as sufficient understanding and freedom to decide the position of a display and sufficient knowledge to know what risks you might be undertaking in putting up and taking down a display and any risks that might be attached to the display itself [16K7–13]. The last thing you want is an object falling on someone or a staple going through a caretaker's hand. You need expertise in mounting, safety concerns, appreciation and evaluations.

It may well be part of your role to renew or create displays for the teacher. You need to know what the intention of the display is, but you also need to learn some skills to help you [16K4]. For instance, choice of backing paper and ways of framing pupils' two-dimensional work can make a difference to whether the display is eye-catching or not. The kind of lettering and its size matters as well as what is written about the work. Three-dimensional displays can be interactive – allowing pupils to touch and examine objects or just for visual effect. Care with paper trimmers, scissors and glue shows care of pupils' work. Teachers should give you plenty of advice on what they are hoping to achieve; most of them have become very skilled at it [16K1–3].

Where possible involve the pupils in ideas of what or how to display their work. Year 2 children are perfectly capable of using a paper trimmer given guidance and can have ideas about the look of a display [16K5]. Older primary children would be able to arrange items on a flat sheet or contribute to 3D displays. Interactive displays can be

PHOTOGRAPH 8.5   A tactile display using space outside the classroom

particularly effective in creating interest and stimulating investigation. They can range from a few questions put among the labels on a flat classroom display to the Science Museum's highly successful Launch Pad. There are ways of simulating design on computers, some of them in 3D. The more children are involved in what goes on walls and surfaces and understand why it is there, the more likely they are to use it [10.5P1]. Commercially produced posters, put up to inform in the absence of the pupils, are merely wallpaper. In this materialistic, fast-moving large-screen world, where shops outdo each other to attract, children are well used to colourful walls and merely accept them as normal unless involved somehow.

PHOTOGRAPH 8.6   A special display in the hall, but interactive with 'post-it' notes and a clipboard

Sometimes the display can show work in progress of the children. These will not be tidy displays, with a polished finish, but will show process as well as end product and will value what is done. Some children, if clumsy, colour blind or just uninterested in art and design, can be put off trying to produce anything for display if everything in the classroom is commercially produced or highly finished, so keep a watch out for this and ensure you can see their success in some other venture, as you would with a child who doesn't achieve in PE or some other subject [10.3P5; 16K6].

Look at at least three different areas in the school including areas within and outside classrooms

- What display is there? What is it for?

- What condition is it in? How long has it been there?

- Is it looked at by the pupils?

- Is it two- or three-dimensional? Why?

- If you feel it is effective, try to note why.

- What colours have been used in addition to the items being displayed?

- What other materials – fabrics, paper, framing – have been used?

- Is the display cluttered or relatively bare?

- Are the items in straight lines?

- Is there any explanatory text added by the displayer?

- What tools, equipment or materials might be needed to create such a display

  - staple gun, pins, scissors, paper trimmer, framing equipment, paper, fabrics, artefacts, books?

- Do you know where to find all of these and how to use them?

If you want to further this interest, look at displays in shop windows, art galleries, museums, advertisements and libraries to pick up ideas on how the displays are made eye-catching or informative. Practise with your pictures or ornaments at home. If your responsibility is great in this area, it might be an idea to undertake some kind of visual arts training. See if there are courses or evening classes in your local centres.

Making and maintaining equipment, resources and materials

It may also be part of your role to ensure that things are ready for the pupils [1P2]. Tasks can range from photocopying, making games or worksheets, through to fully fledged technician status in a laboratory, technology department or ICT suite. In these latter cases, you will need specialist training, as the equipment will be specialist, expensive and possibly dangerous. You may be given the role of ensuring there are always adequate supplies of basic classroom resources such as paper and pencils and that they are in good condition. Establish a routine of checking, and find out where and how you get renewals [3.1P1–4].

Photocopying

- Ensure you know how to work the machine.

- Check the copyright rules.

- Check the paper tray – and always try to leave it ready for use by someone else who might be in a hurry.

- Can the items be double sided, thus saving paper?

- What will you do if the machine runs out of ink? Stalls? Runs out of paper? Has a paper jam?

- Check the position of the master and the enlargement, and select the number of copies needed.

- Do one to start with to check the contrast, then do the run.

- What do you do if the quality is not as you would wish – blurred, pale, streaky?

Creating a tape or disk library

This is rarely done now, with hard disk storage and easy wireless access to the internet from interactive whiteboards available in most schools. If you are required to create such a library, note that there may be old sound or videotapes, CDs or DVDs, pre-recorded or blank.

Ensure you know:

- Where the recorded tapes or disks are to be stored.

- Where to find blanks.

- What is to be recorded and that copyright is not infringed.

- Where the recording/burning equipment is kept and how it is used.

- Whether anyone else wants to use it when you do.

- Practise using the equipment so that you are familiar with it and can record at the correct speed, with the minimum of waste tape or disk space.

- Keep full and accurate records of what is recorded, preferably in some kind of publicly available filing system so that teachers can access it easily.

- Label the tapes and disks clearly, possibly also using some kind of numerical or alphabetical code so that they can be returned to their correct places.

- Check the required shelf life of the recording with the teacher requesting the item and reuse tapes and disks whenever possible.

Tools and materials

If you are made responsible for any of these, you may be in charge of the paper stock cupboard or of scissors, pencils and paint pots or more sophisticated items [3K5].

The crucial things are to keep them:

- tidy – check regularly

- accessible to other staff in a hurry – organise them suitably, keep items on shelves or in labelled boxes

- complete and functional – do not let stocks run out, so find out the system for renewal, and find out about disposal of broken or torn items

- sharp and safe – find out about maintenance procedures and read all safety precautions

- secure – ensure that expensive items are dealt with as the school wishes: some may be under lock and key or even fitted with an alarm. Where possible involve pupils in looking after things and using them properly.

Planning and preparation

Unfortunately, the introduction of TAs to many schools was done as a result of earmarked funding for individual pupils, and the funding came in multiples of pupil contact hours associated with particular pupils. This has led to the 'Velcro' approach to learning support, a misunderstanding about entitlement to provision and with TAs paid only for these hours. Effective support cannot take place without some planning, preparation and reflection on the process both by the teacher and by the TA [1.1P1,2; 1K6]. This needs time outside the pupil contact time although not necessarily a lot. Alternative ways of communication other than meeting can be devised, but are really second best [1.1P3]. Dialogue to form proper relationships and ensure thorough understanding is essential. Some schools and LAs have recognised the need for paid non-contact time for both partners in line with the 'highly recommended' guidance circulated in the *Education (Specified work and registration) (England) Regulations 2003 and (amended) regulations 2007*:

39 Support staff undertaking specified work will be directed and supervised by a qualified teacher. If they undertake this work with a number of classes/groups they are likely to be subject to the direction and supervision of several teachers. The nature of the direction and supervision may vary according to the level of 'specified work' undertaken.

(WAMG 2008): 17

41 Supervision arrangements for all staff undertaking activities to support teaching and learning should include time for teachers and support staff to discuss planning and pupil progress within the contracted hours of the support staff.

(WAMG 2008): 18

Given STL 1.2P1, 1.3P1 and the above recommendation, it is difficult to see how any candidate could achieve a Level 2 qualification without dedicated, paid non-pupil contact time with the relevant teacher for planning and feedback.

There are still some parents and pupils who think they have to have so many hours one-to-one support each week. The Code of Practice clearly states that 'this may not be the most appropriate way of helping the child' (DfES 2001: 53). Is the most appropriate help when the most challenging pupils have support from the least experienced and trained member of staff? Individual support also often increases dependency rather than increasing independence. If you have concerns about your particular role, you should discuss these both with your line manager and with the teacher concerned.

Teachers plan for the long term so that pupils do not cover the same material year after year. Together they have developed yearly schemes of work to plan out curriculum coverage over the time the pupils are in the school. It is unlikely that you will need to see or understand these, but you will soon recognise the differences between what goes on in each year group as you work in different classes. The changes are also based on the understanding that pupils learn some things better at different ages, and there is more about this in the next chapter.

Individual teachers or sometimes year groups of teachers then plan for the medium term, usually a term ahead. These plans should be available and you will find them helpful and interesting. By looking at them you will know what kinds of things will be coming up in the term and whether there are any contributions you could make or ideas you could contribute. There may be field trips, visitors or specific activities planned on dates which you could put into your diary. As you get to know the teachers and work with them, they may ask you to join them in composing medium-term plans.

They then produce short-term plans covering the detail of each week's work, how they are adapting the curriculum to the needs of the pupils and how the pupils have been dealing with the work to date. Figure 8.1 indicates the planning process in diagrammatic form.

The short-term plans should incorporate your role in supporting the pupils' learning. Within these short-term plans, the staff may produce some individual lesson plans. Where managers and teachers are concerned about best practice you will be timetabled and have systems of communication which enable you to understand not only what you have to do before you are to do it, but also why. Ask the teachers you work with what their system is. Some teachers produce special plans for their TAs, and others expect the TA to do their own planning given the teacher's outline plans. This is where it is vital to have formed a relationship with the teachers you are working with so that you know what you are going to do.

Arriving at the classroom with the pupils and taking verbal instructions is not good enough except, of course, in emergencies. The very first performance criterion asks that you 'offer constructive and timely suggestions as to the support you can provide to a planned activity'

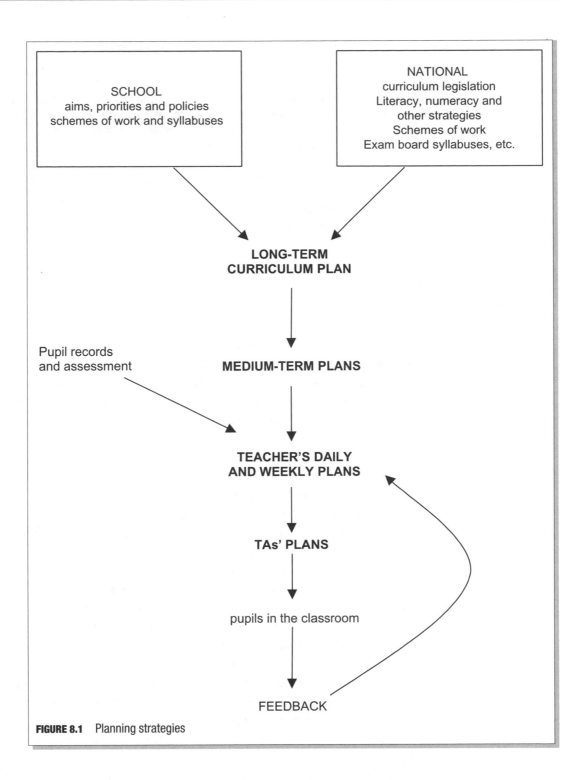

FIGURE 8.1 Planning strategies

[1.1P1]. To do this you will have to have time and opportunity to discuss the teacher's plans with him or her [6.1P1; 6.2P2; 9.1P1; 12K8]. Standard 1K4 asks that you relate your experience and expertise to the plans: this means that you should be sure that you know what you are going to do and that you are capable of doing it. Do make it clear to a teacher if you are unsure. Remember that it is the pupil who will suffer from your deficiency if there is one, and that is not fair. This kind of discussion can cause a little friction especially in secondary schools if teachers are not used to discussing their planning with anyone. If there is a problem, talk it over with your line manager and try to find some strategies to make the

TABLE 8.1   Ofsted judgements in relation to the deployment of support staff

Outstanding	Good	Satisfactory	Inadequate
Very well managed teaching assistants reinforce and support learning extremely effectively.	Adults relate well to pupils in the classroom and expect them to work hard. Teaching assistants and other classroom helpers are well directed to support learning. Good relationships support parents/carers in helping pupils to succeed.	Teaching assistants are adequately managed and are effective in enabling pupils to learn.	Teaching assistants and parents/carers are inadequately managed and therefore do not support pupils' learning as effectively as they should.

suggestions. Lesson plans will contain the learning objectives and some indication of the teacher's expectations of what the outcomes may be [1K5]. All learning objectives have steps to success. It is good practice to share and/or generate this with the pupils. Pupils need to have a clear understanding of the teacher's expectations. Success criteria can take the form of a checklist for pupils to assess their own and others' progress towards learning objectives. When supporting pupils, feedback should be focused and success criteria provide an opportunity to determine next steps clearly. Class teachers have an accountability through the Ofsted framework to deploy other adults effectively (see Table 8.1). Your role should be clearly identified on planning, and the objectives and desired outcomes should be shared prior to the session.

Some examples of planning formats can be seen in the strategy materials; ask your English or mathematics coordinators to go through the materials with you. You need these plans at least the night before, and then you need time (again preferably paid) to prepare what you need for the lesson(s).

Schools have a variety of approaches in this area to help you to understand what you are doing. In some instances you may be invited to attend planning meetings. This is a very useful thing to do as it will give you a clear opportunity of hearing what it is the teachers want the children to learn, in particular any specific group you may be working with. Some teachers have a TA's folder. This usually lives on the teacher's desk. Teachers use it by writing out for you clear expectations of the work you will be doing in any given session. These instructions may include the names of any children you will be working with in the shared part of the hour and will let you know the kind of support needed. Not every part would be filled in every time as often work is ongoing. Some schools ensure that TAs have access to copies of such plans by putting them in folders in the staffroom, and in other schools teachers complete notes in an exercise book or produce a separate TA plan for the lesson.

Plans can also include a space in which you can write down what you actually did, and what happened to the pupils while you did it. Did you achieve the teacher's objective with those pupils? This feedback is vital for the teacher to continue planning for the needs of all the pupils in the class and your future role. Stick a polite post-it note on the teacher's desk when you leave the room, or in the pupil's workbook if the teacher is going to see it – not if it is going home. Make time voluntarily to chat and gradually your contribution will be recognised, meetings will be convened and paid planning time will be instituted. This happens in many schools already and is quite clearly the best practice.

You may have to find resources, do some photocopying, check out some equipment and its availability, read up about the subject, find some artefacts or reference books for the pupils, or even ask someone what on earth the teacher is getting at [1.1P4]. You must ask if you do not understand. If you do not understand, then neither will the pupils. Recognise your limitations, but also use your experience and expertise [1.2P2].

Your standards of planning and preparation will set a standard for the pupils with whom you work. Tatty paper, blunt tools, an uninformed you, all mean to the pupils that what they do with you does not matter. It needs to matter or you are all wasting your time.

An example of good practice in planning and preparation

A TA was working with a Year 4 class. The teacher's plans up in the file in the staffroom indicated that the TA was to work with five less-able children in a wet area attached to an open plan classroom. One of the children had recently returned from a speech and language unit and had communication problems. The relationships were good and full discussion had previously taken place about the objectives and the child's need. The task was to carry out some capacity experiments with various vessels, guessing and measuring. The pupils needed to have more hands-on experience of how shape can alter capacity. It was a mathematics lesson, not a science lesson. The TA realised, from working in the school for a few terms, that primary schools now work in litres, not pints as she had done at school. So, after a brief chat with the teacher that evening after school, to check what apparatus was available for her to use, she went home, got out her own measuring jugs and a few containers, and had a go, looking at the 'ml' section on the jug, not the 'fluid ounces'. Luckily, her young son came home in the middle of this and she had to explain to him what she was doing – a process which subsequently helped her explain to the pupils in her group what they were to do. She actually wrote down a few words that she found useful in the process. Next morning she felt ready to help the children, got out the equipment while the teacher explained the various tasks to the class, and performed the required task with her group. Afterwards, she had a brief word with the class teacher as to which children she felt had grasped the object of the exercise, and the teacher noted this in her planning book.

Pupil contact time

Whatever the planning and preparation, how you actually perform with the pupils in or out of the classroom is going to be the crunch time. This is when your every move and word matter [1.2P1]. Sometimes this is hard, if you are feeling off colour, or the dog was sick just before you left, or your father rang on the way to school and intends calling in that evening for a meal or the washing machine gave up, but you are now a professional, paid to do a job. At the school gate you have to leave your trouble behind (mentally) and concentrate on being a TA. This may mean acting a part, but all professionals have to do this. If things are really bad, you have had a family bereavement or major upset, then be sure you tell your line manager, who will surely help. You should be appropriately dressed for whatever activities you are planning to do, with aprons, gloves or plimsolls if needed, setting a good example to your pupils, who often try to duck such things. Remember simple things like manners: for instance, do not talk with a group of pupils if the teacher is speaking. Always add 'please's and 'thank you's. Work systematically through tasks and ensure you clear up with the pupils, getting them to do all they can. You are a role model.

Many lessons have three parts to them, some more obvious than others – an introduction, possibly with a whole class starter activity, a main activity where pupils get on with some task, and a concluding or plenary section. This is not a time to sit patiently while the teacher takes over. If you have heard the lesson before and are sure of the content of the introduction and plenary, you may be able to undertake preparation or simple marking tasks at this time. Do not work with a child or small group in the same room as this can be distracting for both groups apart from emphasising that the group is different from the rest of their class. The time for differentiation is in the group or task work.

Check out the following:

In lessons you can:

During introduction or oral/mental starter

- encourage reluctant learners to join in

- focus on a group/individual, giving whispers and prompts to give confidence

- model behaviour – look at teacher, refer to vocabulary on wall, show active listening

- alert teacher if special group/individual has an answer

- be discreet – aware of pupils' self-esteem

- ensure you know what the teacher is talking about and know his/her instructions

- perhaps have a similar version of the teacher's resources.

During main activity

- ensure that instructions are understood, perhaps repeat them in simpler stages or with simpler vocabulary [1.2P3; 6.1P4; 6.2P4]

- provide really focused teaching with a small group/individual – see below

PHOTOGRAPH 8.7   Enabling independence by standing back but keeping a watching brief

- prepare pupils for the plenary, perhaps helping them to be able to report back

- help other pupils as and when appropriate [1.2P4]

- praise and encourage pupils in their work where possible [1.2P5; 6.1P4]

- watch and listen to pupils' responses so that you can provide feedback later [1.2P6]

- time your activity to try to ensure the pupils finish what the teacher requires

- ensure you have alternative or additional activities to interest or follow up what the teacher has set if you need them [1.2P7]

- seek help if you need it [1.2P8].

During plenary/concluding/summing up

- whisper prompts

- sit near less confident pupils

- encourage participation

- mention particularly good work.

Teaching

When you are with the pupils in the main activity, you will actually be teaching in the wider sense of that term. Teaching consists of many integral parts, some of which happen concurrently and some at different times.

See if you can see teachers using the following so that you can role model similar behaviour:

(Listen to their speech but also take good note of their position in the room and of body language)

- instruction – telling

- demonstration – showing, using artefacts or interactive whiteboard

- exposition – explaining, describing

- performing – acting a role

- using eye contact, gesture, movement round the room

- listening – this may seem passive but is essential to monitor the understanding of the pupils [1.2P6; 10.1P1; 15.1P3]

- waiting – giving time for thought

- questioning – direct questions for which there is only one answer, but it is a way of involving the pupils in the exposition/instruction mode

  - open questions – can elicit a variety of answers designed to make pupils think

  - asking for further details to ensure understanding

  - challenging

- praising – celebrating good work or right answers, encouraging [1.2P5]

- chairing a discussion

You will be able to give much more individual attention to certain pupils than the teacher (there is a further description in the section on SEN in Chapter 7), but do ensure that the level and type of attention is what the teacher intends and the curriculum requires [6.1P3; 6.2P3]. You will have more time to listen and for individual communication, recognising the appropriate communication methods and vocabulary that will help the pupils who are with you. For instance, when working with a pupil or two using a computer, it is very tempting to engage in the programme yourself and to participate, but it may be that the pupil needs mouse practice rather than just to get the answers to the problems posed. You will enable the pupils to read instructions, explain, instruct, listen, ensure they take turns or share, ensure that the quietest get a time to speak and the extrovert gives way to the others at times. Explain to enable the pupils to do the task more successfully themselves [11.2P3; 15.3P4]. You can keep them on task without being aggressive, praise their progress, comment on success, assist only where necessary – show by example rather than by doing it for them. You can make things interesting and relevant to their world [12.2P2,3]. Use words they will understand [10.1P4]. Get them to read instructions and labels, trying out the spelling of words and drawing their own pictures. Ask open-ended questions like 'Why did you do that?', 'Can you explain what you did?', 'What might happen if you did that again?', 'What do you think about it?' Challenge their ideas where you can to make them think, but always ensure they are not undermined by such questioning [4.1P6; 10K8; 15.3P2]. So praise whenever you can, but appropriately [4.2P5; 4.3P1–6; 4K6].

Always give some kind of feedback to the pupils [1K12; 6.1P4; 6.2P4; 11.2P6; 11K6; 12.3P3; 15.4P2], perhaps something to aim to do better next time [1.3P1]. Where possible tell the teacher what you have suggested; again a post-it note on the planning sheet or the desk or in the pupil's book will do. You should have established whether you are to write directly

PHOTOGRAPH 8.8 Two TAs working with groups during the main part of the lesson

in pupils' books and what is the approved method of doing this: red or black pen, comments or ticks, corrections procedures, etc. You can say 'You tried hard' or 'That is well done for you', particularly if it fulfilled the teacher's targets for those pupils for that lesson. Saying 'That is marvellous' when it clearly is not does no one any favours [11.1P7; 12.1P5]. If the work is careless, particularly if you know the pupils well and they can do better, get them to do it again, or if there is not time, at least recognise that they can do better. Maybe they are having an 'off' day. Try to ensure they finish the task set, giving them a warning as time gets short. If they finish early, they should have some kind of follow-up task to do. You may need to help them complete a homework diary [1.2P3]. Always ensure the pupils clear up before they leave a task or classroom.

Always seek help from the teacher if you are unsure what to do [1.1P8; 6.1P5; 6.2P5; 11.7P7,8; 15K26–28].

It does not always go smoothly. Sometimes the resources are not sufficient, time runs out or somebody's patience is not what it should be. Do not worry about this. Just remember what would have made it go better, and incorporate that next time you do that activity. We learn more from mistakes than from doing things correctly [1K10].

Improve your practice

Watch teachers and others at work and see how they talk with pupils. With their permission, make notes of their body language, tone of voice, the sort of vocabulary they are using.

■ What seems to work well?

■ Did any of their behaviour seem inappropriate?

Share the notes with those whom you have watched. If they agree, share them with colleagues.

■ Could you adapt any ideas that you see for your own work?

If you are really brave, get yourself videoed and watch what body language and verbal prompts you use. It takes practice, although it looks very easy to an onlooker.

Notice that, in all the above, behaviour management strategies are not mentioned. If the teaching and learning strategies are properly focused on the needs and interests of the pupils as well as imparting certain information, there are far fewer behaviour problems. Interesting, prepared, alert teachers do not have the same problems as some others. They use all of their bodies, stay mobile, use ICT or music or drama to illustrate a point, encourage participation and use humour in the right place [10.1P2]. The pace of the lesson is important. Dynamic focused teaching is not easy and is physically draining, but not as draining as dealing with bored, recalcitrant pupils.

You will need to be aware that sometimes things that we assume 'everybody knows' are not known by some pupils because we often make cultural assumptions about the curriculum and the prior knowledge pupils bring with them to the school. Fairy tales or nursery rhymes, or in higher-level classes, texts in which there are literary or historical references may be alien to some cultures or some homes. During the lesson it may mean that you will have to explain the topic or item.

You should not be put in charge of a large group and certainly not a whole class at the level you are aiming for. If the group is meant to be working together cooperatively, you

PHOTOGRAPH 8.9   Keeping the place tidy

PHOTOGRAPH 8.10   Even early years' children can clear up

may need to ensure that shy pupils speak and other more vocal pupils do not dominate. Act like an informal chairperson. Some groups, however, may be meant to be working independently, so your role may be to stop the irrelevant chat to enable them to complete their tasks. Enabling pupils to cooperate and challenge each other is giving them a most valuable life skill. You might be the only adult in the room for a short emergency period, but you should be under the supervision of a qualified teacher at all times.

Supporting EAL in the classroom

To support the pupils' language development, it is very important that learning is supported visually with hands-on activities, pictures, story props and other visual prompts. If these children are just talked to, they are unlikely to learn much but if learning is linked to visual or active learning, EAL pupils can make good progress. For example, if the focus of a lesson is volcanoes, an EAL pupil is much more likely to be engaged if pictures with clear labelling are used (or if the internet is used to show real-life examples of volcanoes). In the first part or introduction to a lesson, the early stage learner of English may gain little from the teacher's explanation unless this includes the use of relevant visual aids. Whispering to the pupil to try to help in the introduction, even in the child's first language, can be very distracting for the rest of the class. You should be able to use a different text at a more appropriate language level, remembering that for older children the text does need to be age appropriate.

If you are working with beginner EAL pupils in a small group, you can, for example, use picture cards to teach basic vocabulary such as classroom objects, science equipment, etc. Remember that children don't always have to respond orally to your question or prompt. They can point or take the right card or picture or carry out an action. These activities can be made into a lot of fun using a variety of games such as Kim's Game or 'Simon Says'. These strategies may also be useful for any slower learner. If you are using words like 'translucent' and 'transparent', have objects with you that show the meaning of the words.

EAL children should not feel that they cannot use their first language in school. A child's first language is clearly an important part of who they are as a person and it should be seen as a valuable skill to support learning. If there are other children in the class or school who speak the same language, they may be able to support each others' learning and understanding through the use of the first language. If you or another adult in the school can speak the child's first language, it can be very supportive to do this to support learning and to give the child an opportunity to talk about how they are getting on in school. Remember that beginner EAL pupils are learning English and they will make 'mistakes' or developmental errors. It is important when you are working with them to focus on communication and not over-correct pupils, particularly when they are speaking. The main focus on correction to begin with is if you don't understand. Developing confidence and fluency in using English is very important.

Observation strategies [STL 9]

If you are undertaking a course it is very likely that you will be expected to make some structured observations of pupils learning, or a teacher may ask you to watch a pupil for a particular purpose [9.1P1]. Observation is now considered so important that a whole standard, STL9, is devoted to it, although STL 9 does cover the informal observations that you might undertake in monitoring and assessment as part of your normal work. There is more on this later in the chapter. You need to understand the purpose of the observation – just interest, or concern over progress, or concern over social interactions within a group. Even if you are not asked to observe, it is always worth spending a little time watching pupils. In this way you will begin to broaden your concept of the normal range of development briefly described in Chapter 5 [6K2; 9K1,2]. You should ask the class teacher of the pupils you want to watch first, and find time to discuss the issues and protocols of observation before you start anything formal, as well as spending time with them afterwards discussing your observations [2.1P2; 12.2P1]. There are suggestions for ways of observing in many books. Wragg's book on classroom observation has all the kinds of examples you might want [9K6,7] (Wragg 1994).

You can notice all sorts of things at random, just by being in a class with small children or young people, but it will sharpen your perceptions if you do this in an organised way [2.1–4P1; 2K1,2; 9.1P1]. You should make notes in as structured a way as possible, and this means you would be making records on someone else's child, for whom a class teacher is responsible. It is important that your observing does not become intrusive for the pupil or disrupt any other class activity [9K3]. Your act of observation may change what is happening [9K8]. If pupils see you writing or using a camera they could immediately behave differently. This is less likely to happen if you do this regularly or if other adults are also in the habit of observing them [9K4,9]. The role of the observer – inspector, assessor, trainee teacher or TA or appraiser – may also influence the process, as will the background of the child. Observing means either taking time out of your paid time or doing it voluntarily. You need some agreed ground rules.

Possible protocols to consider for classroom observation [9.1P2,3; 14.3P1,3]

The following need to be discussed between the TA and the class teacher where any observation is to take place:

- The purpose of the exercise is to . . . e.g. understand more about . . .
- The adults involved will be . . .
- The pupils involved will be . . .

The head teacher/department head/line manager has been told what is happening, and has agreed. It needs to be checked that:

- anything written is to be shared first with each other, so that comments can be made and points of accuracy checked [9.1P6; 9K6]
- any comments to be seen by others will be anonymised, or amalgamated with others to preserve confidentiality
- the main audience of any summary written material will be . . . e.g. the teacher, other members of a course, or an outside reader
- the people observed or interviewed can have a copy of the notes made if they so wish [14.3P4]
- you know what will happen to any written records [9K11]
- the intended outcome of the activity is . . . [9K10]
- you know what you will do if the observation shows up anything within the classroom or school that someone wishes to address or celebrate
- if others get involved, they will be covered by the same sort of protocols
- someone seeks permission of the parents of the children closely involved
- either side should be able to make comments at any time in the process if there is any discomfort or suggestion about what is taking place or being said.

(Watkinson 2002: 39)

Observing

You can use a sheet of A4 paper on a clipboard, a spiral-bound memo pad or an exercise book. Make yourself as inconspicuous as possible [9.1P3–5].

Focus on one area of interest, one pupil, and observe at regular times, e.g. every 30 seconds or every minute. Decide on a part of their body which is of interest, such as their hands. What they are saying?
Do this for five minutes.

- Did they keep still? Did they touch any resources? Did they touch another pupil? Whom did they speak to? Was it about their work?

- Did this tell you anything more about the pupil, the table or desk they are working on, or the children they are with? Repeat the exercise with a different pupil at the same desk/table, or with the same pupil in a different context or classroom.

- Did the same thing happen? How was it different?

OR [9K7]

Note every five minutes what they are doing, and, if they are talking and you can hear what they say, put that down.

- What have you found out about this pupil? [9.2P3]

THEN

- What did the pupil do during that period?

- Was it anything to do with what the teacher intended or not?

- Did the pupil learn anything new during the time you were watching?

- Did they understand anything better?

- Did they practise anything that they had done before?

- Did anyone talk to them or help them? Who did this – the pupils sitting near them, or adults?

- Could you have made things easier for them if you had been sitting there, or if they had been in a different place, or had different resources? In what ways?

Find an opportunity to talk through what you saw with the teacher. [9.2P2–4]

You can develop grids with names and headings of what you are particularly looking for, such as asking or answering questions, or with time markers [9.1P6; 9.2P1]. Some can be found in the TA Induction File (TDA 2006a, 2006b:2.36, 2.37). If you are going to question the pupils, you can prepare some questions beforehand.

Feedback to pupils and teachers

You need to monitor, even informally, how the pupils are progressing and what achievement they make in a lesson, often to make adjustments to what you are doing as you go along, but also then to feed back to the teacher [1.3P1–4; 1K12; 9.1P1–6]. Assessment information is best when gathered against the objective for the session, so it is doubly important that you know what this is. It would also be useful for the teacher to know how well pupils are progressing towards their targets, particularly in literacy or in an IEP, as these are likely to be specific and short-term; what their behaviour is like, especially if a behaviour programme is in place; and what unexpected things you noticed [9K7]. Feedback can be much more informal than the planning process; sometimes just a verbal comment, at the end of a lesson before the TA and teacher separate, in the corridor on the way to the staffroom, or even in the car park on the way home, can help the teacher plan the next step for the pupils with whom the TA has been working. You may have already alerted the teacher if you have had problems during the lesson, but it is better, if you can, not to interrupt him or her and just leave your comments to the end. In one school, the TAs themselves devised a separate written feedback system that would have some consistency for the teachers [13K9]. Another school had a diary system for noting improvement and problems. TAs also use teachers' assessment forms, after training and guidance, and these forms can be ticked when things are achieved. You could stick a polite post-it note on the teacher's desk when you leave the room, or in the pupil's workbook if the teacher is going to see it – not if it is going home. Make time voluntarily to chat, and gradually your contribution will be recognised, meetings will be convened and paid planning time will be instituted. Feedback can usually be done on the move. This has happened in many schools already [6.1P6; 6.2P6].

Assessment, testing and examinations

All the time teachers work with pupils they inwardly make small judgements. This is called informal formative assessment. You will find yourself judging, but without training you may not recognise what you are seeing, so beware of jumping to conclusions too rapidly. You will soon recognise what is realistic to expect of certain pupils, and what is a fair judgement. If the teacher asks you to make a particular assessment or judgment, you must spend

PHOTOGRAPH 8.11 TA checking written work towards the end of the lesson

time with them making sure you agree about what you are looking for, and what lesson or part of the lesson would be best to watch for what the teacher is hoping to see. You may be convinced a pupil has real difficulties where the teacher may have assumed they were just being lazy, or you might consider a pupil was pretending to be slow in order to get your extra help. You must deal with this professionally, be certain you can justify what you are saying and have evidence to support you; and where relationships between you and the teacher are good, and you have pre-agreed the method and criteria to be used, there should not be a problem. *Form*ative assessment is about in*form*ing the teacher about what step the pupil needs to make next [2.4P1].

You may be asked to complete more formal assessments as part of your job. These may be simple reading tests or part of the Standard Assessment Tests or Tasks (SATs) which take place regularly. Again, get full instructions about what is required, ensure you look for strengths as well as weaknesses, and be brief, concise and accurate. These tests are part of what is called summative assessment. Test results depend very much on how questions are asked, particularly where understanding is needed as well as memory, such as in science. Pictures, or seeing and handling the actual materials about which questions are asked, and being able to enquire about the meaning of the questions, all influence how correct the answers will be. Many of us can remember taking tests or examinations when we did not feel very well or the weather was exceptionally hot. These things can all affect our recall and performance, and thus our test results.

The things that teachers want to assess are the knowledge gained, the understanding that has developed, the skills learnt, and the attitudes to learning that are influencing the pupil. Some of these factors are easier to see or measure than others. Tests and examinations tend to test knowledge and understanding; practical skills have to be observed in action as well as by examination of an end product, and are more usually seen as part of a vocational competence assessment. Attitudes are really only seen in the way pupils cope with learning as it happens. In all of these assessments some kind of standard has to be established and then monitored in order that results from one teacher or class or school are comparable with those from other places. Clearly pre-school children will not undergo written examinations, and there is still some concern about the formal testing procedures inflicted upon seven-year-olds with the Standard Assessment Tests or Tasks (SATs). Science is not tested externally until Year 6, and even here there is much debate about how investigative, experimental and explorative work can be tested by written tests. Practical work is not tested until secondary school, and there is still much contention about the use or misuse of project work. Increasingly, misuse of materials available on the internet such as exemplar essays or examination responses is causing problems for those setting formal examinations. External examinations are usually undertaken only by those in secondary education, although some children of primary age in your care may be taking common entrance examinations for independent schools or music grade examinations, for example.

Any kind of assessment procedure needs careful handling by those conducting it, whether it is an informal observation for interest or a formal external examination. If you think back to your own experiences, you may remember a lot of 'hype' among your peers, stern faces from your teachers, the classroom furniture all rearranged so that you would not cheat. The fuss did not make you feel confident and give of your best. You need to minimise the disruption to normal school life, yet ensure quietness and freedom from interruptions. Even simple assessments, such as hearing pupils read in the infant class, can achieve better results in a calm, friendly atmosphere. Most teachers will welcome questions and suggestions you have about procedures to get the best from pupils, provided you offer them in the usual spirit of constructive support. Some families and cultures are particularly keen on examinations and these will create tension in the home, and many schools now practise for external tests, sometimes to the detriment of covering the curriculum in other areas. The tension can be counterproductive. Some pupils (and adults) are very sensitive about being observed, hence the need for protocols and care about your presence in the room doing something unusual.

In undertaking official invigilation duties you will be given the examination guides to follow, setting out a certain procedure [STL 17]. It is important for validity that you follow these instructions, but you can do this without being officious. Particularly if you are supporting a pupil with SEN, you may be asked to read a test paper to a pupil, or encourage a small child to respond to particular questions. Again, the calm, friendly approach will enable the pupils to give of their best. Most of the instructions for supervising such activities will be common sense and want you to follow the guidance you would use for any lesson in terms of health and safety, emergency procedures and working environment. However, supervision of things like seating arrangements, timing, checking equipment or papers, allowing talking and dealing with disruptions must be followed to the letter [17.1P1–11]. Your conduct of the procedures must be exemplary and record keeping must be immaculate. Remember, someone's future may be at stake. There is no excuse whatsoever for mislaid papers or lack of any other attention to detail if you are responsible in this area. Standardisation of practice across settings as far as is physically possible is the only fair way for such procedures to take place [17.2P1–7]. It is more than ever important that you report any problems and discuss any discrepancies or suspected malpractice with the appropriate person as soon as possible. If necessary make a written record of your actions, and sign and date it in case of any subsequent investigation.

As well as ensuring that the pupils do their best in any kind of assessment or test, you must always remember that you have to operate within the framework of the school policies and under the guidance of the teachers [17K1–22]. Confidentiality about the process and the results is really important.

Records

Pupils' and staff records will be kept under lock and key somewhere centrally usually, although some of the running records will be in the pupils' classrooms [3.2P6]. You must find out the systems and procedures for your school, and what your roles and responsibilities are within those [1.3P4; 2.2P7; 2.3P5; 13.2P10; 14.3P10; 15.4P5; 15K29; 17.2P7; 17K22]. Maintain their safe and secure storage at all times, and do not leave important documents on the photocopier. It is easily done. Another trap is the use of paperclips. Single sheets of paper can easily get attached to the wrong set of documents with these [2K4].

The safe storage of data also applies to material kept on computers [9K11; 12.3P4]. All material kept on adults or pupils on computer hard or floppy disks is subject to the Data Protection Act which means that it must all be kept securely, and the subject of the item stored should have access to what is being stored. If you are asked to enter data into pupils' records on a database, ensure that you know the procedures your school adopts to conform with this Act. In principle, only the minimum personal information necessary is stored, and it should be as accurate as possible and only held for as long as necessary. Individuals have a right to see what is stored about them except in very limited circumstances where 'access would prejudice the prevention or detection of crime' (DOH, HO and DfEE 1999: 115). Security measures include not just the physical security of the equipment but the existence of appropriate levels of staff access. Never divulge passwords to office equipment unless requested to by the senior member of staff responsible for the recording systems.

Using your initiative within the boundaries of your role

As you can see from the above, you may be given quite an amount of leeway to interpret instructions, carry out activities, prepare materials and report back. Teachers usually appreciate having people to work with who have ideas, who ask questions, who are prepared to do things 'off their own bat'. But all teachers will vary as to the extent to which they are happy for you to do this. This is where your sensitivity must come in. You have to judge how far you can properly go in any situation in any classroom. What will help you is to talk it through whenever you can with the teacher, preferably beforehand, but if not make sure any unilateral action on your part is reported back to the teacher as part of your feedback [1.3P2; 6K11].

One teacher may be very happy for you to give permission for a pupil to visit the toilet, and another insist all such permission is rarely given in their class, or certainly only by them. Use of certain materials not specified in the planning might need permission – or not. The whole issue of boundaries with each class teacher for whom you work has to be worked out between the pair of you [1K2]. It really does help to be as explicit as possible about such boundaries. Written policies may help you, but many of the issues will be ones of individual idiosyncrasies and relationships.

Supporting the curriculum

The curriculum itself

ANY TASK THAT you are given to do with pupils will not be just to occupy them, but will be designed to help them learn something. What actually goes on in the classroom for the pupil learner depends on the match between what the teacher wants them to learn – the curriculum; the learning style and characteristics of the pupil; and the activities of the adults teaching and supporting the learning. See Figure 9.1.

A curriculum can mean a course of study at a school but really the word covers everything that goes on in a school or early years' setting. The formal part, the part that is now written down, is what most people think of when they refer to a school curriculum. But much more is learnt when in school. You may remember things you learnt at school that were not prescribed, about other pupils and teachers themselves, about how friendships work and how to keep out of trouble. These aspects are sometimes called the 'informal' or the 'hidden' curriculum. The informal curriculum covers the bits that everybody knows go on between lessons: in the corridors or the playground, in assembly or clubs; and the hidden curriculum covers the bits about relationships and climate, the way you feel when you work or visit a place. Early years' curriculum used to seem very informal with its emphasis on play but good provision was always well planned, 'delivered' and assessed just as it was in the more obviously formal curriculum of mainstream school. The match of provision to children's needs was much more dominant, however, with the changes made in the setting environment supporting the learning in a much clearer way.

The formal curriculum

This covers what schools hope to teach. If you work in a state funded school, this includes the National Curriculum (NC) as a legal requirement in English and Welsh schools. Independent schools are free to set their own curriculum, although some follow the NC or parts of it. The NC is dictated by government, and is an entitlement for all children of statutory school age (5–16). Scotland has an advisory NC and Northern Ireland has its own version. Children under 5 years of age do not have to go to school or any other provider. There are no legal requirements on parents or carers to provide any kind of formal curriculum in the home for under fives. For all provision outside the home such as nurseries or child minding there is a statutory framework backed up by inspection. The way this is presented is changing so that by the time the new NOS are in place – September 2008 – the single statutory framework for the under fives will also be operative (DCSF 2007b).

The National Curriculum

Making the curriculum a legal requirement means that everyone has a right to be taught certain subjects at certain ages, and it ensures there is a breadth and balance, coherence and

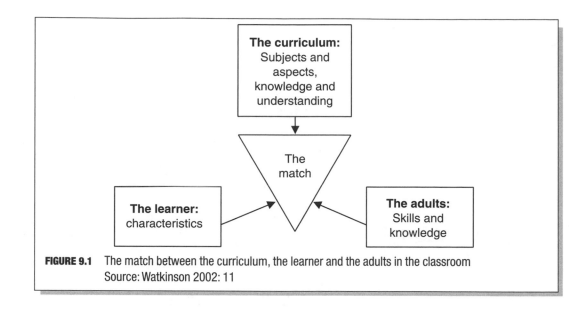

FIGURE 9.1 The match between the curriculum, the learner and the adults in the classroom
Source: Watkinson 2002: 11

consistency, relevance and differentiation. These long words are all written into the legal descriptions of the NC. All schools will have copies of the documents and it is well worth reading the introductory pages (DfEE 1999a, 1999b: 10–13) on 'Values, aims and purposes', and the requirements made of schools and teachers including its structure and timing. The NC can also be found online at www.nc.uk.net which is a website called National Curriculum online. This gives you not only the curriculum itself but also some very useful summaries and descriptions and links to resource sites. Curriculum 2000 stated the aims of this NC as:

Aim 1: The school curriculum should aim to provide opportunities for all pupils to learn and to achieve . . .

Aim 2: The school curriculum should aim to promote pupils' spiritual, moral, social and cultural development and prepare all pupils for the opportunities, responsibilities and experiences of life . . .

The four main purposes of the National Curriculum: To establish an entitlement, to establish standards, to promote continuity and coherence and to promote public understanding.

(DfEE 1999a, 1999b: 13)

The original documents laid out the subjects of a NC that had to be studied in England: English, mathematics and science, which it denoted as the core, and the foundation subjects of design and technology, information technology (IT), art, music, PE, history and geography and after age 11 a modern foreign language. Religious education (RE) was included in a basic curriculum, and cross-curricular linked areas were described later. Welsh was made an additional subject for pupils in Wales. The NC aimed to challenge expectations and raise standards and broaden the range of subjects studied. Spiritual, moral, social and cultural education, citizenship and environmental education are now more closely defined by the new Curriculum 2000. This chapter will be describing the English system so any readers from Scotland, Northern Ireland or Wales will have to check the legal requirements for their own countries. The principles of support for a curriculum are the same, whatever the framework. The framework is set out in Figure 9.2.

We do not have legislation that insists on the same material being delivered in the same way at the same time on each day of the week, each week, month and year. We do not have standardised, centrally legislated and produced lesson texts from which we all work. Some countries do. We have recommended schemes of work which many schools adhere to. These, along with the various strategies also not legally required but recommended, have created the impression of a stereotyped curriculum with certain elements having to be 'got through' in a

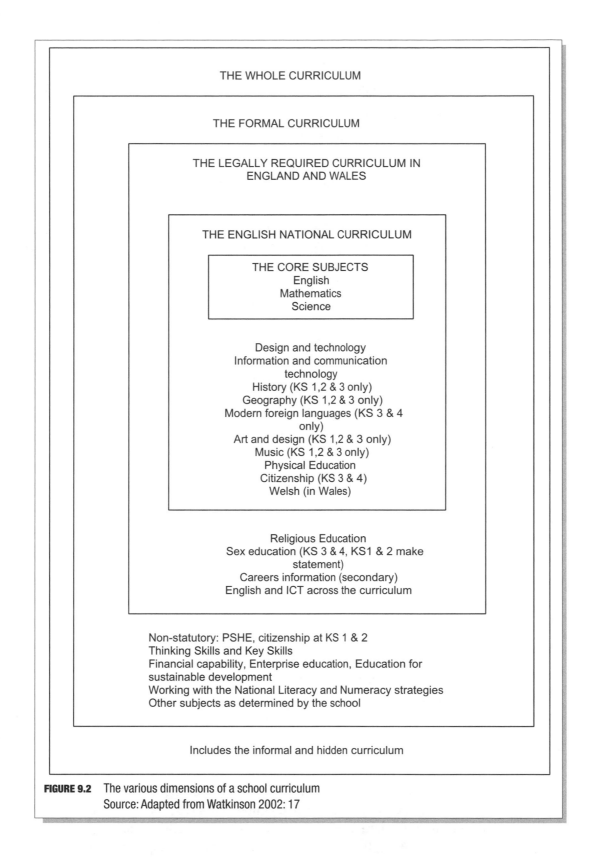

FIGURE 9.2   The various dimensions of a school curriculum
Source: Adapted from Watkinson 2002: 17

certain time at a certain age. Secondary school curricula with their focus on syllabuses for examinations have always seemed that way. However, the current moves are to free schools to adapt their work more to the needs of their pupils – to personalise their curricula.

You may find the jargon of the NC hard, but it will help to understand a few technical terms.

Children between three and five years old are said to be in the Foundation Stage, Four key stages give a structure of years running throughout the statutory school system. Year 1 contains those children who were five before the end of August. If they were in school before 1 September, they were either in a nursery class or in a reception or foundation class.

- Key Stage 1 contains Years 1 and 2 (infants).
- Key Stage 2 contains Years 3 to 6 (juniors).
- Key Stage 3 contains Years 7 to 9.
- Key Stage 4 contains Years 10 and 11.
- Sixth forms, if they exist, will contain Years 12 and 13 (very occasionally referred to as Key Stage 5).

Some authorities still have First, Middle and Upper schools where the key stages do not fit. Middle schools straddle Key Stages 2 and 3 for instance. Their formation was based upon child development theories rather than an artificial curriculum definition, the rationale being that children between seven or eight and the early teens are ready for laboratories, gymnasia, technology facilities yet still benefit from primary style classes with one teacher and cross-curricular planning. With the current trend for rigid subject planning, externally marked SATs at 11, league tables and changes in programmes of study at each key stage the trend has also been to reverse the middle school system to a primary/secondary one in most authorities, despite having designed accommodation for the former. The other major change over the last few years has been the opening of sixth form colleges alongside FE colleges providing a mixture of academic and vocational courses. This sector has been the subject of much review along with ideas of 14 to 18 being an entity similar to the upper schools. You will have to make enquiries in your own area to sort out how your local system works.

The compulsory levels of delivery for all the NC subjects are only Key Stages 1, 2 and 3. General Certificates of Secondary Education (GCSEs) and General National Vocational Qualifications and their courses are for Key Stage 4. Advanced level work ('A2' and 'AS' level) is usually done in sixth forms, tertiary colleges and FE colleges. The introduction of diplomas first to supplement A and AS levels is being piloted during 2007/8 and may eventually replace them, but this is to be decided later. A new Education Bill is before Parliament which will bring about a change in the statutory school leaving age, changing it from 16 to 18 by 2013. The intention is to increase the availability of work based training supplemented by vocational courses.

Programmes of Study describe what should be taught, the basis for planning and teaching. Attainment targets provide a framework in a nine-level scale for assessment in eight levels and a level for exceptional performance. They set out the 'knowledge, skills and understanding that pupils of different abilities and maturities are expected to have by the end of each key stage' (Education Act 1996). Level descriptions are defined for each level and describe the types and range of performance that pupils working at that level should show. They provide the basis for making judgements about pupils' performance at the end of Key Stages 1, 2 and 3, and so provide the basis for teachers to make their assessments.

SATs are based on level descriptions. The basic elements of learning to read, write, count and explore systematically will be taught in the earlier years. The junior years, Years 3 to 6, introduce more factual materials and work that needs certain independent fluency with texts and numbers; topic or project work encompasses experimental and explorative work in science and the humanities (history and geography). Skills are taught in the arts and physical education. In secondary schools, Years 7 to 11, subjects are taught separately by specialists often in specialist areas. By Years 12 and 13 (the old sixth forms), pupils are expected to be independent learners able to research texts, question and use skills to an advanced level, whether taking the A-level examinations or vocational courses. The older the pupils are, the more they are able to cope with abstract concepts.

Schemes of work should be drawn up by each school for each subject. They show in which year particular parts of the NC will be taught in your school, the resources available and probably lots of ideas for activities. The Qualifications and Curriculum Authority (QCA) has produced model schemes of work for schools, to save them reinventing the wheel, and while many schools have adopted these schemes, they are not a legal requirement. A syllabus is even more detailed than a scheme of work, and sets out exactly what should be covered. These can be drawn up by schools themselves, based on the NC or on the syllabuses devised by the examination boards for the external examinations.

Ofsted inspects schools and early years' settings using published guidance. This encompasses specific criteria against which the school is measured, which include the way in which the NC or early years' curriculum is planned, is delivered by teachers, leaders and support staff, is received by pupils and under fives, and what are the learning outcomes.

Curriculum 2000

The aims of Curriculum 2000 were 'to provide opportunities for all pupils to learn and to achieve . . . to promote pupils' spiritual, moral, social and cultural development and prepare all pupils for the opportunities, responsibilities and experiences of life' (DfEE 1999a, 1999b:12) and are based on a statement of values about the self, relationships, society and the environment (pp. 148, 149). These pages should be compulsory reading for all school staff as they are the principles on which all the work on the curriculum is based. Do find a copy and read them, or find them on the online curriculum site.

Curriculum 2000 provided an inclusive framework aiming that:

The learning across the curriculum should promote:

- spiritual, moral, social and cultural development

- personal, social and health education and citizenship

- skills development across the curriculum

  Key skills:
  - communication
  - application of numbers
  - information technology
  - working with others
  - improving own learning and performance
  - problem solving

  Thinking skills:
  - information-processing
  - reasoning
  - enquiry
  - creative thinking
  - evaluation

- financial capability, enterprise education and education for sustainable development.

It also said that:

Teachers, when planning, should adapt or modify teaching and/or learning approaches and materials to provide all pupils with opportunities to succeed:

- Setting appropriate challenges

- Providing for the diversity of pupils' needs

141

- Providing for pupils with special educational needs
- Providing support for pupils for whom English is an additional language.

ICT and RE became designated as part of the legally required core for all children, although English, mathematics and science are still called the 'core subjects'. RE documents are not included within the main set of NC books, but are published as a 'locally agreed syllabus'. All community and voluntary controlled schools in England and Wales have to use these. Foundation and aided schools can make their own decisions, but have to have an agreed syllabus of some kind. Guidelines for teaching citizenship along with personal, social and health education (PSHE) became part of the NC documentation.

Each subject in the NC is set out in the same way; each has a different colour. As they are now all in one document for either primary or secondary, you would find it useful to obtain a copy for yourself. If you are in a middle school, you may need to refer to both. Some subjects only have one part to them but English, mathematics and science all have separate parts – each with different attainment targets. You need not read and learn these in detail, just refer to them when they are relevant or you are particularly interested. The colour codes are:

- English: orangey-yellow
- mathematics: deep blue
- science: scarlet red
- design and technology: green
- ICT: plummy red
- history: purple
- geography: brown
- art and design: orange
- music: pink
- PE: pale blue
- PSHE, citizenship, environmental education and modern languages: white

The stages by which an average pupil is expected to reach each level are:

- End of Year 1: Level 1
- End of Year 2: Level 2
- End of Year 4: Level 3
- End of Year 6: Level 4
- End of Year 9: Level 5
- End of Year 11: Level 6

Brighter children reach the levels earlier, and slower learners spend a longer time getting to each level. There are some pilot projects running during 2007/8 where it is possible for the participating schools to test their pupils when they think they are ready, i.e. at that certain level, rather than testing all of them at the same age regardless of their progress.

After Curriculum 2000

Curriculum 2000 has been revised for secondary schools. It will be phased in from September 2008. Year 7 will be using the new programmes of study from September 2008, year 8 from September 2009 and year 9 from September 2010. The requirements for Key Stage 4 will come into force as the new GCSE qualifications in the relevant subjects begin. Citizenship and PE begin implementation in 2009 and English, Mathematics and ICT in 2010. Details can be found on the QCA website: www.qca.org.uk. The revised curriculum will have less pre-scribed content than Curriculum 2000, enabling schools to be more flexible in determining their own emphases. The purpose is again to help raise standards and help learners 'meet the challenges of our fast changing world' (QCA 2008). The authors suggest their 'challenge is to create a curriculum' that:

■ raises achievement in all subjects particularly English and mathematics

■ equips learners with the personal, learning and thinking skills they will need to succeed in education, life and work

■ motivates and engages learners

■ enables a smooth progression from primary through secondary and beyond

■ encourages more young people to go on to further and higher education

■ gives schools flexibility to tailor learning to individual and local needs

■ ensures that assessment supports effective teaching and learning

■ provides more opportunities for focused support and challenge where needed.

(QCA 2008)

The revised programmes of study share a common format:

■ *an importance statement* describes why the subject matters and how it can contribute to the aims of the curriculum

■ *key concepts* identify the big ideas that underpin the subject

■ *key processes* identify the essential skills and processes of the subject

■ *range and content* outlines the breadth of subject matter from which teachers should draw to develop knowledge concepts and skills

■ *curriculum opportunities* identify opportunities to enhance and enrich learning, including making links to the wider curriculum.

(QCA 2007): 4

A new set of aims which incorporates the ECM outcomes has been the starting point for the changes. 'The curriculum should enable all young people to become:

■ *successful learners* who enjoy learning, make progress and achieve

■ *confident individuals* who are able to live safe, healthy and fulfilling lives

■ *responsible citizens* who make a positive contribution to society'

(QCA 2007): 6

The level descriptions have been changed so that they fit with the new programmes of study. The QCA website http://curriculum.qca.org.uk has links to each subject to download the new programmes of study, and hardcopy can be ordered from http://orderline.qca.org.uk. Any TA supporting a subject specifically in the secondary school would find it helpful to have their own copy of the relevant materials to refer to. You can then talk with the subject leaders and teachers about any implications the changes might have for your work with young people, preparation of resources or background reading.

Cross-curriculum dimensions were identified in the early 1990s but were rarely used by schools, but these have been revived in the 2008 secondary curriculum under slightly different titles. It is important for learners to see where what they are learning in school fits into the real world, because otherwise it becomes a pointless exercise. The real world is complex and subjects interlink, so the cross-curriculum links are an attempt to make sense of the school subjects. The new list includes:

- identity and cultural diversity
- healthy lifestyles
- community participation
- enterprise
- global dimension and sustainable development
- technology and the media
- creativity and critical thinking.

(QCA 2008)

The new curriculum also identifies the skills that young people need apart from those that relate to specific subjects. These include the functional skills of English, mathematics and ICT and the personal, learning and thinking skills. These latter are identified as enabling young people to become:

- independent enquirers
- creative thinkers
- reflective learners
- team workers
- self-managers
- effective participators.

(QCA 2008)

Curriculum 2000 will remain relevant for those students not affected by the categories mentioned above and for those in primary schools. There is a slight change to the primary curriculum following the review of reading undertaken by Sir Jim Rose and his team, which identified the importance of synthetic phonics in learning to read (Rose 2006). This is now part of the programme of study for reading in English. Rose has also been appointed to lead a team looking at a wholesale review of the primary curriculum under The Children's Plan (DCSF 2007a): 10. This is a ten-year plan setting goals for 2020 following the ten years of Labour government initiatives including the ECM agenda. It is an attempt to be more responsive to the needs of children, young people and their families, and yet another attempt to raise standards. The chapters are partly based on the outcomes of the ECM agenda, being healthy and safe, yet achieving high standards. They hope to produce a curriculum that helps 'children move seamlessly from nurseries to schools, from primary to secondary and then to work or further and higher education' (DCSF 2007a): 10.

The strategies

Alongside the definitions in the NC of what must be taught came the twin strategies for literacy and numeracy. Many of you may now be employed to work in especially supporting pupils in these areas. English includes literacy – reading and writing – but it also includes speaking and listening. For some of the younger children with whom you may be working, this area is so difficult that they will need help with it before they will be able to read and write with any understanding. The National Literacy Strategy (NLS) (DfEE 1998c) was introduced into primary schools in 1998, and the National Numeracy Strategy (NNS) (DfEE

1999c) in 1999. For some of you, working with the strategies involves the use of specially written materials, such as Additional Literacy Support (ALS). These materials were usually introduced with specific training and are well covered in the DCFS induction training modules. If you are not able to attend any of these sessions, do ask what training you can attend as some of the requirements of the programmes are quite technical. The strategies were also introduced to Key Stage 3, and TAs are now working with materials especially written for them for English and mathematics in secondary schools. There is more detail on the implications of using the materials in Chapter 10. Some of the catch-up programmes and materials used for booster classes are also available in schools, but you will be given directions for all these materials.

The strategies have resulted in a much more formal teaching approach to the subjects, with suggested structure to lessons, and in the case of the original literacy material even recommended times to be taken over each part of the lesson. However, it is at the discretion of the school to determine the way in which these strategies are used in other subjects, additional experiences beyond those set out, the style of resources used and the time of day that these subjects are taught. Much more didactic class teaching has resulted where the TA's role can be a bit ambivalent, and this needs clarifying early on with the class teachers with whom you work so that you are not sitting around waiting to do something useful. Do try to attend any staff meetings associated with the strategies, and get a copy of the handbooks for yourselves. There is also a lot of additional material, some of which is written especially for TAs to use. Some of this is described in Chapter 10.

A downside of the strategies, which have been very successful in creating consistency in planning and teaching in schools, is that in some schools too much time has been spent on literacy and numeracy, squeezing out the other subjects. Also, the curriculum coherence that came with topic-based teaching in the 1980s was lost. Separate subjects became the norm in primary schools. The idea of a broad and balanced curriculum, accessible to all, enabling all children to experience success, has not yet been realised for some pupils but it is possible (Ofsted 2002). Partly in response to this, a more flexible Primary Strategy was introduced in 2003 (DfES 2003a). It encourages schools to be more innovative and develop a broader and richer curriculum. The withdrawal of groups for specific support can have implications for inclusion, although the children usually enjoy the activities. It is possible that a child receiving specific support in Year 1 may need support throughout their school career, exposing them to a constant diet of being boosted and depriving them of other experiences. Hard decisions have to be made by schools and parents. The current directives are to return to topic-based curriculum for all the foundation subjects, to ensure the English and mathematical skills are well taught both separately and in the context of the other subjects. In the new secondary curriculum assessment procedures, teachers are encouraged even to assess areas like this in other subjects where possible and to link and plan subjects together to prevent overlap as well as to make taught matter more interesting and relevant.

Curriculum for the under fives

Legally, of course, children do not have to be in any setting outside the home until the term in which they have their fifth birthday. From September 2008 there will be a *Statutory framework for the early years foundation stage*, setting the standards for learning, development and care for children from birth to five (DCSF 2007b). This is the result of an amalgamation of three existing documents: *Curriculum Guidance for the foundation stage* (DfEE 2000), *Birth to three matters* (Surestart 2003) and *Arrangements for the childcare of children aged under eight* available from the Surestart website (www.surestart.gov.uk) as a word document (undated). These three documents will be available in the relevant early years' settings and may have useful references to resources and reading matter, but their general contents are all subsumed into the one 2007 framework. The ECM agenda underpins the whole new framework. The aim is to set standards, provide for equality of opportunity, create a framework for partnership working, improve quality and consistency and lay a secure foundation for future learning. It gives both the legal framework and practice guidance. It can be downloaded from www.standards.dfes.gov.uk; www.teachernet.gov.uk/publications or www.everychildmatters.gov.uk.

The four distinct but complementary themes running through the document are:

- *A unique child* – recognises that every child is a competent learner from birth who can be resilient, capable, confident and self-assured. The commitments are focused around development; inclusion; safety; and health and wellbeing

- *Positive relationships* – describes how children learn to be strong and independent from a base of loving and secure relationships with parents and/or a key person. The commitments are focused around respect; partnership with parents; supporting learning; and the role of the key person.

- *Enabling environments* explains that the environment plays a key role in supporting and extending children's development and learning. The commitments are focused around observation, assessment and planning; support for every child; the learning environment; and the wider context – transitions, continuity and multi-agency working.

- *Learning and development* recognises that children develop and learn in different ways and at different rates, and that all areas of learning and development are interconnected.

You can see from these descriptive words how closely the early curriculum follows the development of the child and talks of meeting their needs [10K4]. The older the child, the less the developmental stage of the child is taken into account; actual age and individual subjects become the yardsticks for defining what should be taught. The curriculum match to children's needs seems of less importance than the match to the teacher's planning and assessment as the children get older.

The early learning goals, previously for those aged 3 to 5, are now set out for the whole age range but cover some similar headings. STL 15 is highly dependent on the philosophy and practice outlined in this document.

- Personal, social and emotional development
- Communication, language and literacy
- Problem solving, reasoning and numeracy
- Knowledge and understanding of the world
- Physical development
- Creative development

instead of

- personal, social and emotional well-being
- positive attitudes and dispositions towards their learning
- social skills
- attention skills and persistence
- language and communication
- reading and writing

- mathematics

- knowledge and understanding of the world

- physical development

- creative development.

On-going formative assessment will take place throughout the child's time in any setting, but an end of stage profile will be compiled to sum up the development and achievement on 13 scales derived from the early learning goals. This will have to be completed by the end of the term in which the child reaches 5 (or 30 June in the summer term) – which is the statutory starting school age.

Appendix 2: Areas of learning and development is a most useful and detailed guide to support early years' practitioners [STL15]. All of you who work in that sector would be well advised to get your own copy for reference. You may not be responsible for any planning, resourcing or assessing, but the 'development matters' sections will give useful information and the 'listen and note' lots of ideas when observing children in the setting. The effective practice section will help you in developing your own skills in supporting more senior members of staff and the children in your care. This is done for six stages of development:

birth to 11 months
8 to 20 months
16 to 26 months
22 to 36 months
30 to 50 months and
40 to 60+ months.

You can see how each group overlaps with the two adjacent groups, recognising that children do not all develop at the same rate and norms need to be flexible [10K9–12].

Other aspects of the formal curriculum

Schools have to have policies for sex education and behaviour management and can set out anything else they want to teach in their prospectuses. If you have a copy of the prospectus for the school in which you are working, have a look at what they say about their curriculum. They are also supposed to set out how they intend to teach this formal curriculum. Some books talk about 'delivering' the curriculum, but it is probably clear to you, to use the old saying, 'You can take a horse to water but you cannot make it drink'. Children and young people are not containers to be filled with knowledge. Delivery alone is not enough, the contents have to be understood and used. We must also recognise the importance of individual achievements, and the value of encouraging pupils to want to learn, to value themselves and of stimulating curiosity and creativity. A challenging task!

Each school will have its own curriculum policies, laying down how each subject is to be taught, resourced and assessed in that school. If you are regularly helping in particular lessons you need to obtain a copy of the relevant policy and see how your presence fits in with what the school wishes to achieve. Try to attend the staff meetings associated with that subject. If you are in a secondary school, it may well be advisable to consider taking a GCSE in the subject if you do not already have one. This is especially true of science and geography where the technical language is specific to the subject and can be the source of confusion for the student. You need to be sure of your own facts and skills before you can help others.

You need to be able not only to read worksheets but to interpret them for students with learning problems; you need to be able to show students how to use apparatus safely and accurately. This goes from using rulers through to using complicated specialist equipment. You need to know when accuracy matters, or numbers of results. It is hoped that all TAs have GCSE or its equivalent in mathematics and English or are in the process of attaining them, in order to be able to help pupils adequately and accurately, as numeracy and literacy underpin recording and communicating information in all other subjects. While these qualifications are compulsory only for HLTAs, all TAs are working with pupils using basic literacy and mathematics. It is possible to study for a qualification in English and mathematics and get a Level 2 qualification in these subjects paid for by the Learning and Skills Council. Enquire at your local FE or AE college for information or look at the LSC website www.caretolearn.lsc.gov.uk.

Age-related aspects of a curriculum

If you look at STL2 K10–13 depending on the age range of the children you are working with alongside a copy of the NC or the early years' framework stage document you will begin to understand how they were constructed. The choice of subjects for the NC was made by politicians who had largely been educated in the private sector and reflected their personal experiences. However, each subject document of the NC was drawn up by teachers and experts in education who based each programme of study and attainment targets on their understanding of how children learn at each level. To get an idea of progression in the NC documents you have to look at each key stage description in turn. Key stages are also quite big jumps compared with the progression outlined in the document for the early years. Look at the introductory paragraphs at the beginning of the subject in which you are interested and the key stage in which you work. They briefly describe the expectations of what a child of that age should be able to do and understand.

The informal curriculum

Because the informal curriculum is not set out in legal requirements, every school will be different in what it expects of this area. The behaviour management systems fall in this area as well as in the classrooms. Unless there is a consistency of approach 'this is how you behave when in the school environs' which is dealt with by any adult passing, the pupils soon consider out of classroom areas as 'muck-about' areas and show lack of respect for any adult who ignores them out of the classroom. Schools have found it useful to employ male TAs or midday assistants in an otherwise female school or in a secondary school in order that the boys' toilets do not become a 'no-go' area. Where children and young people know that once inside the school gates certain rules of courtesy and a lack of tolerance of bad language apply and are enforced, their behaviour can change as they walk in the gates or door.

One of the results of the ECM agenda is the highlighting of the need for extended schools. At first glance the use of this expression seems to indicate major changes but most schools have always run lunchtime or after-school clubs. Many schools have extended these to breakfast clubs, or other early morning before school activities where the background of some of the children has indicated this would benefit their learning. Community schools are not new: the village college movement was well established in Cambridgeshire from before the Second World War. Here, the buildings of a local secondary school – secondary modern at that time, now comprehensive – were deemed a community resource, and a warden was appointed to work alongside the head teacher, responsible for the out of school hours activities. All kinds of adult activities went on into the evening or the school holidays, using the resources of the building and grounds, and the staff where they wished. It needs a lot of give and take for resources to have multiple uses in this way but the benefits for the community are huge. Extended schools in the twenty-first century are expected to go beyond just opening the school facilities for longer hours but also to provide centres for multi-agency working. These can be activities from child minding to health and counselling provision. It is not about add-on activities but seeing the school as a core organisation for people, especially the young people in the community. Outreach to parents and families can be much easier where they are used to using the same building and see professionals also working as teams, not disparate entities.

The extended school movement also sees increased partnership between providers – the police, health and social services – and partnership between pre-school provision, primary schools and the secondary schools in community clusters, schools being the focal points. There is no 'one size fits all': rural areas will have particular problems in making links. Head teachers will have to work more closely together and in some cases federations have been formed with an executive head. Usually, your LA will have appointed someone to coordinate the movement in your area. New schools are being built with libraries, rooms for the elderly or the new mothers to meet, rooms for health inspections or interviews, or community talks to take place. Increasingly TAs are running or involved with one of the clubs or caring activities outside the classrooms. You need to know how it fits in the scheme of things for your school and ensure you understand all the health, safety and emergency implications of such a responsibility and that you are well trained and up to date in the programming and resourcing of whatever you are involved with.

TAs are also made responsible sometimes for a physical area outside the classroom, such as the library or entrance hall. You can use your talents for display and organisation here and be a real influence on the climate and culture of the school. As mentioned earlier, surroundings have messages; tidy, well-organised, attractive entrance halls, corridors and communal facilities indicate a caring and professional staff, and a well-run institution, whether it is a hotel, railway station, hospital or school. Staff rooms that have clean mugs, accessible resources, comfortable chairs and ready refreshments give a real boost to staff morale. 'Just making the tea' is not a job to be undertaken lightly: how it is done can make a real difference.

One of the areas of the school which has suffered neglect in recent years is the outside environment. Even playing fields in some cases have taken second place to the indoor curriculum, but unless you are actively involved in the sporting activities as an instructor it is unlikely that you will get involved in maintaining the sporting and PE facilities; grounds people are usually employed for this. But TAs often get involved in environmental or gardening activities. Some schools fifteen or twenty years ago built outdoor classrooms and fenced off areas for wildlife including building ponds. Sadly, these have become neglected in many cases. With the increased understanding of the need for a healthy diet and the impact of our busy lifestyles on the environment, there is now an increased emphasis again on studying, working with and using locally accessible plants and animals for conservation, recreation and food. Sustainable education is in the curriculum. Some schools are even developing their own vegetable plots and planting fruit trees. Some TAs have set up such areas as projects for higher TA qualifications.

The *Learning outside the classroom manifesto* is available from the DCSF website. The teachernet website has links to resources and people involved as well (DfES 2006b). The movement links especially well with the ECM agenda encouraging healthy eating and lifestyles and safe practices. Many children are living highly protected indoor lives, there is even a concern about some suffering lack of vitamin D because of this. While children are transported from their cocooned, warm, computer dominated lives at home in warm vehicles, to a warm indoor life in school they will lack an understanding of the fundamentals of life in Britain, of seasons, of the wonders of the living world and have no understanding of how to cope with danger when they meet it. Much of the formal curriculum can be taught out of doors [10K7]. The Forest Schools movement (www.forestschools.com) has also taken off in some areas, encouraging children to develop a sense of place in a location away from the schools grounds where they can be themselves, play in a safe way in areas like woodland or other green space. Some schools are linking their science and mathematics into monitoring their energy use and changes they are making to have a more sustainable building. Of course, all new builds have to consider all kinds of energy saving strategies.

Outside, all schools have some kind of play area for break-times even if they have no grounds or green space. Early years' settings should also have outside play areas and those catering for the under threes' day care provision for rest periods [2K10.13]. Some schools still have to walk or even bus their pupils to their playing fields and not all of those are in urban areas. Many of you will not only be a classroom TA but also a midday or lunchtime assistant [10K]. The way in which you relate to children in the dining hall is important. Unfortunately few teachers ever eat with the children to encourage positive social behaviour, and fewer families seem to eat together at tables although more eat out in restaurants together. You as assistants at this time can be a very positive influence on how the meal times go. Serving each other, using table manners, clearing up are all procedures which oil the way we relate to each other and respect how people look after us.

The use of the play areas opens up another whole subject for study. Increasingly, budgets are being set aside to ensure there is additional play provision for these areas, or quiet spaces. Some schools allow their children to eat outside in the summer, trim trails or activity areas with safety matting or bark beds have been built. Ideally, areas for dens and imaginative play are constructed from hedging or under trees. Special training should be available for supervisors of this outside space. You need to know about time out areas, friendship bus stops, using any facilities painted on the ground (do you know how you actually play hopscotch properly?), using singing games, skipping ropes and areas for ball games. All the usual things apply about care of apparatus, clearing up and appropriate behaviour management rules for such informal area. This may sound very primary school orientated but secondary children also need a break, and stretches of boring tarmac are asking for domination by football, opportunities for conflict. Access to quiet areas, reading materials, even study areas should be considered [10.4P3–7; 10.5P2; 10K5,17,25].

Outdoor play for the under fives is built into the curriculum but is sometimes seen as an extended version of the primary school playtime – everybody puts coats on, gets the bikes out and has a race around. Outdoor play should be available most of the time by choice, and have a changing range of activities which have been designed with as much care as the indoor range. The bikes can become space transport or pizza delivery vehicles, with play houses as space stations or restaurants; the sand and water trays can become places to explore certain containers or build a town. It should all be planned and evaluated for the needs of the children at that time and with a thematic approach, just like the indoor curriculum. Mathematical areas with large shapes to climb on, sensory areas to walk on or listen to or smell can all be built into the outside area. If you are working in an early years' setting you will need to make a special study of the outdoor provision.

Play can be built into the formal curriculum at any age, it is important for encouraging curiosity, problem solving and exploration, all possible in the virtual world that so many youngsters inhabit. However practical play also encourages social learning and the development of physical skills and interests not possible with ICT [2K10.8–11; 10K22].

The hidden curriculum

Things that used to be implicit in the way schools worked are becoming more and more explicit, so less is 'hidden'. Things like politeness and care of property used to be taken

PHOTOGRAPHS 9.1 AND 9.2 Provision for constructive and interesting outdoor play

for granted, but now sometimes have to be part of the explicit behaviour policy. Treating everybody with courtesy, whatever their needs, colour, creed or race is spelt out in equal opportunities and anti-discrimination policies. Enjoyment and attitude are all part of a school's culture and climate. Emotional development and behaviour of learners is reported on, as well as the learners' spiritual, moral, social and cultural development and their ability to stay safe and healthy. An Ofsted inspection of a school recognises these less definable areas, and other aspects of personal development. They also look at how well the school ensures a pupil's welfare, health and safety, provides support advice and guidance for pupils and seeks to involve pupils in its work and development (Ofsted 2007a).

Note how many aspects of the hidden curriculum appear in the following list.

Inspectors will report on:

- description of the school
- overall effectiveness of the school
  - effectiveness and efficiency of boarding provision
  - what the school should do to improve further
- achievement and standards
  - personal development and well-being
- quality of provision
  - teaching and learning
  - curriculum and other activities
  - care, guidance and support
- leadership and management
- the extent to which schools enable learners to be healthy
- the extent to which providers ensure that they stay safe
- how well learners enjoy their education
- the extent to which learners make a positive contribution
- how well learners develop workplace and other skills that will contribute to their future economic wellbeing.

The following is the description of what is considered good in terms of personal development and well-being:

> Learners' spiritual, moral, social and cultural development is good and no element of it is unsatisfactory. Young children are learning to understand their feelings. All learners enjoy school a good deal, as demonstrated by their considerate behaviour, positive attitudes and regular attendance. They feel safe, are safety conscious without being fearful, and they adopt healthy lifestyles. They develop a commitment to racial equality. They make overall good progress in developing personal qualities that will enable them to contribute effectively to the community and eventually transfer to working roles.
>
> (Ofsted 2007b: 14)

You know when visiting schools, maybe on your first visit to the school you are now working in, that schools have a climate. They try to define this in words, describing their 'ethos', but it is hard to legislate for happiness. While 'to be a happy place' cannot be the first aim of a school (we could say that about homes or social clubs), pupils will not learn if they are unhappy and staff will not work with a will if they are miserable. Once you are a member of staff you will also be part of that school and a little responsible for its climate. Respect and support are needed by you, but you will have your part to play to give it to all the other staff as well as the pupils. Your relationships, spelt out in Chapter 3, taking responsibility for your own actions, and the actions of others with pupils as well as staff all contribute to this hidden curriculum.

Freiberg and Stein (1999) said:

School climate is the heart and soul of a school. It is about that essence of a school that leads a child, a teacher, an administrator, a staff member to love the school and look forward to being there each day. School climate is about that quality of a school that helps each person feel personal worth, dignity and importance while simultaneously helping create a sense of belonging to something beyond ourselves. The climate of a school can foster resilience or become a risk factor in the lives of people who work and learn in a place called school.

(p. 11)

Supporting English and mathematics

BOTH THESE SUBJECTS have been under the spotlight for the last ten years with the publication and dissemination of vast resources for their teaching into schools. The aim has been to raise the standards of literacy and numeracy which were considered very low once the results of national tests became the norm. The NC attainment target levels at Level 4 are considered the basic minimum needed for an adult to function in today's world and many children were not attaining that. Both subjects are needed in order to understand and function in most other areas of the curriculum. Even performance areas may need them in order to attain the higher levels. So, national strategies were launched based on the known evidence for best practice. You need to know how this is interpreted in your school [6.1P1; 6.2P1; 6K1]. The strategies have raised standards but there is still work to do. All the materials mentioned in this chapter unless separately referenced are available on the strategies website www.nationalstrategiescpd.org.uk or www.standards.dfes.gov.uk. The Primary Framework is predominantly web-based and both TAs and teachers need to be competent and confident in their use of the computer, internet and in particular to be able to navigate the Primary Framework site.

Both are areas in which TAs are heavily used to support teachers to raise the adult–pupil ratios in order to give more individualised help. One concern is that TAs themselves may have struggled, particularly with mathematics, when they were at school and may not have the curriculum knowledge or confidence to help as well as they could. One suggestion if you are in this category is that you study for a GCSE yourself in either or both subjects. Don't try to hide your insecurity, teachers have also had the same problem and will be only too willing to help and support you [6K11].

Also, all the things mentioned in previous chapters about how children learn, about supporting pupils in lessons and about helping the teacher apply to English and mathematics: you need to know the teachers' objectives; planning and preparation are crucial; there are appropriate ways to support pupils to preserve their self-esteem and retain the independence, yet challenge them to achieve their best; appropriate praise and good feedback are needed; you may have to simplify the stages in which the pupils undertake a task or the vocabulary you use in order to help them complete it; ask for help when you need it and feed back achievement and concerns to teachers [6.1P4; 6K8]. You should have your own copy of the school policies in both areas, and have read them and understood them [6.1P1; 6.2P1; 6K1], and you need to discuss anything you don't understand either with the class teacher, the subject head or coordinator.

You should be told if there are particular problems with any of the children with whom you are working [6K10]. When dealing with specific problems then you should be able to see the pupil's IEP. This will deal with the specific areas the pupil needs to work on and will give a measure of past targets met. The areas may be general or very specific. One instance of the latter might be that you would work with a pupil with poor spelling skills when other areas of learning present no problem. You may get a chance to discuss it with the SENCO

[6K6]. However, there could be a short-term problem such as an ear infection which could mean that a pupil is not hearing clearly, or they may have been involved in some kind of emotional upheaval.

EAL learners of English and mathematics [6K7]

EAL pupils who have been learning English for two years or more can come across conversationally like native speakers and have excellent accents particularly if they started learning English at a young age. The English language is, however, quite complex grammatically with many exceptions to rules and it is full of cultural references and nuances. This means that EAL pupils have a lot to learn and can sometimes be seen as having low ability while in fact they are still learning English: it can take between five and seven years for EAL pupils to grasp English fully to the level of a native speaker.

The implications for the classroom are many. Lessons need to be planned with a clear focus on vocabulary and language structures and skills to be taught clearly identified. In English you need to model language clearly either orally or in writing to support the lesson objectives. EAL pupils also can benefit considerably from activities that provide opportunities to develop spoken language. It is important that you know from the class teacher the key phrases that need to be learnt although pupils may of course come up with their own. You also need to try to develop an awareness of possible cultural gaps that pupils may have. You may assume that everyone understands or knows about Guy Fawkes, about the story of Cinderella or has cornflakes for breakfast but this may not be the case. As with early stage learners of English, EAL pupils' understanding can benefit considerably from the clear use of visual and kinaesthetic approaches to learning. The use of video clips can support the understanding, for example, of Shakespeare plays or of war poetry (and trench warfare).

Pupils who have EAL may have considerable ability in mathematics. If they are new to your school and speak little English, ask if a first language mathematics assessment can be done to see what level of maths they were working to in their previous country/school. The teacher needs to check the child's mathematical knowledge in terms of number problems to start with and then other aspects of maths such as algebra as appropriate. Although, initially a beginner EAL pupil may not know the language of mathematics in English, they will need to be challenged in terms of their ability in order that they are put in a correct grouping.

It can be very useful to use maths as a focus with a beginner EAL pupil. They will need to know how to say and listen to numbers, and to know the specific terms used for the addition, subtraction, multiplication and division. Ensure that you will be teaching the correct vocabulary. There are also many hands-on activities, games and active learning and software programs which can very effectively support maths development for EAL pupils. Doing class surveys can be a great way for beginner EAL pupils to talk to their peers and to develop/practise skills such as making various forms of graphs. They can also practise questioning skills and notation. One area of greater difficulty can be problem solving because of the language content required to understand the mathematical problem.

SUPPORTING ENGLISH

English is an entitlement for all pupils of primary age and should be taught for a minimum of five hours per week; at secondary, a minimum of three hours. In primary schools, however, it is becoming less common for single lessons to be an hour in length each day. This is due to a shift in culture, meaning that more schools are teaching through cross-curricular methods. Literacy is the ability to communicate and understand language through spoken and written text. English in primary schools is called literacy.

Cross-curricular teaching combines several subject areas in one session. For example, the objective of the lesson may be to write a letter (literacy focus) but in order to do this, pupils need to employ their History and ICT skills as the letter is from Henry VIII to the Pope and will be word-processed. Themed approaches are deemed to enable pupils to have a broad and balanced curriculum and to focus upon the teaching of skills that can be used across all subjects. Therefore in primary schools, practice has changed. The five hours minimum literacy entitlement is often delivered flexibly; some days' sessions are longer than an hour, some shorter. For younger pupils literacy may be taught in short sessions delivered throughout the school day. It is imperative that language skills taught in literacy are practised when talking, reading or writing in all subjects.

The NLS gave teachers a real focus for English teaching. In a drive to raise standards, teachers in all key stages had to teach age-appropriate objectives and have much more rigorous word (vocabulary and spelling) and sentence (grammar and punctuation) level teaching and understanding. The NLS is over ten years old and supplementary documentation has been published to support teachers and pupils further. The strategies are evolving in light of new research and social and technical changes. The strategies for primary schools have been revised and updated and renamed the Primary Framework. This online resource has been developed to assist teachers further in raising standards, providing more opportunities to meet the needs of children in primary classrooms today.

The Primary Framework – Literacy

Teaching objectives for the Primary Framework have been categorised into 12 strands (see Table 10.1). The objectives are no longer confined to a specific term but are end of year age-related expectations. For example, the objectives in Y2 refer to the standard that the pupils need to reach before moving into Y3.

The objectives are age-related, in line with national averages [6K5]. Age-related expectation at the end of Key Stage 2, for example, is Level 4 so the objectives for Y6 in the Primary Framework are set at this level. Age-related expectations for Y2 pupils are Level 2 by the end of the year, and therefore, the objectives in Y2 are of a Level 2 standard. Standards in learning govern the framework. Age-related outcomes should be achieved by all pupils with the exception of those who have specific cognitive difficulties. Many pupils should exceed these outcomes. The published league tables show this data. Schools with high percentages achieving Level 4 and 5 by the end of Key Stage 2 are perceived in the public eye to be 'good' schools. National average for the number of pupils achieving Level 4 is approximately 80 per cent. Schools that have Key Stage 2 results showing a percentage below the floor target (65 per cent) are perceived to be schools requiring support to raise standards. In secondary, published league tables represent the number of pupils achieving 5 A*–C grades at GCSE. Mathematics

TABLE 10.1 The 12 strands of the Primary Framework for Literacy

1 Speaking	2 Listening and responding	3 Group discussion and interaction	4 Drama
5 Word recognition	6 Word structure and spelling	7 Understand and interpret texts	8 Engage with and respond to texts
9 Creating and shaping texts	10 Text structure and organisation	11 Sentence structure and punctuation	12 Presentation

and English are core to this and these subject areas must be two of the five. There is a constant push to raise expectations to ensure even more pupils achieve the recommended standards.

Assessment for learning

Statutory testing takes place at the end of each key stage:

Foundation stage: age-related outcome 6 points across the 6 areas of learning.

Key Stage 1: Y2 age-related outcome Level 2

Key Stage 2: Y6 age-related outcome Level 4

Key Stage 3: Y9 age-related outcome Level 5–6

Key Stage 4: Y11 (GCSE) Level 7–8 (grade B/C)

The goal, at present, is for all pupils to make two levels of progress across a key stage.

Pupils are assessed against the foundation stage profile at the end of their first year in school. English in the foundation stage is called CLL (communication, language and literacy). A child achieving 6 points at the end of the foundation stage is 'on track' to achieve age-related outcomes throughout their education. Tracking the progress of pupils in relation to age-related outcomes is of a high status in all schools. Teachers predict where pupils will be at the end of the year and monitor progress towards the end of year expectations based upon the previous teacher's assessments. Support for pupils who are not identified as SEN is often allocated based upon accelerating progress towards achieving or exceeding age-related expectations. Teachers have a greater awareness of the need to differentiate (provide activities appropriate to ability). Often differentiation is by the adult support allocated to the pupils.

The present educational climate has increased the accountability of teachers regarding the progress of pupils in their class. Performance management monitors and challenges teachers' ability to add value to the academic progress of the pupils they teach. When working with groups of pupils the teaching assistant's role is to support the learning, thus assisting the teacher to contribute to the children's academic progress. Increasingly, you need to be familiar with the current academic level of the pupils and the targets they are working towards.

Intervention

Assessments inform the next steps pupils need to take. For many pupils interventions have to be planned in order to help them get back 'on track' and 'catch-up' with the rest of the class. Primary published interventions are:

Year 1: Early Literacy Support (ELS);

Year 3: Literacy Support (Y3LS);

Year 5: Further Literacy Support (FLS).

These intervention programmes are designed to be delivered by teaching assistants at the delegation of the class teacher. Each programme is aimed not at SEN pupils but at pupils who are at risk of falling behind. The interventions are a supplement to in-class literacy teaching and need to happen outside the literacy whole class session. Small group intervention such as this is known as wave 2 intervention.

Wave 1: whole class, quality first teaching – providing sufficient differentiation

Wave 2: small group intervention

Wave 3: one-to-one specific catch-up based upon gap analysis

Wave 3 intervention can be delivered by the teaching assistant, again at the delegation of the class teacher. The sessions will be planned for by the teacher. *Reading Catch-Up* is a widely used wave 3 intervention for literacy. The programme is very structured with specific guidance for the delivery of the sessions. The principle of wave 3 intervention is that the pupils make twice the recommended progress while engaged in the programme.

All interventions designed to get pupils 'on track' to achieve age-related outcomes should only be used once per child. For example, a child who did ELS in Year 1 should not do Y3LS in Year 3. The intervention model has not worked if they are still falling behind. The theory behind this is that the intervention programme would mean that pupils are back working at an age-appropriate level with the rest of the class and quality first teaching should now meet their needs. There are booster materials available for Year 6 pupils to further support the achievement of age-related expectations.

For secondary pupils, interventions are again at the discretion of the teacher to delegate to the TA. *Intervention Tool Kits* are available for use to support pupils who are at risk of not meeting age-related expectations. There are *Literacy Progress Units* for moving pupils from Level 3–4 to be delivered outside of the existing English lessons. *Targeting Level 4* reading and writing materials can be built into lessons delivered by the teacher.

Intervention for the more able is to give high-achieving pupils the opportunity to understand ideas and themes more broadly and deeply. The role of intervention for gifted and talented pupils is to enrich their learning.

Subject knowledge

The NLS underlined the need for pupils and adults supporting them to have secure subject knowledge. Technical vocabulary has become a core part of language teaching.

Phoneme: a single unit of sound e.g. *mood* has 3 phonemes *m-oo-d*

Grapheme: how the sound is represented in letters

Digraph: 2 letters making one sound *–oo*

Trigraph: 3 letters making 1 sound *–igh* in *night*

Noun: subject/object – *car, Devon*

Verb: action – *write, run*

Adjective: description – *red, small*

Adverb: describes the action – *quickly, softly*

Determiner: focuses upon the noun – *a, the*

Preposition: explains where – *in, at, with, over*

Pronoun: stands in the place of the noun – *he, they, who*

Conjunction: can join clauses together in sentences – *and, because, when, although*

Sentences are made up of clauses.

- *Simple sentences* contain just one clause.

  The pupils ran.

- *Compound sentences* consist of two or more main clauses loosely joined by conjunctions – *and, but, or.*

  The pupils ran and the teachers shouted.

- In *complex sentences*, clauses are linked together in ways which show the interrelation-ships of ideas. Complex sentences are built up of main clauses and subordinate (minor) clauses. The subordinate clause does not make sense alone

When the pupils ran in the corridor, the teachers shouted.

(subordinate clause)   (main clause)

When supporting pupils, at any age, you need to have a clear understanding of the level of subject knowledge required to assist the pupils accurately and effectively [6K11].

Accuracy in articulating letter sounds and in using grammar, spelling and punctuation is essential for ensuring that pupils have the most appropriate level of support. There is a wealth of documentation to ensure the adult's subject knowledge is always at least one step ahead of the pupils. You need to have access to this information and have a responsi-bility to ask questions if the required subject knowledge is unfamiliar. The majority of new, recent publications and those in current use are available to read online or download on the *Primary Framework* website www.standards.dfes.gov.uk/primary frameworks. This site has professional development materials for adults to use to develop their own subject knowledge. One problem a TA may encounter is if their own spoken English is ungram-matical. Some dialects, such as estuarine English include phrases like 'them things' which are in common usage. TAs should be role models yet need respect for their background just as any other member of the school community. It is a sensitive issue for any manager to deal with, so try to recognise your own foibles and do what you can to speak correct gram-matical English but retain your local accent if you suspect a problem. If you know you have this problem, talk with your line manager. Ask them to observe you and listen to you at work if you are brave enough and to point out where the particular problem lies.

Different text types are now used in class. A list is found in Table 10.2.

Using visual and multi-modal texts is becoming commonplace. Pupils are engaging with and reading film and responding to and creating texts which combine more than one mode e.g. pictures, text and sound.

The teaching sequence (see Figure 10.1) has been developed to ensure pupils have a fuller understanding of the text type and the skills required for quality writing. It is expected now that pupils have an extended time preparing to write before writing. In its most basic form, phase 1 is reading, phase 2 is analysis and phase 3 is writing. Each phase should take approximately a week but this is dependent upon the desired outcome for the writing and the age of the pupils.

TABLE 10.2   Different text types

Narrative	Non-Fiction	Poetry
Stories/Prose	Instructions	Limerick
Myths	Report	Narrative poetry
Legends	Recount	Performance poetry
Traditional tales	Explanation	Haiku
Familiar stories	Discussion/argument	Kenning
Mystery	Letter	Free verse
Adventure	Persuasion/advertisement	Shape poetry
Play-script	Labels, captions and lists	Sonnet

THE TEACHING SEQUENCE FOR WRITING

READ ⟶ ANALYSE ⟶ PLAN ⟶ WRITE ⟶ REVIEW

READ	1 Writers have a real audience and purpose with an established outcome.	**CONTINUAL ASSESSMENT FOR LEARNING**
	2 Writers are immersed in a broad, rich and engaging reading curriculum including picture books, graphic novels, ICT and film.	
	3 Writers engage, experience and empathise through planned drama, speaking and listening opportunities.	
ANALYSE	4 Writers actively unpick the features and characteristics of a chosen test/genre.	
	5 Writers own and understand the success criteria of the agreed outcome.	
PLAN	6 Writers use the features of the text and the success criteria to plan their writing.	
	7 Writers are guided through modelling, demonstrating and supported composition with the teacher and through peer assessment.	
WRITE	8 Writers use their knowledge of reading to help them compose their writing.	
REVIEW	9 Writers receive clear feedback linked to the success criteria and understand the next steps in developing their writing.	
	10 Writers reflect on their outcome against original audience and purpose and plan for future learning.	

FIGURE 10.1   The teaching sequence for writing

Practice

Speaking and listening

English/literacy is not only reading and writing but speaking and listening. Pupils are assessed in this area also. Adults supporting pupils in literacy should have high standards of oracy. Talk for writing is a key element of phase 1. Children's ability to communicate and listen effectively to others and to structure and articulate thoughts verbally has a great impact upon the quality of the written outcome. Talk partners are encouraged to enable pupils to have time to prepare answers and discuss ideas. Pupils have the opportunity for focused talk upon a specific objective. Teaching assistants provide the class teacher with another person to model the process with and the teaching assistant can initiate discussions with less confident pupils and monitor and re-focus talk.

Modelling

Best practice is to model the desired outcome and the process for pupils. Modelling in writing is to write in front of the pupils and articulate the process. Share how to check for sense, spelling, how to edit and improve. In reading, articulation of re-reading for sense, flow and clarity and how to link ideas together is required. Share, for example, how to refer to own experiences and to question characters' actions to gain a greater comprehension of the text.

Questioning

Questioning is the first point of assessment. Often, the questions we ask pupils are closed. Closed questions have a pre-determined answer that the adult already knows. Closed question are used more frequently because of the element of control provided. Open questions have no predetermined answer, and therefore higher level thinking skills need to be employed and the questioner has less control over the answer. During reading there are three tiers of questioning: literal, inferential and deductive, and evaluative.

Literal questions are closed, e.g. 'what happened?'

Inferential and deductive questions are higher order, open questions: they show the need to 'read between the lines'.

Evaluative questions are higher order, open questions, e.g. asking why the author has used particular words or phrases.

It is recommended that pupils have enough time to think about the question in order to give the best answer. Ten seconds thinking time sounds short and in practice feels longer but it is essential to allow for it, particularly when asking higher order questions.

ICT

Advances in technology have led to major changes in the teaching of literacy. Cine-literacy, reading through film, has been developed to engage and motivate learners. Reading in print and reading on screen are skills required at all stages of education. Teachers are using interactive white boards to support teaching and pupils are presenting work electronically. ICT skills are becoming more and more embedded in practice. Pupils use and create electronic images, sounds and texts. Supporting learning in literacy is now more likely to require ICT skills.

Guided reading

This is a key role for teaching assistants. Guided reading is a planned session for the teaching of reading skills. Teachers in the first instance should lead guided reading sessions and teaching assistants delivering a session do so at the direction of the teacher. Table 10.3 gives the teaching sequence suggested. The aim here is to encourage and extend independent reading skills.

Key principles

- Pupils grouped according to ability
- Same group text selected by teacher
- Text accessible to all pupils in group, less than 1 in 10 miscues
- Objectives set based upon teaching specific reading strategies
- Teacher leads session.

The simple view of reading represented in Figure 10.2 shows the two skills we employ to enable us to read: our ability to decode the words and read them, and the ability to understand what they mean. Pupils need to work towards having good decoding and comprehension skills. This is why the teaching of reading relies heavily upon good early reading skills employing the use of phonics. The *Rose Review* (Rose 2006) has driven many of the changes for teaching early reading.

TABLE 10.3   Teaching sequence for guided reading

Book introduction	Prepare the pupils. Orientation/discussion drawing on recent experiences, topics of interest, title, author, illustrator, etc, cover illustrations, first impressions, genre. Build confidence – the pupils need to know they can read the book successfully.
Strategy check	Be explicit about the focus of the session – share objectives/targets. Build upon prior knowledge of reading strategies such as what to do when you get stuck on/don't understand the meaning of a word.
Independent reading	Be clear about how much of the text you want the pupils to read and explain/share the questions that will be asked afterwards. For pupils who finish early, remind them of other things they can do, e.g. re-read the best/most difficult part again, carefully prepare an answer to a question you have asked.
Returning to the text	Discussion – check that the pupils have understood the text 'literally'. Time to praise – tackle misconceptions, possibly hear a couple of pupils read aloud a sentence or paragraph to the group/partner/adult.
Response to the text	Discussion, answers to questions valuing contributions from all pupils. Adult to select questions specific to the text – identifying how to use the text to support ideas/feelings.

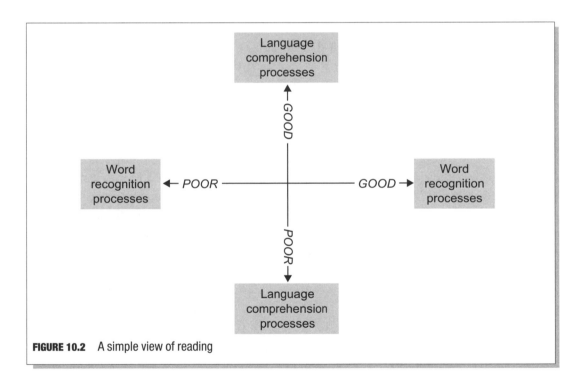

FIGURE 10.2   A simple view of reading

Phonics

Phonics is the knowledge of sounds to enable both reading and spelling. In Foundation Stage and Key Stage 1, phonics is taught for a minimum of 15 minutes daily as a supplement to the literacy session. The *DCSF Letters and Sounds* published materials have a structured six-phase programme for teaching phonics. There are many published materials to support the teaching of phonics and all focus heavily upon clear articulation of phonemes. The approach to teaching phonics needs to be multi-sensory to ensure that pupils have the best possible access to learn, practise and apply their skills. Good phonics subject knowledge now has a heightened status with regard to supporting all pupils to read and spell the English language.

Guided writing

This is a small group session, again planned by the teacher to raise standards in writing and to teach skills identified through assessment for learning. Pupils are grouped together by ability or more specifically, by need to develop writing skills. The key focus is upon developing, extending and refining for quality writing. Clear objectives and success criteria are essential. During the session pupils have the opportunity to see modelled writing, and to discuss, practise and review their own writing in relation to the learning objective. Teaching assistants supporting pupils during guided writing need to have the appropriate subject knowledge which should be provided by the teacher but it is the responsibility of the supporting adult to ensure the objective is taught accurately. The DCSF published materials, *Improving Writing with a Focus on Guided Writing*, have clear guidance on the content and structure of guided writing.

SUPPORTING MATHEMATICS

All the appropriate methods you will need are outlined in the NNS handbook or equivalent folder for Key Stage 3 [6K8]. Each class/subject teacher has one, and you should have ready access to a copy or be able to download the relevant materials. Two other books produced by the NNS are essential: *Teaching Mental Calculation Strategies* and *Teaching Written Calculations* (QCA 1999a, 1999b). You must be able to use the methods, formal or informal, currently being employed with the class. Do watch and listen to the teachers in your school and ask about anything you feel unsure of.

Vital to your success is the correct use of language and vocabulary. The NNS *Mathematical Vocabulary Book* (DfEE 1999d) lists most of the vocabulary the pupils need; it is age/stage-related and new words are highlighted within the text [6.2P5]. Many schools involve TAs in the delivery of catch-up programmes of the NNS such as Springboard 4 and Springboard 7 and you will have to ask where and when these are used in your school. The pace of change within our schools is unrelenting and with it the role and perceptions of how you should and could operate. TAs are well established in many secondary school classrooms, carrying out a variety of tasks, many simply mirroring those undertaken by primary colleagues. The revised/renewed primary framework and the introduction of PPA time put significantly more responsibility in the hands of TAs. You are now expected to have a much greater working knowledge of the planning structures and progression within mathematics teaching and learning.

The framework website contains a vast amount of extremely useful material and is being constantly updated and added to. Searching the site will give clear guidelines on what is to be taught, when it could be taught, how it can be expanded or simplified, where it came from and where it leads to. All support materials are contained in the site as are many useful additions such as assessment for learning materials, key questions and activities to assist in the learning and teaching of mathematics. It is very much in your interest and, of course, that of the students with whom you work for you to be able to find and use resources from within the framework site. One way to acquire the expertise and confidence is to explore a little at a time and do it often. You will find a pad of 'post-it' notes very useful to jot down the pathways you are following and therefore have a route back to find materials on other occasions. Competence with the 'new technologies' is an increasing requirement within our schools and you need to be able to use resources such as interactive whiteboards, screen projectors, and at secondary level you need a good working knowledge of scientific or even programmable calculators such as graphic calculators. Your school should be able to offer practical assistance in all of these areas including providing calculators for your use. The curriculum for secondary schools is undergoing revision: the mathematical content will not change much but more emphasis will be placed upon the using and applying of mathematical skills and processes.

The mathematics/numeracy policy

Explicit in these policies will be how the NNS is to be used. The NNS radically changed the teaching of mathematics in many schools and it will almost certainly be very different from the way you were taught at school. In order to understand the scope of the learning objectives you need to be fully aware of the developments that have taken place within mathematics in recent years [6K5].

■ TAs operating with children in the early years need to be fully conversant with the Foundation Stage curriculum, including Early Learning Goals, as well as having a working knowledge of the Key Stage 1 curriculum.

■ TAs working in Key Stage 1 need a working knowledge of the Foundation and Key Stage 2 curriculum and to be fully conversant with the Key Stage 1 curriculum.

■ TAs working in Key Stage 2 need to be fully conversant with the Key Stage 1 and 2 curricula and have some knowledge of Key Stage 3.

■ TAs working in secondary schools will need to know of the methods used at Key stage 1 and Key Stage 2 as well as having a working knowledge of Key Stage 3 and possibly Key Stage 4.

■ All TAs need to be able to use and understand the range of methods, both mental and written, that children are expected to use.

You need to be aware of:

■ The informal methods for subtraction, the use of the empty number line for counting up which leads to counting up using a vertical method.

■ The formal written method for subtraction (decomposition) and the use of the expanded form. This method might well be familiar to many people but the understanding comes in the use of the expanded form.

■ The grid method of multiplication and how to move children to the standard written format.

■ Chunking for division and the use of the standard written method.

■ The variety of mental methods that children could use to approach a calculation.

■ Language level, appropriate use of mathematical language and, with older children, something of the symbolism and ways of setting out working.

It is particularly important to encourage children (KS2 and KS3) to record their thinking and where appropriate to use diagrams or sketches to support their thinking. If you model processes the children will follow your example. It follows that you should show consistency in the methods you use with children and this is developed by keeping the skills fresh for yourself.

Developing numerate pupils

There are some children who seem to have a good grasp of the mathematics involved in any given situation. This is often called having a good 'feel for numbers'. They seem to know automatically if they have done something wrong or which strategy is suitable for calculations. For example, in KS1 if a child who is asked what 93 − 89 is equal to realises that the numbers are very close together they will approach the calculation in a very different way from the child who just sees two numbers that bear no relationship to each other.

The aim of the NNS is for all children to have a 'feel for numbers' and to be numerate. To be numerate a person needs to know more than just the four rules. A key point would be being able to apply their knowledge. Being numerate includes knowing algebra, shape and space, measures and data handling. Mathematics is essentially a social, practical activity and as such should involve pupils in using practical apparatus and enjoying problem-solving activities. These types of activity can present more difficulties than the more straightforward practice of calculations.

The daily mathematics lesson

This is now firmly established within both primary and secondary schools.

Oral and mental starters (OMS)

Within the OMS, you should work primarily with those pupils needing greatest support. Model with these pupils the activity being run by the teacher. You should have any resources needed readily to hand, such as

- white boards and marker pens
- number cards
- hundred squares
- calculators
- counters
- number lines [2K11.9].

Your involvement greatly assists the teacher in maintaining pace and in providing a brisk, interactive and meaningful start to the lesson; the interaction between the teacher and TA is seamless. The TA usually sits at the back of the class with a cohort of less able pupils. Other pupils who are not always very confident tend to gravitate towards the TA, dipping in and out of the support as and when necessary. This prevents the distinctive 'labelling' of pupils. All the class see you as a resource to be used. It is important that the support is confidence-building or strategy-giving, not doing the work for the pupils by giving the answers. In secondary classrooms you are most likely to be working with a targeted student or a small group, depending on how the class furniture is arranged.

The main part of the lesson

It is here that there is most variance in practice at all key stages. In lessons with a substantial teaching element, that is where a new topic is being introduced, you can sit with and assist the less able group of pupils or targeted student, modelling for them the teaching being delivered. Once the direct teaching part of this type of lesson is complete and the pupils are engaged upon some other activity (written or other) you will probably remain as direct support for the less able pupils. In this way there is a significant support structure in place for those very pupils who need most support when learning new concepts or skills, this being the case in secondary classrooms too.

If the lesson is a follow-up lesson or a consolidation lesson, with minimal input from the teacher at the start of the second phase, you should not be restricted to working with the less able pupils; even if your brief/contract is for a specific child you should give support to others if and when needed or directed. There is a requirement that the class teacher works with all pupils within a class and this means that the teacher has to spend at least one of the week's mathematics lessons working more closely with the least able pupils. On such occasions you should operate with other groups, including the most able. Sometimes you could even hold a watching brief over two groups, thus providing less intensive support but monitoring and intervening as and when appropriate.

You need to pay particular attention to:

- ensuring that the children are using the appropriate mental strategies and formal written methods for calculation;

- ensuring that the children fully understand the mathematical reasoning. For example, when multiplying by ten many children will say 'add a nought' but this will not work with decimals;

- extending children's knowledge by effective use of open questions and allowing children to spot patterns and rules;

- ensuring that calculators are being used appropriately (schools should have a policy on the use of calculators, but it is often under-use rather than over-use that is the problem);

- enabling children to estimate the answer and use appropriate strategies for checking the results of calculations.

During each week all pupils need time to work unaided, as they need to develop as independent learners. One of the most recent changes in education policy has been the change to the national key stage tests (SATs). From 2003 more using and applying questions have been used. You need to allow children to explain their answers verbally and in writing – usually in that order. Make sure that you have seen exemplar questions from the national tests in order to familiarise yourself with the expectations.

The plenary

One of the main purposes of the plenary is that it provides the teacher with an opportunity to assess the learning that has taken place during the lesson, and you can assist the teacher in this objective. You need to use the plenary to obtain and use information about a pupil's ability to understand and use numbers. You can also, by use of questions and prompts, help these children to cement the learning of the lesson, to firm up their ideas and to help cancel out any misconceptions which have arisen during the work part of the main teaching activity.

Good use of language, questions and vocabulary is clearly vital and you may need the same sort of resources as in the OMS, plus blank paper for jottings and vocabulary cards to assist the children with formulating answers using the correct words.

Assessing understanding in mathematics [6.2P7]

One method of obtaining information about a child's ability is observing and taking notes during the oral and mental starter or the plenary. Another is to analyse children's SATs. These tests cover the range of work that children are expected to do in a year. The tests are statutory in Years 2, 6 and 9 and optional in Years 3, 4 and 5. There are also SATs papers for Year 7 and currently a pilot project is under way to look at the use of single level test papers in both Key Stages 2 and 3. The results of this pilot project could be that SAT papers become a thing of the past and teacher assessment is used to determine children's levels of progress. This has future implications for the further development of your role and may make it necessary for you to have an even greater working understanding of mathematics. The drawback is that these tests only give information about what a child does or does not know.

What you really need to be aware of is why a child is getting something wrong. You should be aware of how teachers use the two days' 'assess and review' lessons at the end of each half term to carry out assessments. The NNS materials include a useful book called *Using Assess and Review Lessons*. As the lessons are activity based rather than pencil and paper tests, they enable the teacher or assistant to ask the children questions which help gauge their understanding.

Central to all the activities is the role of discussion and the importance of children's explanations. Valuable insights are provided by children explaining how they arrived at the correct answer (or the incorrect answer). On many occasions, what seems like a completely wrong answer is hiding a misconception, which, when corrected, will enable the children to get the right answer. For example, when calculating 48×16, the child might give the answer 336. It is only by asking the child how they did it that you would ascertain that the child was multiplying 48 by 1 rather than 10 (then adding it to 48×6).

A point you need to be aware of is that children's ability in numbers can vary widely from their ability in shape, space and measures. It is not uncommon to find an able child who finds it difficult to look at a shape and, for example, work out whether it has a right angle, particularly if the shape is orientated differently from usual.

Mathematics resources

Most primary schools have a maths area where large resources are kept; for example, different types of scales, trundle wheels, metre sticks, weights and capacity jugs. Class teachers often have smaller resources either in their year group or their classroom. You should have your own box of resources, including devices to develop understanding of shape and space. Particularly useful would be geoboards or pegboards for children to make 2D shapes. Secondary maths departments often have an office in which is kept some equipment and each teacher may have their own supply of resources. It will be different in each school, so you should enquire as to what is available and where it can be accessed.

An excellent resource is the *Springboard* materials (KS1 and 2) available on the framework website and in paper form within schools. These are intervention programmes that are used to support children who are falling slightly behind their peers but are not on the SEN register. These materials only support number work and complement the daily lesson. Most schools are using these intervention strategies and you will find the materials useful to look at, particularly as they include video demonstration of lessons. At Key Stage 3 equivalent materials are provided through the national strategy.

Strategies for supporting mathematical development [6K5]

Possibly the most crucial strategy is enabling children to experience practical activities (this need does not diminish as the child ages and practical experiences are important at all key stages). This starts off in Reception classes when using cubes for addition and subtraction. However, there can be a danger that children will rely on the physical object for too long. For example, rather than committing to memory the number bonds to ten, children often continue to use their fingers.

Practical activities are also vital when working on shape and space. Children need to have experience of making shapes on geoboards and then drawing them. You must be very clear about the properties of shapes as this is an area of common confusion. For example, a square is a special rectangle. Purchasing a mathematical dictionary, or *Mathematics Explained for Primary Teachers* (Haylock 2001), would be a good investment.

Do be aware of how powerful the use of the empty number line is to model and explain various mental strategies, for example when working out $93 - 19$. See Figure 10.3.

The number line is also used to show repeated addition and subtraction with its links to multiplication and division. In terms of mathematical development, the most important

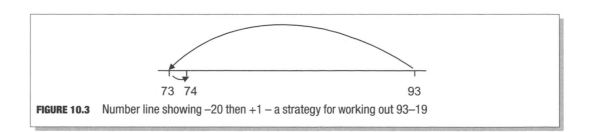

FIGURE 10.3   Number line showing −20 then +1 – a strategy for working out 93−19

aspect of primary and early secondary teaching is children's understanding of the number system. For this, children need to be able to see, and you need to help them see, the connections between various areas of mathematics. For example, children need to see and use the relationship between ¾, 75% and 0.75.

Estimation is a key developmental point. There are problems in estimation. Children are often conditioned to get the correct answer and can see estimation as the teacher wanting them to get the answer deliberately wrong. Using measures is an excellent way to teach estimation and it is crucial that children have plenty of experience of practical measuring activities. Once estimating skills are established they can be extended to areas of numbers. For example, a child estimating 43×56 could work out that the answer would be somewhere between 2000 (40×50) and 3000 (50×60) and then hone it down to estimate that the answer would be about halfway between the two numbers.

The most difficult but potentially the most rewarding lessons for you are those involving the solving of problems. With the classroom teacher, think very carefully both about the questions you will ask children and about the type of recording children will use to solve the problem. The intervention questions need to be carefully graded in order that the answer is not virtually given to the child. They should give the child who is stuck a clue which enables them independently to access the task. This is particularly appropriate for children with different learning needs.

Problems in mathematical development

Some of the difficulties that occur as children develop mathematically are ironed out as they get older but there are some key areas that hinder their progress [6K10].

The first of these is the issue of place value. Children need a thorough and regular grounding in place value work. Part of the original intention of the oral and mental starter in the NNS was to include regular counting activities. While these are still regular occurrences in classrooms, TAs need to be aware of the purpose of counting. Just as in any other part of mathematics, areas of misconception should be targeted. For example, most children by Year 2 can count in twos and tens (starting from zero) up to quite large numbers, but the area of misconception would be counting in tens, starting from a non-multiple of ten, and crossing the hundreds' boundary, e.g. 171, 181, 191, 201, 211, etc. It is often counting in tens that confuses children and you need to deliberately target this in your support.

Another area of common confusion, and possibly the most important, is how children learn mental strategies and how they move to written calculations. There is a difference between rapid recall of facts and mental strategies. Rapid recall is the calculations that children are expected to just 'know', whereas mental strategies are calculations that need to be specifically taught and applied according to the situation. For example, double 35 = 70 is a fact that should be known by Year 4 whereas knowing that a quick way to calculate 35 + 36 is to double 35 and add 1 would be a strategy that needs to be applied. The booklet *Teaching Mental Calculation Strategies* (QCA 1999a) is an excellent resource and explains all the strategies and age expectations.

Parents (and some teachers) often comment that children are expected to learn too many strategies. You should understand why there is this expectation. If one was presented with the following calculations: £8 − £ 2.99, 45 + 46, 16 × 7, 55 + 37, 135.4/10, 428 × 2, 900 − 500, 36 − 18, 78 − 32, one would reasonably expect that they could be answered mentally, but the strategies used would all be different. Children need to be taught different strategies and then, crucially, when it is appropriate to apply them. For example, if you were supporting pupils in a lesson that was concentrating on using near doubles, you would give the children practice examples that were appropriate for this strategy, e.g. 30 + 31, 24 + 25, but at some point in the lesson you could ask the child what 55 + 37 is. Using near doubles would obviously not be a good strategy to work this out. What you are doing is leading the child to look at the numbers first and see if there is any connection between them before attempting the calculation.

It is a clear intention of the NNS that by the end of Key Stage 1 children should be able to mentally answer any two-digit addition or subtraction question. When children move into Key Stage 2, the focus switches to written calculations. The intention of the NNS is that by the end of Key Stage 2 children should have a standard written method for all four rules of numbers. This means one standard written method for each operation. A small but significant number of children have not mastered these techniques by the time they enter Key Stage 3 and the TA within the secondary school needs to be able to call upon the methods used in KS2 to assist these children with their mathematical development.

The difficulty that children experience is how they move from mental to written calculations, particularly in Years 3 and 4. *Teaching Written Calculations* (QCA 1999b) explains this in detail. You can support this movement from mental to written by ensuring that the children think about what method they are going to use. For example, if a child was given 2001 − 1999 to calculate, it would be inappropriate and inefficient to set it out as a written calculation when the child could easily count up 2. The first question to ask when supporting a child with a calculation is 'Can you do it in your head?' If the calculation is inappropriate to work out mentally, the child should use a standard written method at Key Stages 2 and 3.

Another problem that could arise is recognising when it is appropriate to use a calculator. Guidance is given on the role of the calculator in the NNS framework.

Links between mathematics and other subjects

In the Foundation Stage it is commonplace for links to be made between mathematics and other subjects. This becomes less commonplace in Key Stage 1 and certainly by Key Stages 2 and 3. Excellent guidance is given in the introduction to the NNS framework, page 16. Several secondary schools are in the process of revisiting maths across the curriculum and a policy should be in place within the school. Many schools have produced materials to develop the links between maths and science, art, music, geography etc.

Questions to ask yourself

- How did you feel about learning mathematics at school?
- Are you confident in supporting pupils in mathematics?
- Do you need to further your own knowledge and skills outside the school scene?
- Are you able to participate in the school INSET programme for the numeracy strategy?
    - If not, why not?
    - If your circumstances are the problem, can you reorganise some regular events in your life in order to be able to understand the school mathematics practices better?

Supporting ICT and practical subjects including play

SUPPORTING ICT

SOME OF THE NOS relating to ICT relate to the general principles of supporting pupils and teachers as outlined in the previous chapters, and safety measures as described in the health and safety sections, plus some of the items mentioned in the next section on supporting practical activities. For instance, you will need to provide equipment and resources required by the teacher; know the sort of equipment and resources that are available and their location; know the school procedures that must be followed in its use and maintenance; and be familiar with the reporting of faults or problems. Helping the pupils means maintaining interest, independence and self-confidence in pupils. Some TAs have even become ICT co-ordinators for their school although this should be considered to be working at the level of an HLTA and paid accordingly. One ICT standard is the same for Level 2 and Level 3, so stands alone in terms of expertise. There are clearly some specific items relating to ICT that must be considered. First, note that ICT does not just refer to the use of computers and the use of hardware and software, but also, as the scope of the NOS makes clear, to filming and projection equipment, and to recording and playback equipment such as tape, video and DVD recorders and cameras. All equipment associated with computers and recorders such as disks, tape, paper, networks, whiteboards, printers, mobile phones, programmable equipment and digital measuring equipment and that are in use in many schools are also included.

The use of technologies in schools is rapidly changing and the NOS are intended to encompass new and emerging technologies as they become available. ICT is increasingly becoming part of our daily lives. This is illustrated by the use of mobile communications, games consoles, digital cameras and other technologies in the home, school, workplace and community. For the younger generation, technology is now an integral part of their life and the educational system needs to ensure it reflects this.

In June 2003 the then Secretary of State for Education, Charles Clarke stated: 'ICT can make a significant contribution to teaching and learning at all stages and across all areas of the curriculum. ICT should be embedded in all our education institutions and in the teaching that takes place there' (Clarke 2003). It is therefore no longer acceptable for any adult working in the education system to state 'I hate computers and don't want to work with them'. It would be unheard of for school staff to say 'I don't like books' or 'I don't like working with numbers'. ICT must be viewed in the same way [7.1K1].

The first task for anyone supporting ICT in schools is to read the school policies or check with the head teacher, coordinator or subject leader to ensure clarity of procedures. These will be discussed in more detail in the section 'Health and Safety'. ICT resources will cover a large range of equipment and technological devices: programmable toys, phones, videos, DVDs, timers, keyboards, keypads, computers, software, digital cameras, interactive whiteboards, projectors, temperature/sound/light sensors, mobile technologies, online resources, etc. You will need to know and understand the sorts of ICT resources available within the school and where they are kept [7.1K2,4].

ICT is increasingly used to enhance the education of all learners, but for some, the use of digital resources may present barriers because they have special needs or disabilities [8.2P2]. Schools will want ICT resources to be accessible to all their learners – and have a legal duty to make 'reasonable adjustments' to ensure that learners who are disabled are not put at a substantial disadvantage. The ECM agenda highlights this [8K14,25].

Electrical safety and security

One of the things all the above have in common is the need for electrical power in the form of connection to the mains or the use of batteries [7.1K8]. Both of these have safety risks which must be understood in their use and particularly in the supervision of pupils using the equipment. A very useful couple of pages can be found in *Be Safe* (ASE 2001) and a full account of dealing with electrical matters safely can be found in the electricity chapter of the secondary safety handbook, *Safeguards in the School Laboratory* (ASE 2006), which should be found in every school. Mains electricity must always be treated with care and you should be constantly alert and regularly check for faulty switches, broken sockets or plugs, frayed flexes and any defects in apparatus which could lead to problems. Faulty appliances should never be used. You should label them as dangerous, take them out of use and report their existence immediately, so an early item will be for you to identify the person to whom to report such problems [7.1P8,9; 7K5]. All apparatus should be tested annually for electrical safety and should be date marked to indicate this has taken place. For more information try www.pat-testing.info/ as a source [7.2P6]. ICT equipment is still very costly so security measures for its safe storage must also be understood and carefully followed [8.2P1].

Pupils should be trained from the beginning of their contact with any apparatus in its proper use, and the ways of dealing with sockets, switches and connections according to the policy of the school [7.2P2]. Some primary schools, for instance, will not allow any pupils to connect or disconnect anything to the mains, and others teach the older pupils about switching off first before disconnecting and are happy for pupils to do this. Pupils should be taught from an early age that water and electricity are dangerous together, so wet hands or floors are to be avoided when dealing with any of this equipment. Make sure you know where the nearest fire extinguisher for use with electrical equipment is, and where master switches are in cases of accidents. Always switch off the power, if necessary at the mains or the meter, before dealing with any incident or breakdown. If there is an electrical incident, send for help. If you have to act without turning off the power, insulate yourself by standing on a pile of dry paper and use a wooden pole or chair to get the victim away from the source of power [7K23].

Batteries need replacing or recharging and may contain toxic materials. Recharging should be done with care, and dud batteries disposed of where indicated by any school procedures. Bulbs are made of fragile glass, a possible hazard in itself. Projector bulbs are especially fragile when hot, one of the reasons projectors are fixed to ceilings, the other being security. Appropriate storage is important both for the equipment and for things like batteries, film, tape and bulbs. It needs to be safe and secure as most of the items mentioned are expensive and sought after.

All items will have come into school with a handbook for their safe and proper use [7.1P3; 8K17]. Find the location of those associated with the equipment you are to use and make yourself familiar with them. Much of the equipment you may already have at home and be familiar with its use, except perhaps projectors. It is still worth checking that the school equipment is similar. Switches may be in different places or the sequence of operation may be different. Always use the appropriate consumables [7.1P4]. Cheap tape, ink cartridges or paper for some machines can be damaging. Follow the setting up and operating instructions indicated for the machine you are using; again some actions can damage equipment. For instance, projectors should not be moved until the bulb cools down, as doing so will certainly shorten the life of the bulb but can even cause it to explode. A certain routine for switching off is often essential to prevent damage [7.2P7].

In order to minimise risks, also be alert for things like the use of the correct furniture. Use of low chairs for computers can cause eye or back strain for the user, and trailing flexes through furniture can be hazards. Some flexes are encased in rubber treads where they go across the floor to prevent people tripping; computers, screens and printers should be near the power source. You may need to talk politely to the teacher in charge of the ICT lesson or the ICT coordinator if you have a concern [7.2P5,6; 7K9; 8K18].

Preparing yourself

Before you work with pupils using ICT equipment, there are several things to do. Check your job description to see what is expected of you and make sure you have copies of any policies or procedures for dealing with and obtaining ICT equipment [8K9,10]. Get hold of a copy of the ICT policy for the school [8K1]. Somewhere there will be instructions as to the storage and maintenance, the use of various sorts of equipment by pupils (or not), who has access and when, how equipment or consumables are allocated and what requirements the school has of anybody using the equipment [8.2P7]. There may be signing out procedures for players, for instance, or a booking procedure for the video camera [7K3]. The policy also should have some kind of references to the legislation of which users should be aware, and how the school deals with such matters. For instance, software CDs and DVDs are often used under licence; you should never use your own disks from home, unless they are approved by the school. The policy should have information about virus control on computers and the use of personal devices like mobile phones, ipods and the like in school [7K25].

The same copyright procedures used for photocopying may be indicated for scanning and printing materials or downloading music using a computer [7K7]. The Data Protection Act covers any use of data for compiling databases, say in a class survey [8K13]. While most schools will operate a firewall preventing inappropriate incoming data getting to the pupils from the internet, there may be the possibility of child protection issues when pupils start communicating with each other or with other schools [8K20]. Ensure you understand the school policies and procedures for dealing with virus control and any kind of internet or email access, use of passwords or other possible sources of problems. Becta, the British Educational Communications and Technology Agency, the government agency for ICT use in schools, have some useful booklets giving advice in this area, all of which can be downloaded from their website www.becta.org.uk/schools/safety. It states 'The Internet is vast and unregulated, and, in common with all communication media, there remains the concern that it can be abused'. Teachers, support staff and pupils should be aware of the issues surrounding the use of the internet for education, just as with television and video [7.1P7; 8K19].

Every school should ensure they have a suitable internet filter which would block inappropriate materials being viewed from the internet. However, on occasion a site gets past the filter. Schools should have procedures in place within their ICT internet policy in dealing with these issues and it would be wise to familiarise yourself with these processes prior to supporting pupils. Pupils also need to be taught about email safety in line with the school policy. They must never give their full name or arrange to meet anyone they only know through the internet [7.2P5; 7K10–12].

173

You will need to spend a little study time in self-tuition in the use of any equipment with which you are not familiar, and if you are supporting ICT in the secondary school you may need to undertake further study at a local college to be able to support the secondary ICT curriculum requirements [7K6]. While pupils with SEN with developmental problems in secondary schools may be operating at levels more usually found in primary schools, and one of the requirements of the secondary curriculum is increasing independence, some of the sophisticated uses of data logging, spreadsheets, email, creating web sites, video-conferencing, even film-making may need you to understand such techniques.

You may need to familiarise yourself with programmes used by the school [7K2,14]. If you do not have a computer at home, ask if you can borrow one for a limited time, or use the school machines for practice. Remember there may be a problem with insurance as such equipment is valuable and portable. Do check. If you are not familiar with fax machines, using the internet or sending emails, see if there are ways of practising. No member of staff in a school these days can plead ignorance in this area, such is its importance in every field of the school's work [8K21,25]. Try out equipment like players or recorders before you use them; nothing is more embarrassing than being given a task that the pupils will be really keen to do and then finding something does not work, or a battery is flat, or you have run out of disks or tape [7.2P1].

Another area of self-study that may be useful is to refer to a copy of the NC for the age group you are working with. Look at the programme of study for the key stage, and at the attainment targets at the end of the NC book (DfEE/QCA 1999a; DfEE/QCA 1999b). This is probably more useful in the first instance for the programmes of study than the slimmed down new version for secondary schools as it will give more detail. Just check the level descriptions with the new secondary version: Level 2 should describe the achievement of an average seven-year-old, Level 4 an average 11-year-old, Level 5 an average 13-year-old and Level 6 a GCSE equivalent. There is not much reading involved and it will give you some insight into what to expect when you work with pupils [8K11]. The school may also have a scheme of work or syllabus which will help you know what will be taught in each year group.

General age/stage-related expectations [7K17]

Children in early years' settings should have access to ICT equipment in order to become familiar with it as a source of communication. Children from birth can show an interest in things that incorporate technology. They will increasingly explore toys and simple mechanisms and imitate the use of things like cameras in their play. Children as young as 22 months may show an interest in ICT equipment and may well develop the basic skills of turning on or operating equipment such as the television. By four years old they can use a simple programme on a computer and many can come to school knowing how to use a mouse and keyboard. On the other hand, 20 per cent of homes still do not have their own computer, so that unless these children have attended pre-school there will still be children coming into school at five years old who have had no experience of computers or other sophisticated ICT equipment. There are a few children who may be banned the use of ICT equipment by their religion, such as members of the Exclusive Brethren. You must be guided by senior staff as to how you work with these pupils.

The NC indicates that children in Years 1 and 2 will be exploring the use of equipment to become familiar with it. They need to become confident that they can operate machines properly and safely, and start to develop their own ideas. Key Stage 1 children can gather information about their peers and make graphs, enter and store information, plan work and give instructions to things like 'turtles' using logos, and can use a variety of tools and outputs like art programmes or simple databases with lots of pictures. They can describe what they are doing, talk about it, and relate it to what people do outside school in a shop or the home, share their ideas, and review and present their work in a variety of ways. You can encourage all of this talk.

By Key Stage 2, children can use a wide range of tools and sources and begin to use research skills. They should be questioning the plausibility of the information they get and its quality. They can consider the audience of any work they produce, say if using a camera or recording a playlet or a song. They will be able to create databases, classify, check, interpret and think about the information they use. They can organise a variety of sources like word processing and photographic images for simple desktop publishing, monitor different dimensions in the environment, ask 'what if?' questions of simple spreadsheets by changing values – they can get different patterns and relationships. They should be able to share and exchange ideas, and query different ways of doing things.

By Key Stage 3 they are independent users of much ICT equipment, and should be becoming systematic and selective in its use, able to analyse and reflect on what they are doing. They can use different media for testing or problem solving, and produce good-quality presentation fit for their purpose. They will email and format web sites, explore the continually evolving forms of communication and suggest improvements. Key Stage 4 pupils should have developed an holistic approach to using all the various methods currently available, mixing and matching them, and be easily ICT literate in the world outside school.

Working with pupils

All the usual things apply when you are going to support pupils working in ICT. You need to check out the teacher's requirements, learning intentions, assessment and monitoring procedures for the pupils [7.1P1,5; 8.1P1,2,8]. Then check the equipment you are going to use [7.1P2,6]. Then with the pupils ensure they are safe and using safe procedures. On computers you can teach them proper sequences and routines for switching on, setting up, and then saving and closing down. With other apparatus again, routines that are safe and considerate of other users should be reinforced each time you work with the pupils, so that such activities become second nature. You should give them direct guidance on the proper use of expensive equipment; sometimes pupils have developed careless attitudes to property – they think someone else will clear up, replace, clean, put away. You need to disenchant them quickly. Laptops, now frequently found in schools in use in classrooms, are still rather fragile and expensive to replace. Pupils need to be trained in care as the actual task in hand [7.2P8,9].

Pupils should be trying things out for themselves, not just working their way through repetitive, occupying games. You can teach skills on the computer like mouse control, or where to 'click' for certain routines, and how to use the printer. Safe storage of data, film, tape and other materials associated with ICT equipment can all be part of the training. Look at the teachers' schemes of work and planning and where possible discuss with them the general principles that they are trying to teach so that you can follow their intentions. Where TAs switch on, prepare software and just feed pupils through its use, printing off any attempt at word processing or allowing pupils just to copy out pre-written, corrected text, the pupils will not learn the potential of anything except how to exploit a TA [7K20].

As with all school learning, the aim is to get the pupils to think for themselves and act independently of you [7K22]. You can help in ICT by asking questions like 'Why did you do that?' or 'Why do you think that happened?' or 'What happens if you do . . .?' [7.2P4]. One of the problems encountered when Key Stage 2 children begin to search for topic information is their reading ability is not up to the task. They find some of the search engines obscure in their logic; they will ask a question of a programme but the programme can only answer questions put in a certain style; or they find a page of information and just print it off without any critical appreciation of the contents, as it takes too long for them to read it on screen and select the bit relevant to their needs [8.2P4]. You can help them here by ensuring they know what they are supposed to be looking for before they begin – or are they just exploring search methods? [7.2P3; 7K13,24]. Some of the material produced for use on the computers is boring or difficult to access, although another problem is the sheer volume of what is available [8K23,24]. This is where trying out materials beforehand and knowing the interest of the pupils you work with will help. It is important to discuss any problems you encounter with what seem to you inappropriate materials – either too hard or too easy – with the teacher in any feedback. You will automatically be monitoring the pupils' successes and problems as they work, and feedback can be as in any other lesson [8.2P11,12; 8K15,27]. Do ensure you also report back any problems with the equipment itself.

Finally, try to organise the time when you are working with the pupils so that they print off and save work, shut down computers and put away other equipment, rather than you doing it later. It will be your responsibility to make sure all is left safe and secure at the end of any session.

It is not possible in a book of this size to cover all the knowledge and understanding you need to have in order to cover all the performance criteria spelt out in the ICT standards as with many other of the optional standards. You need to have a personal level of skill in using computers, something a book cannot teach you. You will be expected to be able to research the source of appropriate materials for a variety of students, and keep up to date with the range available and the developments in the field, which are rapid [7K26; 8.1P5; 8K7]. The emphasis these days is much more on the use of ICT across the curriculum as a tool rather than the study of ICT as an end in itself, in the same way that literacy and mathematics are. You will also need a good understanding of the pupils you are working with and probably considerable experience of working with the teaching staff and curriculum in your school, in order to adapt machines or materials for the pupils of the age with which you work, and to select and evaluate programmes bearing in mind learning needs, curriculum demands, interest levels and cost [7K15,16,18,19,21,24; 8.1P3,4,7; 8.2P3,5,6,8–10,12; 8K2–6,8,16,21-13,26,28].

ICT to support language learning

An example in the wide applicability of the use of ICT is its use in supporting EAL learners' language and learning development [8.1P6]. The interactive whiteboard which is now common in many classrooms means that there is much greater access to visual support for curriculum areas. There are a wide range of interactive mathematics and language programmes which you can use with EAL pupils. The tasks and activities usually have a clear and controlled language focus which means that you can act as a facilitator to support learning. A widely used resource is called Clicker, used for beginner EAL learners. If you are supporting the curriculum in-class, you may be able to find effective curriculum resources on the internet such as maps, photos, pictures and video clips which will greatly help EAL pupils understand the lesson. Using a laptop with DVD extracts from a key text can be a great way of helping a beginner in English understand even complex novels: or showing a video clip of a rainforest can create a real context for learning. There are now also a wide range of primary stories available on DVD or CDs as bilingual stories. These can be listened to in different languages as well as English.

There are also a number of free web-based translation services such as for example 'Babel Fish'. This means that you can write an instruction or letter home or give homework in

English and it can be translated into a specific language: in a similar way a pupil can write in their first language and it can be translated into English. Similarly there a number of visual multilingual computer dictionaries available which can be very useful and practical for older learners.

If your school has developed an MLE (managed learning environment), try to make sure that you know how to use it and also that newly arrived EAL pupils know how it works. Talk to your ICT Coordinator about this, or the class teacher should know. Using this will enable you, if you have time, to set targeted work for your EAL pupils and to monitor the progress they are making with various aspects of school work.

SUPPORTING PRACTICAL SUBJECTS INCLUDING PLAY

General principles

The general principles of supporting any curriculum subject apply to practical work or play, but with the added component of making sure you are aware of the safety measures you and the pupils need to take [1K10]. Usually pupils enjoy any kind of practical work, whether it means using tools or media, or working with their own bodies as in PE or drama. However, some pupils, particularly as they get older, become very self-conscious about expressing themselves, or being slower or less competent than others, with things like dexterity or clumsiness being more obvious in such subjects [10.4P3; 15K20]. It is important therefore to maintain the fun element of such activities, to be alert for the possibilities of low self-confidence or poor self-esteem in such areas. Many of the skills you may use or techniques you may teach will be of value throughout the pupils' lives, serving as leisure activities or outlets for creativity. Unfortunately, many activities such as performances, matches or field trips have got squeezed out by concerns for safety, cost or completing the more formal, testable parts of the curriculum.

The much-needed move to ensuring a curriculum entitlement for every pupil across the possible range aligned with the strategies' attempts to ensure that the basic skills of literacy and numeracy were taught to every child have unfortunately resulted in a crowded curriculum and a shortage of time. This has meant that subjects like PE, music, art, drama, and even to an extent practical science and DT, have received less attention. This loss has been recognised and timetables are being relaxed in primary schools: cross-curricular, thematic approaches with interest, enjoyment and practical work are slowly returning. Without the exploration and investigation, children will not gain a sense of ownership of their learning or realise the potential of the materials with which they are working – including the potentials of their own bodies [2K12.7; 13.7]. To accomplish a work of art whether in writing, performance or graphic art, you need both skills and freedom to explore the media. Creation or invention takes time, often mistakes, application and appreciation [10.3P1–3].

You need to know the learning objectives of the activity you are supporting in just the same way as for any lesson. The activity should have a shape – introduction, the activity itself and review. You will need to plan and prepare, participate, evaluate and ensure completion and clearing up by the pupils in your group. Pupils need to discuss their work and that of others constructively, whether it is making sand pies in the reception class or doing a sculpture in the art A-level class. They need challenge and success. Science, design and technology can all encourage thinking skills and problem solving while using the skills learnt in literacy, numeracy and ICT lessons. Practical subjects will have elements of skills, knowledge and understanding, just like the more formal activities. If you are unsure of any of these, do ask.

You should be trained by the teacher in any skills with which you are unfamiliar, and if you are supporting pupils at any higher level, say for external examinations, you may well feel more secure if you actually undertake the qualification for yourself. Have a look at the relevant parts of the early years' framework, the NC and any textbooks used by the teacher, not necessarily reading all the words but seeing how diagrams are reproduced for recording, or how certain procedures are carried out. You need to know the degree of accuracy for measuring purposes, whether preparing materials, measuring with the pupils or recording. You must familiarise yourself with any tools or apparatus to be used before you work with them with the pupils. If you are working in PE, unless you are a trained instructor already, do recognise the need for your own training in the proper ways to move or support a movement. Do not do this away from a qualified teacher or instructor: even trainee teachers have to have such people present for PE activities. Gymnastics has proper holds, ball play has distinct skills. Rules and team play need to be taught at the appropriate age or stage [2K12.10; 2K13.11].

Wherever possible, do not do the activity for the pupil. Work alongside the child, discuss the progress and outcomes. Do a separate one and show the pupil how you did it, often known as the 'Blue Peter' approach. This goes for encouraging a baby to sit up, as well as everything from cutting out for the youngest pupils to sophisticated science experiments. Practical skills can only develop when the child or pupil does the work for themselves. Some of the pupils you support will have physical disabilities which make success in such activities difficult, so your encouragement and praise for small steps of progress are important. Remember the persistence that the paraplegic athletes must have, and the long hours of practice that any successful musician puts in, or your own attempts at learning skills; these kinds of examples will encourage those who easily give up. Pupils with learning problems often achieve success in practical subjects when finding more formal learning daunting.

An example of success in practical activities

Stephen had struggled to learn the days of the week for all six of his primary school years. He could not recognise the names of them when written down and could not see the purpose of knowing them. His mother told him whether to get ready for school or not. He was a happy boy, satisfied to work with his friend's horses in the school holidays or after school, and popular with his schoolmates in the playground. However, by Year 5 he was pretty fed up with lessons and could not see the purpose of many of them. Then his teacher introduced a DT project which entailed the use of a glue gun. Stephen was dextrous and mastered this tool's use quickly, and completed his model in record time. The teacher then let him show other less dextrous, if more literate, pupils how to have success with the glue gun in their DT lessons. School suddenly had a purpose for him.

All pupils including those with EAL make excellent progress in their language and learning development in the more creative aspects of the curriculum. For early stage learners in particular, EAL pupils may be able to show particular skills and talents which can increase their self-esteem (rather than finding it more difficult on more language and literacy focused activities). Much of the language used can be directly related to context. In drama, for example, there are many opportunities for pupils to learn the meaning of language from each other, for example, through role play, following instructions and pair/group activities. You can play an important role modelling language and actions for pupils [2K10.14; 2K11.11; 2K12.9; 2K13.8]. With PE activities such as with movement and dance and also in music, pupils will again be able to follow instructions directly linked to activities which can be modelled. In art and technology, activities can again be modelled practically enabling EAL pupils to access the curriculum content. You can support this process very effectively in small groups or on a one-to-one basis if further explanation is needed [10K2].

In the core subject areas, active learning strategies can be very supportive of language learning. Science and Maths can lend themselves to a hands-on kinaesthetic approach to learning where the target language used is linked to practical activities. This can range from carrying out experiments to playing Maths games as simple as snakes and ladders. This is also true for English where the use of language learning games (such as Kim's Game or using a 'Feely' bag to guess an object), focused pair work and practical activities such as book making can very effectively support learning.

All the suggestions made for group working, getting pupils organising, planning, talking, questioning, thinking, reviewing and evaluating hold for practical activities [10.2P1–3]. The booklet *Primary Design and Technology – A guide for teacher assistants* (DATA 1996) has some useful tips for showing children how to do something, talking to children while they are working, supporting practical work, supervising a group (including clearing away), organising and maintaining resources and creating a display. The following are some of their tips for helping children in practical work:

- Don't do things for the children that they can do for themselves, e.g. fetch materials, clear away, use tools

- Encourage them to think about what they are doing and to work carefully

- Remind the children about safe working

- Follow the same rules as the children when using tools or they will soon copy bad habits

- Encourage them to keep their work area tidy, e.g. return tools and equipment which are no longer needed, put unusable scraps in the bin, rearrange equipment and materials on the table so that it is easier to work

- Encourage them to be as accurate as possible, e.g. cutting carefully, measuring food ingredients, marking the position before punching a hole or sticking something down

- Watch how the children are holding tools and how they have positioned themselves and suggest changes if necessary, e.g. you might find it easier to stand up to do that, try holding it like this, use this finger to guide it/keep it still

- Make sure that girls and boys have equal access to tools and equipment – sometimes that is true in theory but not in practice!

- If you need to show a child how to do something, use a spare piece of material rather than their work

- Use the correct names for tools, equipment and materials and help the children to remember them.

(DATA 1996 : 19)

DATA also have publications about health and safety at primary and secondary level as well as guidance for technicians and those working with the early years.

Safety [3K7]

If you are working in a secondary school laboratory, studio, gym or workshop you must ensure that you follow the safety guidelines laid down by the school for staff working in such areas. There are likely to be rules regarding clothing and specialist protective garments, for instance using safety goggles in a laboratory or wearing appropriate shoes in a gym. All staff working in these areas should be trained in the use of any hazardous equipment or when new procedures are introduced. Do not work in these areas unless you are confident you know what you are doing and can help the pupils you are with to work properly and safely without delay. There are likely to be fewer restrictions in primary schools as the apparatus used and the procedures carried out are less risky.

PHOTOGRAPH 11.1   Safe science with a TA

Working in an infant or more particularly a nursery school will mean you are working in a practical way for most of your time, and with young children who are less aware of dangers.

ASE's *Be Safe* (2001) and *Safeguards in the School Laboratory* (2006) are excellent booklets and should be available in most schools. One of the things that is pointed out in the latter is that (referring to pupils): The biggest danger in the lab is YOU! You are a danger whenever you are either ignorant or careless or both. Remember this because the person most likely to suffer from your mistakes is YOU! Report any accident or breakage to your teacher.

There were a useful set of ten rules for behaviour in a secondary laboratory in the tenth edition:

1 Only enter a lab when told to do so by a teacher. Never rush about or throw things in the lab. Keep your bench and nearby floor clear, with bags and coats well out of the way.

2 Follow instructions precisely; check bottle labels carefully and keep tops on bottles except when pouring liquids from them; only touch or use equipment and materials when told to do so by a teacher; never remove anything from the lab without permission.

3 Wear eye protection when told to do so and keep it on until all practical work is finished and cleared away.

4 When using a Bunsen burner, make sure that ties, hair etc. are tied back or tucked away.

5 When working with dangerous liquids or heating things, always stand so you can quickly move out of the way if you need to.

6 Never taste anything or put anything in your mouth in the laboratory. If you get something in your mouth spit it out at once and wash your mouth out with lots of water.

7 Always wash your hands carefully after handling chemicals or animal and plant material.

8 If you get burnt or a splash of a chemical on your skin, wash the affected part at once with lots of water.

9 Never put waste solids in the sink. Put them in the bin unless your teacher instructs you otherwise.

10 Wipe up all small spills and report bigger ones to your teacher.

(ASE 1996: 25) [3K6]

You could be working with a group in a cooking activity, or out on the sports field, or using glue guns or craft knives. All of these must be handled safely by you and the pupils you are with. Electrical safety procedures as described in the previous section of this chapter should always be observed. You may be using chemicals that could be dangerous if eaten or you may be handling soil or pond water.

Precautions for doing these activities should be observed, such as covering open cuts with lightweight gloves and ensuring proper hand washing after use. A list of suitable chemicals for primary schools as well as those that are dangerous is included in *Be Safe*, although it is not comprehensive (ASE 2001: 19). The international hazard warning symbols are on page 21 in *Be Safe* and could be displayed and taught to children. It is also the duty of all staff to point out to a more senior member of staff, any hazards noticed in equipment or procedures with which they are associated.

It is tempting in these days of increased awareness of danger and risks of litigation, for schools to stop doing many of the interesting and even exciting activities, but this should not happen. Children should be taught risk assessment. A good example of how this works is to think of the Green Cross Code. Small children used to be taught this rigorously. However, concern for road safety and 'stranger danger' has encouraged many parents and carers to give their children lifts to and from school and refuse to let them play out or go unescorted until a much later age than, say, 40 years ago. At some point the children will go out unescorted, need to cross a busy road on their own and recognise that dangers can be in the family as well as with strangers. They need to be taught how to cross a road if they cannot 'find a safe place to cross'; how to assess the risk of the traffic levels, the need to walk to a marked crossing or listen carefully on a rural road; and how to say 'no' when they see risk that is more than they wish to take [10.4P1,2; 2K13.5].

They need to be taught that some things are safe if done in the proper way, or wearing the right clothing or if proper procedures are followed. An example of this is that it is perfectly acceptable, indeed desirable, that even small children should handle soil. Like the traffic, many are prevented from doing this at home because of living in a flat or fear of germs or getting dirty. Soil is our basic material: thankfully in this country we have soil, not sand or perennial ice. Our lives depend on someone somewhere growing things. Soil has texture, colour, and variety all worth exploring in their own right. Bare hands are needed to get the feel of it as well as its smell and sight. Children just need to be taught to wash their hands properly afterwards and how to use a nailbrush if they need it.

Good pupil behaviour is essential when doing practical activities, so you should tell the teacher in charge if you have any concerns about any of the pupils you are working with.

Usually, pupils are more interested in 'doing' rather than listening, reading or writing and so often behave better in such lessons, but they can get excited when new activities are introduced. There are many rumours about what is safe practice – or not – that are incorrect. The important thing is that parents should be aware of the nature of activities that will be carried out, the safety precautions that will be taken and the risk assessments that will be carried out, particularly in secondary activities. These will all be spelt out in prospectuses and policies to ensure the school staff are both protected and able to provide an appropriate breadth of experience for pupils.

Working with paint and other art media like clay and glazes, wire and plaster, all bring their own safety precautions but also enable the pupils to be explorative, creative and imaginative. There is a great need for an increase in this kind of activity, so do not be put off by its messiness. Wear protective clothing, have appropriate mops and sponges to hand, and enjoy with the children. Keeping areas clear to enable works of art or craft to dry or remain unfinished until another opportunity arises is also important.

For instance, it is perfectly possible to heat things in primary science lessons, but some sources of heat are not recommended, such as spirit lamps and picnic stoves. Nightlights, hot water, electric rings, microwave ovens, hair dryers and kilns are all suitable for use in primary schools, but must be used with proper procedures and adult supervision, or only by an adult, e.g. the kiln. You should be taught how to use a Bunsen burner properly in a secondary school if you did not do science recently at school, and understand all the guidelines that go with it, such as using hot wires, test tubes, where and how to put down tapers or matches, and hot items.

Use of glass should be avoided in primary school, but even here accidents can happen and children need to be taught the hazards of glass and what to do if they find something broken. You should know how and where to dispose of broken glass, and, where more glass

PHOTOGRAPH 11.2 Creative and derivative art work

is more widely used as in secondary science lessons, the emergency first aid procedures for dealing with pupils with cuts. Knowing the first aid procedures for dealing with foreign objects or chemicals in eyes when in a laboratory or workshop would also be good practice.

Some lessons include using ourselves or animal parts such as bits of skeletons. Here you must be aware of sensitivities over difference between pupils, e.g. shape, colour or size. Tasting and feeling and smelling things should be done hygienically. Examining soft body parts such as offal is both permissible and safe provided they are fresh and fit for human consumption; eyes of pigs can be used but not those of sheep, cows or goats. You may find pupils dislike this kind of handling, or have cultural or ethical reasons for not taking part. They should never be put under pressure to take part, and the teacher should be told of any problems. Live animals can still be kept in schools but clearly some are more suitable than others, and the proper procedures, safety codes and hygiene facilities should be in place.

Micro-organisms such as fungi can be grown in schools but there are proper ways of doing this and of disposing of finished cultures. Yeast growth, yoghurt cultures and examining pond algae are likely to be the extent of work in primary schools, but safe procedures should still be followed. In secondary schools, cultures on special media such as agar will take place and you need to understand the proper ways of dealing with this equipment and its safe disposal. Plants are often grown in schools, both inside and outside in the grounds. Some are hazardous in causing allergies or produce poisonous seeds or leaves.

The external environment

Increasingly, it is recognised that the living environment is not just a source of food. It is known that experience of green spaces has a definite beneficial effect on those with depression or mental illness. Care of living things including wildlife is essential for developing a sense of responsibility as well as looking after our fragile planet. Exploring school grounds, developing wildlife areas, visiting parks and woodlands can enable some children to experience a freedom otherwise denied them. The current initiative known as 'Forest Schools' trains leaders in working with children in such areas. (For more information try www.forestschools.com.) It is known that in seaside towns, only half of the children in school will use the facility that many of us travel miles to experience. Provided the safety boundaries are followed and all adults with groups are properly trained in how to behave in such areas, exploring the natural world is a must for all ages [10.5P3]. More details of the opportunities such work can offer will be found in the *Outdoor learning manifesto* (DfES 2006b). The school will have comprehensive guidance for taking pupils out of school on visits (DfEE 1998d), whether to static displays in museums, fieldwork or on activity trips. The site www.teachernet.gov.uk has links to all the various documents available for training staff going on visits, using a minibus or going near water. If these guidelines are followed implicitly there should be no fear of litigation or blame. Cost of transport is often blamed for the decrease in trips to nature reserves or other locations and that problem is difficult to address.

Play

In good early years' settings the curriculum is about the provision of as varied a diet of equipment and experiences as possible, but not all at once or the same for all age groups. The adult:pupil ratio will be higher than in schools [3K11]. There should be something to stimulate each of the areas of learning, to support physical, linguistic, intellectual, emotional and social development. In a nursery there are usually geographical areas that can be identified with aspects of learning [2K10.8–11,16,17; 2K11.7–9,13,14]. You would be able to see quiet areas with books, tables for drawing or writing, creative areas with paints and modelling media, investigative areas, constructive areas and imaginative areas with facilities for role play. Most physical provision is usually put outside, where some open air and some covered areas can be found so that physical play can take place whatever the weather. Some nurseries have sensory areas with different surfaces to walk on, objects to bang and listen to, plants with different smells as well as areas to dig and climb on.

The aim is to provide the facilities in the setting in a safe way, enabling exploration, development – not suppression – of curiosity, challenging without frightening in adult presence to ensure appropriate boundaries are maintained yet allow freedom of choice [2K10.12; 2K11.10;10.5P4,6,7]. STL 15.4 is entirely about play provision. It should be planned and evaluated as for any other area, be safe, appropriate to age and stage of development, work within a legal framework, be tided up and have progress or changes recorded. The exploration and investigation, the questioning and questing in play is what develops into scientific pursuit given the introduction of a framework in later school life. It also gives a growing child the tools to cope with real life. Adult life is not just a matter of playing with sandcastles but questioning and challenging politicians and statistics, investigating best buys and trying out 'do it yourself' methods. You can see that things like cooking, gardening and sports activities all stem directly from practical and play activities encouraged in formal settings. The foundations of literacy and numeracy are laid with the speaking, listening and manipulative play of the early years. This rather neglected aspect of the formal curriculum is vital for enriching the curriculum at every stage but also in providing the foundations for adulthood. When safety concerns are properly understood and carried out, the range of such activities is virtually boundless.

12

Looking forwards

IN SEPTEMBER 2003, the first of the new workload agreement changes came into force with 24 things that teachers should not do, including photocopying or other administrative type duties. It was followed soon after by the legal requirement for teachers to have 10 per cent dedicated non-pupil contact time for planning, preparation and assessment (PPA) purposes. This has all led to an increasing use of TAs, and, more particularly from your point of view, the defining and training of new higher level HLTAs. The proposals for new standards have been accompanied by comprehensive consultation and suggested new regulations to ensure their continued proper supervision.

However, it has also resulted in some poor practice on the part of managers who have used TAs to undertake class teaching tasks for which they are not properly prepared or qualified, and the malpractice of paying properly trained and qualified people only when they are in charge of a class. While the exploitation of TAs is a concern, it is also important that you recognise your own limitations and that schools – managers and teachers – do not ask of people more than they are qualified or experienced to do. It is up to you to make a stand if you are asked to do something beyond that of which you are sure you are capable – remember, it is the pupils in your care who suffer if you are not up to the job being asked of you. School budgets must not dictate quality of provision in this area. The new regulations introduce the concept of compulsory supervision for all support staff, to be written into the job description both of the support and supervisory staff who would be qualified teachers. The school management must determine the levels of supervision and its nature. This means it should be much clearer what TAs with differing qualifications and job descriptions can or should not do, and what should be the size of groups they can work with and the nature of their tasks and responsibilities. It also should make clear the supervision and performance management situation. While those of you reading this book are not immediately aiming for HLTA status, you should also be clear what attaining this status should mean, but sometimes doesn't.

You may be reading this book as part of a course and be already en route for completing a qualification at Level 2. Some of the possibilities within this level are discussed in the section on Qualifications, page 181. Hopefully, your school will have appointed a mentor or line manager for you when you took up post and you will be able to review your job prospects and competence with an appraiser or performance manager. You will then need to decide what route you wish to take. You need to discuss these implications with your family, your mentor and line manager. You may not go beyond this Level 2, and be quite happy as a competent TA, but you still need contact with others in your profession to ensure you are continually updating your knowledge and skills. In some job descriptions, your responsibility for continuing professional development is built in. Whether or not it is, you need always to be aware of gaining more knowledge, understanding and skills. Education does not stand still, there is always more to learn and we all are lifelong learners. By undertaking reading about your job, attending meetings or courses of whatever nature, you are enlarging your own horizons and providing a role model for the pupils you work with. While registration and compulsory qualifications for all TAs are not part of the above proposals, if you hope to continue working in a school for any length of time in your present capacity, you would be well advised to consider an accredited qualification of some kind.

Continuous professional development

Chapter 2 got you to look at yourself as you were at the beginning of the process of getting to grips with Level 2, how you could organise yourself and how other staff could help you as mentors and line managers. Colleagues are sources of help and support. Performance review or appraisal should have helped you analyse your own development in supporting pupils. But, as with all learners, only you can learn more. The hope is that all staff in a school see themselves as learners so that the school is a learning institution, never satisfied but always seeking new ways to support pupils and each other. You may have had to analyse aspects of your understanding and practice during the reading of the book or the studying for any qualification, and hopefully it has become a habit. The habit of reflecting on practice is one of the best ways to continually develop professionally: you become what is known as a reflective practitioner. Chapter 2 suggested keeping a diary and a portfolio. These are more formal written ways of reflecting, but just thinking about your job on the way home, or sharing thoughts with a colleague in the staffroom will develop your own understanding further. Become self-critical in a constructive way. Be careful not to become so introspective that you lose confidence.

Take opportunities for meeting colleagues from other schools, and if necessary make these opportunities happen. This is how local support groups will be formed. Most head teachers, if approached, would let you have a meeting in the evening in their school, and you could host one and invite TAs from nearby schools. Share ideas, get a speaker in to challenge you all. Take any opportunity to go on external courses. It may mean making special child care arrangements, but it will be worth it to meet other colleagues even if the course itself proves a bit dull. Don't be frightened to ask questions both of the tutor and of your colleagues. The simple ones are often the most telling. You may be worried that a question will show up your ignorance, but you can be sure that someone else in the audience wants that same answer. Talk about the content with your colleagues over any breaks and reflect on your way home.

This book is clearly not able to provide all the information that you need to do your job and certainly cannot provide the practical training that is required by many of the standards at Level 2. In many chapters there are some suggested books which you might like to explore, along with the NC of which you really ought to have your own copy relevant to the age group with which you are working. The internet is a mine of information: in fact, just typing in the subject for which you want information can come up with an almost endless supply of it, more confusing than helpful. Stick to the official sites, again mentioned in the text, until you are confident and check what you find with the relevant teacher before using it or implementing a new idea. The most useful, which have usually been referred to in the text as you went through, are also at the end of this chapter. Discuss what you read whenever and wherever you can so that any ideas that you are formulating are challenged. This discussion process will fix the ideas more firmly in your head – and help you digest them.

Another source of inspiration is television. It has been found that more TAs watch Teachers' TV channel than teachers. As with internet or book information, check before using new material and discuss ideas with colleagues, mentors and line managers.

Progression

The way is set for a recognised profession of teaching assistance, with various levels of responsibility. The NOS, which this book underpins, are already produced in the two levels which correspond to a competent and an advanced TA, Levels 2 and 3. The HLTA status awards are now well established and the original standards have also had a rewrite, as have the NOS and the teacher standards. Some TAs have already got qualifications at Level 4 – that of undergraduate study – and more are now set on the course of foundation degrees in teaching assistance. These are equivalent to two-thirds of a normal degree. The HLTAs standards also indicate a level of expected study to be at second-year degree level.

Only between 10 per cent and 20 per cent of TAs actually want to go on to be teachers; most just want to be good TAs – at whatever level they feel comfortable with. To be a teacher entails having a full degree with QTS, or an NC subject or early years' degree and a PGCE. A few people are able to undertake study towards QTS from the two-thirds degree status while still working. Currently there is funding for people a year to train 'on the job' for a reduced salary through the Registered Teacher route and for graduates to train under a Graduate Teacher route. The TDA website has full details of what you need to enter one of these routes and what is involved. They have a career development framework for school support staff which maps support roles against national training and qualifications in 2005 (TDA 2005). If you are interested in this route, then do talk to a senior manager in your school or to the LA. Foundation degrees for TAs are not available in all teacher training colleges or universities so you will have to make enquiries as to what is available locally for you. There are some very interesting links made by some authorities with universities, colleges and training schools to support TA professional development and qualification routes. Many schools like the in-house routes, as they feel they are 'growing their own'!

Some indication of the levels of responsibilities that might be expected of the Level 3 and HLTAs are summarised in the document *Support staff: the way forward* (NJC, 2003, no. 624) where the expectations of the various levels are spelt out. Table 12.1 gives a summary of this document. Subsequent pages spell out how each job could support pupils, support the teacher, support the curriculum and support the schools, and suggest the experience, qualifications, knowledge and skills that would fit into the particular level being described.

Qualifications

When the TDA came to match qualifications at Level 2 for teaching assistants hoping to gain HLTA status, they found 600 variations on the theme. Well over 200 TA qualifications alone existed before the first definition of NOS to which nationally recognised qualifications would have to match. The NVQs are based on NOS, as are the other qualifications

NVQs are meant to be assessed by work-based assessors, who check your competencies and question you about your underpinning knowledge. College courses will support this process if they are NVQ-based, or you may prefer a more conventional college course with assignments or even examinations. Whatever course you undertake, there will be an element of workplace-based study and competence assessment. The awarding bodies produce detailed information about their courses, which can sometimes be downloaded from their web sites, requested by telephone or sometimes has to be purchased. It is worth looking at the materials before you undertake a course, just to see what you are letting yourself in for. You may be working towards an award from one of the following. If not details can be found on their websites. See p. 183.

TABLE 12.1 Support staff job profile summary (NJC (2003):5)

Expected skill level/equivalent	Induction/basic skills	NVQ 2	NVQ3 specialist knowledge/skills	NVQ4 specialist/higher level TA management responsibilities
Teaching Assistant supporting and delivering learning	**working under direction/instruction supporting access to learning** ■ welfare/personal care ■ small groups/one to one ■ general clerical/organisational support for teacher	**working under instruction/ guidance enabling access to learning** ■ welfare/personal support – SEN ■ delivery of pre-determined learning/care/support programmes ■ implement literacy/numeracy programmes ■ assist with planning cycle ■ clerical/admin support for teacher/department	**working under guidance delivering learning** ■ involved in whole planning cycle ■ implement work programmes ■ evaluation and record keeping ■ cover supervisor ■ specialist SEN/subject/other support	**working under an agreed system of supervision /management delivering learning specialist knowledge resource** ■ lead planning cycle under supervision ■ delivering lessons to groups/whole class ■ management of other staff
Teaching Assistant behaviour/guidance/ support			**working under guidance delivering learning** ■ pastoral support ■ learning mentors ■ behaviour support ■ exclusions, attendance	**working under an agreed system of supervision manage systems/procedures/policy** ■ pastoral support ■ mentoring/counselling ■ behaviour ■ exclusions/attendance
Curriculum resource support	**working under direction/instruction** ■ preparation/routine maintenance/operation of materials/equipment ■ organisational support for teaching staff ■ support/supervision of pupils in lessons ■ general clerical/admin/technical support	**working under instructions/guidance** ■ preparation and maintenance of resources ■ support for pupils and staff ■ specialist equipment/resources ■ routine invigilation/marking ■ general admin/technical support where some technical/specialist knowledge required	**working under guidance** ■ specific support in technical/specialist area ■ preparation/maintenance of resources/equipment ■ implementing specific work programmes including assessment ■ demonstrations/operation of specialist equipment	**working under supervision/management specialist knowledge resource** ■ management team ■ management of budget/resources ■ staff management ■ lead specialist ■ delivering lessons in subject specialism under supervision ■ support special projects ■ advise teaching staff on specialist area/equip/resources
Administration and organisation	**working under direction/instruction** ■ general clerical /admin procedures ■ typing, photocopying etc. ■ maintenance records/data ■ collect/record finance ■ organisational support for staff/schools	**working under instruction/guidance** ■ some skilled work e.g. WP/ secretarial ■ routine financial administration ■ regular interface with public ■ specific curriculum/dept. support ■ record keeping/production data/information	**working under guidance** ■ complex finance ■ operate complex tasks/systems ■ management/analysis of resources/ data/information ■ advice/information/training/supervision of other staff ■ skilled PA/WP etc.	**level 4 manage** ■ budget, resource/systems, people, business, premises **level 4+ responsibility for** budget, resource/systems, people, business, premises

Reproduced with kind permission of Local Government Employers from the publication School Support Staff – The Way Forward

Edexcel at www.edexcel.org.uk,

OCR (Oxford, Cambridge and Royal Society of Arts (RSA)) at www.ocr.org.uk

CACHE (Council for Awards in Children's Care and Education) at www.cache.org.uk

City and Guilds at www.cityandguilds.com

Look at what your local college is providing. There are links to these websites from the TDA website – www.tda.gov.uk – and also to the National Database of Accredited Qualifications – www.accreditedqualifications.org.uk and to the National Qualifications Framework (NQF) at the Qualifications and Curriculum Authority (QCA) at www.qca.org.uk.

The NQF shows you where NVQs fit in the overall scheme of things. This NVQ Level 2 is at the equivalent level of GCSEs and so is often a starting point for young people setting out on their career. Whether you go on to Level 3 or some other form of accredited training, you must go on with your search to do your job well. Anything less is letting the pupils down. Table 1.2 shows the NQF.

Matching pay to competence

Despite the efforts to define levels and provide nationally accredited courses, career progression for TAs remains difficult. The range of jobs has increased which is confusing, reflected in the increased variety of standards in the new set. Pay levels should reflect responsibility and job descriptions, not the level of qualifications undertaken. After all there are a significant number of very highly qualified people working as a TA for whatever reason. It is what you do that should determine remuneration, not your PhD, QTS, HLTA status or NVQ, unless that qualification is seen as essential to the job – as with taking responsibility for a class.

All LAs have also had to come to a single status agreement with the unions in their authority over pay scales relating to job descriptions so that all LA staff other than teachers, whether manual workers or 'blue collar' workers, are paid on a single scale. Some LAs sorted this out early in the century before workforce remodelling, but others left it until the last moment and the negotiations got confused with the changes in job descriptions proposed by those changes. It has caused friction in some areas as heads have insisted on downgrading staff according to provided job descriptions which do not fit what staff actually do. It is important to bear in mind that whatever excuse the heads give for down-grading, all schools have Local Management and can describe and pay any individual on what levels they like, provided they use the levels provided for them. The government also intend to bring in national pay scales for TAs during 2008 after consultation, which should at least make the whole enterprise more equitable across authority boundaries, although management can still use the national scales as they wish. One current issue which may cloud the employment market in the near future is that of equal pay for women. In some authorities, certain pay settlements following court case rulings for this issue, the onus on paying back pay has fallen on the schools. Such is the extent of the award in some schools and areas that staffing levels will be affected. This may also happen following the agreement of national pay scales.

If you are at all concerned about pay issues or other employment issues than join a union. They will give you legal advice and often professional advice as well; again there is a list at the end of the chapter. Currently there is no TA union or association, and the only unions which TAs can join are mainly serving a much wider workforce. Unison and GMB both serve administrative and office staff generally; a few of the teacher unions have a TA section. If you want the rights and recognition given to other professions you must consider some responsibilities beyond just turning up for work to carry out your job description.

Small local associations are being formed, often as part of other consortiums or cluster arrangements, sometimes following a course, and some more regional associations are beginning to spring up. Hopefully, these will soon form a national association of TAs, able to voice opinions and use their expertise to participate in debates about any future developments. Just a small word of warning. There is an organisation called the National Association of Professional Teaching Assistants (NAPTA) in existence which you will find if you type this into Google but they are a subset of the commercial organisation Pearson Educational, a large educational book publisher. They are not representational and they exist to sell a diagnostic tool for TAs considering qualifications. This is useful, but it does not provide further support in your profession or represent you in disputes or consultations.

Being a professional

TAs are an accepted part of school life and are found in all schools. They are no longer the hidden staff and no longer invisible: they are highly valued and recognised nationally. The names still vary, and the details of the role are defined by the job description, but their general role of helping the teaching and learning of pupils is understood by the wider public. To be a professional means taking responsibility for that role, and 'performing' to the best of one's ability. Many think of 'the professions' as limited to the law, medicine and the church, sometimes adding in teachers, but the word 'professional' is much wider and indicates a commitment to a code of ethics and practice that is generally recognised. With the NOS publication and the public recognition of the role, you must consider yourself a professional. Professionalism is defined in the dictionary as a state indicating quality, character, method or conduct, gaining a livelihood and not being an amateur.

You are part of a movement to enhance the teaching and learning of pupils, the adults of the future. Your skills and attitudes matter. I wish you continued success in your career, whichever way it takes you.

USEFUL WEBSITES

www.ukstandards.org.uk for the standards themselves

www.tda.gov.uk for the official guidance to the standards and most material relevant to TA qualifications and information

www.dcfs.gov.uk for official educational information

www.curriculumonline.gov.uk for curriculum support materials

www.fultonpublishers.co.uk or www.routledge.com for useful books for TAs, teaching and learning and SEN specialisms

www.lsc.gov.uk for help with English and mathematics qualification training

www.nc.uk.net for curriculum information and support materials for inclusion, SEN and G&T

www.ngfl.gov.uk for general gateway to educational resource

www.qca.org.uk for support materials, especially schemes of work and assessment information

www.standards.dfes.gov.uk for statistics and strategy materials

www.teach.gov.uk for information on training to be a teacher.

www.teachernet.gov.uk for support materials and documents in general

www.teachernet.gov.uk/teachingassistants for general information for TAs www.tda.gov.uk/hlta for general information about and for HLTAs

www.nationalstrategiescpd.org.uk for information and publications about the strategies

Professional associations or unions being used by TAs

www.unison.org.uk – a union for support staff

www.gmb.org.uk – a union for support staff

www.pat.org.uk – Professionals Allied to Teaching (PAtT): accessible via the Professional Association of Teachers (PAT)

www.napta.org.uk – an association formed by Pearson Publishing to provide services to TAs

The main teachers' associations

www.teachers.org.uk for National Association of Teachers (NUT)

www.teacherxpress.com for Association of Teachers and Lecturers (ATL)

www.nasuwt.org.uk for National Association of Schoolmasters and Union of Women Teachers (NASUWT)

Subject association websites

for subject magazines, conferences and local branches

SEN: www.nasen.org.uk National Association for SEN

English: www.nate.org.uk National Association of Teachers of English

Mathematics: m-a.org.uk and atm.org.uk Mathematics Association and the Association of Teachers of Mathematics

Science: ase.org.uk Association for Science Education

Design and Technology: data.org.uk Design and Technology Association

A general site: www.subjectassociation.org.uk

Also useful is the ICT support website: www.becta.org.uk British Educational Communications and Technology Agency, a UK agency supporting ICT developments

Awarding bodies

www.cache.org.uk

www.city-and-guilds.co.uk

www.ocr.org.uk

www.edexcel.org.uk

Magazines

Learning support for primary TAs: www.learningsupport.co.uk

Times Educational Supplement: www.tes.co.uk

Child Education and *Junior Education*: www.scholastic.co.uk

Nursery World: www.nurseryworld.co.uk

References

Abbott, J. (1996) The critical relationship: Education reform and learning Education 2000 News (March)

ASE (2001) *Be safe: Health and safety in primary school science and technology* Hatfield: Association for Science Education.

ASE (2006) *Safeguards in the school laboratory* (11th edn). Hatfield: Association for Science Education.

Clarke, C. (2003) *Technology can revolutionise education for all learners* (press notice). London: Department for Education and Skills.

Clarke, C., Boateng, P. and Hodge, M. (2003) *Every Child Matters* (Green paper CYPUECM). London: Department for Education and Skills.

DATA (1996) *Primary design and technology: A guide for teacher assistants.* Wellesbourne: The Design and Technology Association.

DCSF (2007a) *The Children's Plan: Building brighter futures: Summary.* London: Department for Children, Schools and Families.

DCSF (2007b) *Statutory framework for the early years foundation stage: Setting the standards for learning, development and care for children from birth to five.* London: Department for Children, Schools and Families.

DCSF (2007c) *The use of force to control or restrain pupils* (Non-statutory guidance). London: Department for Children, Schools and Families.

DfEE (1998a) *Excellence for all children: Meeting special educational needs* (Green Paper). London: Department for Education and Employment.

DfEE (1998b) *Meeting Special Educational Needs: A programme for action (MSENPAS).* London: Department for Education and Employment.

DfEE (1998c) *The National Literacy Strategy Framework for teaching.* London: Department for Education and Employment.

DfEE (1998d) *Health and safety of pupils on educational visits (HSPV2).* London: Department of Education and Employment.

DfEE (1999a) *The National Curriculum: Handbook for primary teachers in England; Key Stages 1 and 2.* London: Department for Education and Skills and the Qualifications and Assessment Authority.

DfEE (1999b) *The National Curriculum: Handbook for primary teachers in England; Key Stages 3 and 4.* London: Department for Education and Skills and the Qualifications and Assessment Authority and the Qualifications and Curriculum Authority.

DfEE (1999c) *The National Numeracy Strategy: Mathematical vocabulary book.* London: Department for Education and Employment, Standards and Effectiveness Unit.

DfEE (2000) *Curriculum Guidance for the foundation stage* (QCA/00/587 ed.). London: Department for Education and Employment.

DfES (2000) *Working with teaching assistants: A good practice guide* (DfES 0148/2000 ed.). London: Department for Education and Skills.

DfES (2001) *Special Educational Needs: Code of Practice.* London: Department for Education and Skills.

DfES (2003a) *Excellence and enjoyment: A strategy for primary schools* (Advice DfES/0377/2003). London: Department for Education and Skills.

DfES (2003b) *Raising standards and tackling workload.* London: Department for Education and Skills with Workforce Agreement Monitoring Group (WAMG).

DfES (2003c) *The education (Specified work and registration) (England) regulations 2003.* London: Department for Education and Skills.

DfES (2004a) *Every child matters: the next steps.* London: Department for Education and Skills.

DfES (2004b) *Role and context module: Induction training for teaching assistants in primary schools.* London: Department for Education and Skills.

DfES (2006a) *Safeguarding children and safer recruitment in education* (04217-2006BKT-EN). London: Department for Education and Skills.

DfES (2006b) *Learning outside the classroom*. London: Department for Education and Skills.

DoH, HO and DfEE (1999) *Working together to safeguard children*. London: The Stationery Office: Department of Health, Home Office, Department for Education and Employment.

Freeman, R. and Meed, J. (1993) *How to study effectively*. London: National Extension College and Collins Educational Ltd.

Freiberg, H.J. and Stein, T.A. (1999) 'Measuring, improving and sustaining healthy learning environments'. In Freiberg, H.J. (ed.) *School climate* (pp. 11–29). London and Philadelphia: Falmer Press.

Gibbons, P. (1991) *Learning to learn in a second language*. Available through NALDIC, South Herts EMA Centre, Holywell School site,Tolpits Lane, Watford, WD18NT: Primary English Teaching Association, Australia.

Goleman, D. (1996) *Emotional intelligence*. London: Bloomsbury Publishing plc.

GTC (2002) *Code of professional values and practice for teachers* [www.gtce.org.uk/gtcinfo/code.asp]. General Teaching Council for England (accessed June 2006).

Haylock, D. (2001) *Mathematics explained for primary teachers* (2nd edn). London: Paul Chapman.

LGNTO (2001) *Teaching/classroom assistants National Occupational Standards*. London: Local Government National Training Organisation.

NJC (2003) 'Support staff – the way forward'. London: Employers Organisation for the National Joint Council for Local Government Services.

Northledge, A. (1990) *The good study guide*. Milton Keynes: The Open University.

Ofsted (1993) *Handbook for the Inspection of Schools*. London: Her Majesty's Stationery Office

Ofsted (2002) *The curriculum in successful primary schools* (HMI 553). London: Office for Standards in Education.

Ofsted (2007a) *Every Child Matters: Framework for the inspection of schools in England from September 2005* (September 2007 edn). London: Office for Standards in Education.

Ofsted (2007b) *Using the evaluation schedule: Guidance for the inspection of schools* (September 2007 edn). London: Office for Standards in Education.

Pollard, A. (2002) *Reflective teaching: Effective and evidence-informed professional practice*. London and New York: Continuum.

QCA (1999a) *The National Numeracy Strategy: Teaching mental calculation strategies: Guidance for teachers at Key Stages 1 and 2* (QCA/99/380). London: Qualifications and Curriculum Authority.

QCA (1999b) *The National Numeracy Strategy: Teaching written calculations: Guidance for teachers at Key Stages 1 and 2* (QCA/99/486). London: Qualifications and Curriculum Authority.

QCA (2007) *The new secondary curriculum: What has changed and why*. London: Qualifications and Curriculum Authority.

QCA (2008) *The secondary curriculum: a curriculum for the future*. Qualifications and Curriculum Authority (accessed 6 January 2008 from www.qcq.org.uk).

Rogers, B. (1991) *You know the fair rule*. Harlow: Longman.

Rogers, B. (1994) *Behaviour recovery*. Harlow: Longman.

Rose, J. (2006) *Independent review of the teaching of early reading* (0201-2006 DOC-EN). London: Department for Education and Skills.

Surestart (2003) *Birth to three matters: An introduction to the framework*. London: Surestart, Department for Children, Schools and Families.

TDA (2005) *Career Development Framework for school support staff*. London: Training and Development Agency.

TDA (2006a) *Teaching assistant file: Primary induction*. London: Training and Development Agency.

TDA (2006b) *Teaching assistant file: Secondary induction*. London: Training and Development Agency.

TDA (2006c) *Pre-course information for teaching assistants: Primary induction*. London: Training and Development Agency for Schools.

TDA (2007) *National Occupational Standards in supporting teaching and learning in schools* – Levels 2 and 3 available as download only from www.ukstandards.org.

WAMG (2008) *Regulations and guidance under S133 of the Education Act 2002*. London: Department for Children, Families and Schools for the Workforce Agreement Monitoring Group.

Watkinson, A. (2002) *Assisting learning and supporting teaching*. London: David Fulton Publishers.

Watkinson, A. (2003) *The essential guide for experienced teaching assistants: Meeting the National Occupational Standards at Level 3*. London: David Fulton Publishers.

Watkinson, A. (2005) *Professional values and practice: The essential guide for higher level teaching assistants*. London: David Fulton Publishers.

Wragg, E.C. (1994) *An introduction to classroom observation*. London and New York: Routledge.

Index